Faversham in the Making

The Early Years: The Ice Ages until AD 1550

Patricia Reid

with contributions from
Michael Frohnsdorff and Duncan Harrington

WIND*gather*
PRESS

FAVERSHAM SOCIETY ARCHAEOLOGICAL RESEARCH GROUP

F·S·A·R·G

This book is dedicated to all the members of FSARG (the Faversham Society Archaeological Research Group) whose dedicated and skilful work has made much of this book possible.

Logo derived from an Early English Delft tin-glazed carinated dish found in *Tanners St* in 2005.

Windgather Press is an imprint of Oxbow Books

Published in the United Kingdom in 2018 by
OXBOW BOOKS
The Old Music Hall, 106-108 Cowley Road, Oxford, OX4 1JE

and in the United States by
OXBOW BOOKS
1950 Lawrence Road, Havertown, PA 19083

© Windgather Press and Patricia Reid 2018

Paperback Edition: ISBN 978-1-911188-35-3
Digital Edition: ISBN 978-1-911188-36-0 (epub)

A CIP record for this book is available from the British Library

Typeset in India by Versatile PreMedia Services. www.versatilepremedia.com

For a complete list of Windgather titles, please contact:

United Kingdom	United States of America
OXBOW BOOKS	OXBOW BOOKS
Telephone (01865) 241249	Telephone (800) 791-9354
Fax (01865) 794449	Fax (610) 853-9146
Email: oxbow@oxbowbooks.com	Email: queries@casemateacademic.com
www.oxbowbooks.com	www.casemateacademic.com/oxbow

Oxbow Books is part of the Casemate group

Cover illustrations: front: The view from the west door of Davington Parish Church,
formerly Davington Priory; back: Left: Faversham's Nautical Festival in 2012, its first
year. Right: Looking across Faversham Creek up to the town, the Town Warehouse
(c. 1450) in the foreground, the churchtower in the background.

Contents

Contributors

Patricia Reid, Ph.D, has worked in community archaeology for the last 23 years and in 2004 founded the Faversham Society Archaeological Research Group (FSARG). She has written numerous reports on the archaeological projects undertaken by FSARG in Faversham which are available on the FSARG website www.community-archaeology.org.uk. She has also contributed articles to Faversham local newspapers. Articles on community archaeology have been published in several publications such as Current Archaeology and London Archaeology.

Duncan Harrington is both a Fellow of the Society of Antiquaries and the Society of Genealogists, and President of the Kent Family History Society. He is a free-lance research historian and compiles the Kent Records, New Series, for the Kent Archaeological Society. With the late Patricia Hyde, he produced several important books on the history of Faversham including *Faversham Oyster Fishery* and *The Early Town Books of Faversham*. He is currently engaged in publishing the Faversham Abbey Leiger Book.

Michael Frohnsdorff, M.A. (Cantab.), has carried out a considerable amount of research into medieval Faversham, with special attention paid to the history of the Maison Dieu, Ospringe. Michael has researched, lectured, and published on Saxon as well as medieval Faversham and translated the Abbey Charters for publication.

Acknowledgements

The great majority of the photographs in the book were taken by members of the Faversham Society Archaeological Research Group (FSARG), especially by Jim Reid. Elsewhere, I am particularly indebted to the following for permission to use their copyright material: The Faversham Society; The Kent Archaeological Society for permission to use material from Archaeologia Cantiana; Karl-Ernst Behre of the Lower Saxony Institute for Historical Coastal Research, Wilhelmshaven for use of his indispensable sea level change graph for the Southern North Sea; Department of the Environment for the use of LIDAR: Dr Brian Philp for permission to use material from his account of the Faversham Excavations 1965; The Geological Survey for use of the Faversham area geological map; Historic England for permission to photograph artefacts at the Maison Dieu, Ospringe; St Mary of Charity, Faversham, for permission to photograph aspects of the interior and to the Faversham Camera Club for helping with the photography; Maureen Wickham of FSARG for immaculate original diagrams: Irene Andrews for the photograph of the Argosy site.

I am very grateful to the many people who have offered contributions, advice and help, but any errors are entirely mine as editor.

Acronyms and abbreviations used in text

Arch. Cant.	*Archaeologia Cantiana*
ASC	*Anglo Saxon Chronicle*
BL	British Library
CAT	Canterbury Archaeological Trust
CCA	Canterbury Cathedral Archives
CPL	Calendar of Papal Letters
CPR	*Calendar of Patent Rolls*
DNA	Deoxyribonucleic Acid
FGW	FSARG website: www.community-archaeology.org.uk
FSARG	Faversham Society Archaeological Research Group
KAFS	Kent Archaeological Field School
KAS	Kent Archaeological Society
KCC HER	Kent County Council Historic and Environment Record
KCC SMR	Kent County Council Sites and Monuments Record (replaced by HER)
KHLC	Kent History & Library Centre
KHTS	Kent Historic Towns Survey (2003)
LIDAR	Light Detecting and Ranging
LTR	London Topographical Record
PAS	Portable Antiquities Scheme
SSARG	Sittingbourne Society Archaeological Research Group
SWAT	Swale and Thames Survey Company
TNA	The National Archive
VCH	*Victoria County History*

Foreword

The great historic cities of England such as London, York and Winchester deservedly receive much attention from high-powered historians and archaeologists. Small towns keep a much lower profile, their stories attended to usually by local societies. Nowadays, although professional archaeological units visit to record findings from development sites, they rarely communicate with local communities, and information remains fragmentary. Yet these small towns can be very ancient indeed, with powerful and deep-rooted senses of identity.

This book is an attempt to tell the story of one such small settlement, the Borough of Faversham in north Kent. An exceptionally wide range of sources has been used, and these are described in Chapter 1. Because of the wealth of material, this volume is limited to the early years, up to AD 1550. This is a far from arbitrary date, and the book ends with a quick look ahead at the implications for the town after this date: Chapter 10 is titled 'Epilogue' but could well be a prologue.

This account concentrates mainly on the period from the last advance of ice around 11,000 years ago until AD 1550. For most of this time span, evidence comes from the work of archaeologists with major contributions from geography, ecology and anthropology. Chapters 1–5 and 9 are my work as an archaeologist, based on the many sources that are increasingly being woven together through the labours of FSARG, the Faversham Society's community archaeology group. Chapter 6 on the invasion period (AD 811–1100) was created through a joint effort from myself and local historian Michael Frohnsdorff.

Chapters 7 (AD 1100–1400) and 8 (1400–1550) on medieval Faversham, come from historian Duncan Harrington, who has worked with Patricia Hyde on many highly professional document-based historical publications on medieval Faversham. Anyone who thinks rural medieval history is a dry and uneventful period of docile peasants tilling fields needs to read the colourful, dramatic and ever-changing story of Faversham during these times. Chapter 9 looks at the medieval period from the archaeological angle, with special attention to the medieval 'standing remains'.

This book is aimed at an interested non-specialist readership, but the underpinning and references are designed to take more academic readers further in. All assertions are firmly rooted in evidence, whether physical or documentary, and preferably both.

Finally, I extend a welcome to any readers whose interest becomes aroused in reading about this example of a small English town with roots going back thousands of years. Do not, however, expect a glossy, gentrified place: Faversham is, as it always has been, a working town with an exceptionally large voluntary sector. There are Open House Days, Open Gardens, and, unsurprisingly, several Museums and the best times to come are on market days, Tuesday, Friday and Saturday, with special markets regularly. The times, however, when that powerful sense of identity is at its strongest are the festive days – the Nautical Festival, Hop Festival, carol singing at Christmas in the Market Place. Enjoy.

Dr Patricia Reid
Community Archaeologist for the Faversham Society

CHAPTER ONE

Welcome to Faversham (or Feversham, Febresham – choose from 20 alternatives)

....

Introduction

Let us start with a look at Faversham in 2017.

Arriving by car, you would probably come via the M2, leaving at junction 6, turning left onto the Faversham to Ashford road, and driving past ribbon development to the busy Canterbury Road. Crossing at an awkward junction, you drive down a tree lined road with late Victorian houses of familiar type. The road snakes to the left to go underneath a railway bridge. Then you swing to the right and take the first left turn: you are now in Preston Street, the closest Faversham possesses to a High Street. At this point, park and walk and be joined by visitors arriving by rail. Going down Preston Street, you meet another awkward T junction but to the left you will see the stilted Guildhall and, if this is a Tuesday, Friday or Saturday, the bright pavilions of market stalls selling fruit and veg, fish, baked goods, clothes, flowers, bric a brac.

What have you made of the town so far? Not large (the population at the 2011 census was 19,316) with modest shopping facilities and, so far, no particularly large buildings. There are no up-market boutiques or fancy delicatessens or trendy, expensive, children's clothes shops, but there are plenty of well-kept pubs, small restaurants, charity shops and small specialist shops run by enthusiasts.

If you turn right at the Guildhall you will go along wide, cobbled Court Street and then into Abbey Street. Now there are some large buildings. In 2017, those on the right house a TESCO and an ASK restaurant. Tucked away are many attractive apartments. On the other side of the road, very imposing if you have come into town via the Ospringe Road, is another set of large and complex buildings, and these are still in their original use as the Shepherd Neame brewery: the buildings occupied by TESCO on the eastern side were owned originally by Rigdens brewers, finally Whitbreads, closed in 1990, to be converted sensitively to these other uses.

Along a side street to the right is the parish church, St Mary of Charity: it has an unusual openwork spire and lots of fascinating features. The sheer size of St Marys, the largest parish church in Kent, might seem over the top for such a seemingly modest little town.

Walking down Court Street and Abbey Street, you will begin to see many handsome brick houses and some timber framed ones with jettying. Finally, turning left opposite the *Anchor* pub brings water into view: you are now on Standard Quay, with black wooden warehouses and moored barges on Faversham Creek, all very picturesque. You will probably notice that the inner warehouse although timber framed with a brick finish, rests on a stone foundation wall about 1 m high.

So far, you have a charming little town, not particularly wealthy or fashionable but comfortable in its identity. It has no walls, no castle or cathedral: medieval foundation, you might assume. Now, however, let us rewind and look at your route into town with other eyes.

The turnoff at the M2 motorway (built 1962) takes the visitor onto an ancient route way, a droveway across the North Downs from Faversham to Ashford. As you drive on northwards towards Faversham, about 300 m on your left is a medieval manor, Perry Court, listed in the Domesday Book nearly 1000 years ago. In the back garden of one of the houses on your right, a boy digging a hole for fun in 1965 found late Iron Age pottery, over 2000 years old.

You turn briefly onto the Canterbury road. This is no ordinary road. This is that most famous of Romano-British Roads, Watling Street. It ran from *Londinium* via *Durobrivae* (Rochester) and *Durovernum Cantiacorum* (Canterbury) to *Rutupiae* (Richborough) and *Dubris* (Dover). There have been many important Roman occupation period finds nearby, and about 1 km to the west was an informal Roman street settlement known as *Durolevum*. Turning right into the Mall, you are driving along what used to be the top end of Preston Street until the coming of the railway in 1858–60. As if the arrival of the railway was not dramatic enough, in the process of excavating the embankments an exceptionally rich early Saxon cemetery was uncovered. Large scale brickearth removal in the same area in the second half of the nineteenth century yielded yet more precious loot – gold and garnet brooches and buckles, gold headdresses, swords, necklaces.

So far, then, we have Late Iron Age, Roman, pagan Saxon and Saxo-Norman and you have not even reached the town centre.

The Guildhall dates from 1574, with the current superstructure dating from 1819. The market itself, however, has a much longer history: Faversham is listed in Domesday as one of only two Kentish towns to have a market. Faversham was also at that time a Kings Manor and the lead town for an Anglo-Saxon Hundred. The first documented use of the name and its identity as 'the Kings little town' is in a charter of King Coenwulf dated to AD 811.

The regal connection gets stronger. Remember that stone wall at the base of the warehouse on Standard Quay? There is no natural building stone in the Faversham area apart from flint nodules: this stone was mostly imported from near Maidstone with some yellowish pieces coming from quarries near Caen in Normandy. This is recycled stone from a high-status Norman building. Five hundred years ago, just south-east of Standard Quay, were the cloisters and functional buildings serving a huge Abbey Church in which King Stephen, his wife and son were buried. The great Royal Abbey of St Saviour, founded in

AD 1148, dominated the town (or tried to) for nearly 400 years. Now only the splendid Abbey Barns (to the east, about 300 m/300+ yds away) and the Abbots Lodge (you passed it along Abbey Street) survive to tell the tale although the stones can be found in many a nearby wall as well as the one on Standard Quay.

Finally, there is that attractive waterway Faversham Creek, with plenty of leisure craft at moorings and an ever-increasing amount of waterside housing. Yet only 50 years ago, the area opposite Standard Quay was occupied by a shipyard, where boats were launched sideways into the creek. Photographs of the creek from the early 1900s show large ships bringing up cargoes of wood for the timber yard or coal for the Gas Works at the Creek head. Only 20 years ago, in 1997, the creek on the town side and around the Basin was still lined with industry.

The long-term importance of Faversham as a port is marked by its membership of the Cinque ports. Faversham has been a 'limb of Dover' for at least 800 years and enjoyed the independence and duties of such a position. Yet back in Roman times, sea level relative to the land was lower than now. Go back further in time to just after the last Ice Age – which is only around 11,000 years ago – and the sea was far away. Our knowledge of the people living around here at that time is much cloudier than that of the medieval Favershamites, but that they were here is beyond doubt, proven by the abundant flintwork they left behind.

In short, what looks at first glance an unpretentious small market town, probably founded like so many small Kentish market towns around AD 1200, is shown at the quickest second glance as something more special and unusual. It is easy to overlook places like Faversham, especially as ten miles away is one of the United Kingdom's most famous historic towns, Canterbury. This book is an attempt to bring together the earlier narrative for this small place and its hinterland: the voice of small and indomitable towns will be heard.

Voices with names

Nowadays the inquisitive can examine any part of the world in detail without leaving their computer screen. Census documents can be pulled up online, ancient newspapers studied, old aerial photographs and maps summoned. Yet it is the voices of people that speak to us, long dead friends, and colleagues, who bring the past alive.

Voices from 400 years ago: Leland, Lambarde, Camden and Philipot Senior

John Leland (1503–1552) has been described as the father of English local history. Living through the tumultuous time of the Dissolution and great social changes, he dedicated himself to collecting antiquities, books and manuscripts and aimed to complete an *Itinerary of Britain*. In this, he intended that Kent, 'the key to all England', be the first chapter. Although his work was not gathered together and published until 1710, his documents circulated and were consulted by those who followed, such as Camden. Leland, our first named voice, describes Faversham as a market town with a 'great Abbey of Blake Monks'. He also mentions the 'Meason de Dieu that now belongs to St Johns, Cambridge' and tells us that 'Faversham has a Creek for vessels up to 20 tons and a great Key called Thorn that takes big vessels'. Leland lists fishing for oysters, mussels, and mullet as important local occupations (Leland 1710, section 58).

The earliest published description of Faversham, however, is contained in William Lambarde's *Perambulation of Kent*, published in 1576. This was the first published county history. Lambarde originally intended to cover the whole of Britain but he learned that William Camden was already carrying that out. Lambarde was born in London in 1536, son of a high-status draper and, like several of these voices, qualified as a lawyer. He ended up as Keeper of the Records in the Tower and died in 1601.

Lambarde says of Faversham: 'this town is well peopled and flourisheth in wealth at this day, notwithstanding the fall of the Abbey ... this is a very fruitful area, the very garden of Kent and has a commodious tidal creek'. Lambarde is keen to say that in his view the benefits of the water were important long before the building of 'that Abbey'. This favourable judgement is backed up by values given in his many lists of the places of Kent. Thus, with the total value of the tenths and fifteenths of the various hundreds of Kent, Faversham Hundred at £52 is exceeded only by Milton (£110) and Kingsland (£103) (Lambarde 1576, 228–32, 281).

Lambarde's compatriot Camden (1551–1623) achieved that aim of recording all of Britain in a series of accounts of the different counties. His masterwork, *Britannia*, was published in Latin in 1586 and proved very popular. The English language version came out in 1610. Camden was particularly keen on looking for traces of the past in the existing landscape, just as we observed the stone in the Standard Quay warehouse. Camden (1610, 334) says about Feversham:

> ... Very commodiously situate for the most plentifull part of this country lieth round about it and it hath a creeke fit for bringing in and carrying forth commodities, whereby at this day it flourisheth amongst all the neighbouring towns. From above Feversham the shore runneth on plentifull of shel-fish, but especially oisters.

Camden had as companion on many journeys John Philipot (he was born Philpot in 1589 but inserted the extra 'i' to give his name a touch of class). The Philpots came from the Folkestone area but John moved to London as apprentice to a draper and through marriage contacts rose high in the College of Arms, becoming a 'Rouge Dragon puirsuivant-in-ordinary' and gaining the title of Somerset Herald. John Philipot collected a great deal of information on Kent and on his death bed in 1645, he begged his son Thomas to publish his findings. This Thomas did in 1659 and 1664 as *Villare Cantianum: or Kent surveyed and illustrated* but under his own name. We will meet Thomas Philipot again later in this chapter.

John Philipot was the first to translate that early AD 811 document of King Coenwulf as calling Faversham the 'Kings little town' and the phrase has passed into the popular story of Faversham. Philipot goes on to give an account of the various rows and riots of the Abbey versus town period, these also becoming accepted as gospel by subsequent writers.

In Thomas Philipot's accounts of the other parishes nowadays reckoned to be part of Faversham – Preston, Ospringe, Davington – he is most interested in the names of the families involved in the successions of ownership of the manors. He does, however, have some interesting comments to make about the Maison Dieu in Ospringe, which he assigns to the Knights Templar. He is surprisingly evocative about the ruins he saw – Mackenade manor being '… almost gasping in its own ruins being crushed into disorder by the rough hand of time' and the Maison Dieu being '… that neglected heap of ruins wherein the ancient fabrick is visible' (Philipot 1659).

These writers would call themselves Topographers and Surveyors rather than historians, and four hundred years later it is their descriptions of the town as it was in their time that are valuable. Thomas Philipot, however, writing in the next century and using his father's research, is much more interested in the past, a tendency that is characteristic of the next phase.

Voices from 350 years ago: Southouse, Philipot Junior, the Rev. Lewis and Defoe

The Rev. John Lewis was born in Bristol in 1675 and followed a church career. Retiring to Canterbury, he devoted himself to research and writing mainly on religious topics but sometimes on topographical subjects. Thus, he produced an account called *The History and Antiquities of the Abbey and Church of Faversham*. Edward Jacob who, 100 years later, was to publish the first comprehensive account of Faversham, believed, however, that the Rev. Lewis had derived most of his information from a modest little book called *Monasticum Favershamiense in Agro Cantiana; or A Survey of the Monastery of Faversham in the County of Kent*, by Thomas Southouse. This was published in 1671, with Lewis's account following in 1727. Both are dedicated to Lord Sondes, Lord of the Manor of Faversham at that time (Southouse 1671; Lewis 1727).

Southouse, unlike Lewis, was a Faversham boy. His account, written, he claims, using the ledger of the Abbey, is very engaging. He aims, he says, to 'unhoodwink your eyes' about the truths of the Abbey 'with which yourselves (with shame let it be spoken) are unacquainted'. The book is enlivened with poems, a very flowery one being penned by our friend Thomas Philipot. The two Thomases are both working at Grays Inn at this stage and clearly friends: both Southouse's book on Faversham Abbey and Thomas Philipot's treatise on *The Chemical Causes of the Tides* (1673) were printed at the *Sign of the Three Bibles* on London Bridge.

For such a small book, *Monasticon* is crammed with information. Southouse lists the manors the Abbey owned, the houses it rented out in Faversham itself, knights fees for a range of places, details of the Custumal and the impact of Mortmain statutes in the thirteenth century. For the modern reader, however, the most valuable section concerns that which is still standing in Southouse's day. He describes the refectory as still entire though being used for storage of ladders and 'other little fruiterer's trumpery'. The bake house, brew house and malt house survive only as 'tattered skeletons', a vivid phrase which crops up in later versions of this story. The kitchen, he tells us, is all gone, its foundations dug up in 1652 to pave Court Street. They did, however find the sewer that drained the kitchen though he tells us that many people thought it was a passage to the nuns at Davington. Finally, the palfrey stables survive next to where 'Lord Sonds hath lately built his farmhouse'.

Unlike the Rev. Lewis who is very anti Papist, Thomas Southouse's musing on the end of the Abbey is as a young man of the Enlightenment. He says, 'Thus we have seen, Reader, that bodies politick as well as natural bodies can die' (Southouse 1671). Sadly, Thomas himself died not long after, in 1676 at the age of 35. His son Filmer carried on with his father's studies but he too died young at the age of 31. Thus, they never achieved their aim of completing a study of the town itself and this was left to Jacob.

FIGURE 1.1. Daniel Defoe, an eighteenth-century voice (From an engraving by M. Vander Gucht)

The last link through to the eighteenth century is Daniel Defoe (Fig. 1.1) who published the first volume of his entertaining, snobbish, and acidic version of a Perambulation – *A Tour Through the Whole Island of Great Britain* in 1724. He describes Queenborough, near to Faversham, as 'a miserable, dirty, decayed, poor, pitiful fishing town ... consist(ing) in ale houses and oyster catchers'. With Faversham, however, he is much more admiring, describing a large, populous and 'as some say' a rich town. Defoe draws attention to 12 large Dutch hoys at anchor there and although they are ostensibly there for the oyster trade, he tells us that this is only a disguise for 'the most notorious smuggling trade from which the people hereabouts are arrived at such proficiency that they are grown monstrous rich from that wicked trade'. (Defoe 1724, letter II) (Fig. 1.1).

Voices from 230 years ago: Jacob and Hasted

The published denial of Defoe's smuggling accusation came from Edward Jacob, born in Canterbury in 1710, but living in Faversham from the age of 25, serving as mayor three times and dying in Faversham in 1788 (see Pl. 1a). By profession he was a successful surgeon, serving Lord Sondes and the Gunpowder works, amongst other responsibilities. At heart, however, he was a collector and researcher, with interests ranging from plants and fossils to antiquities and literature. Jacob's book *The History of the Town and Port of Faversham*, published in 1774, was the first comprehensive study of the town in its own right and is the model and source for later studies. His pre-Ordnance Survey detailed map of the town remains invaluable. As with Southouse and Lewis, the book is dedicated to Lord Sondes, Lord of the Manor of Faversham.

Jacob explains that his problem has been to select from the mass of material the appropriate pieces for his book, a problem familiar to all historians. His chapter headings cover the early history of the town, the Abbey, Maison Dieu and Davington Priory, the parish church, Grammar School, Market, Guildhall, Port or Creeke, the civil governance after the Charter of Henry VIII, the companies of Dredgers and Mercers, the inhabitants, Gunpowder works, cultivation of madder and 'miscellaneous matters' e.g. the paving of streets. Lengthy appendices include lists of Mayors, burials etc and accounts of some of the lively events of the town such as the Arden murder and the nasty experiences of James II in Faversham. Illustrations include Roman coins, the surviving Abbey gate, and Arms in the windows of St Mary of Charity. Jacob says firmly that he wishes to 'convince us of the ridiculousness of the repeated assertion that this town is notorious for smuggling'. Instead he emphasises the huge contribution made to Faversham's fortunes by the ever-increasing London market and the ease of transport thereto of corn, fruits, gunpowder etc, and he portrays a prosperous and up to date town which he is proud to serve.

Hasted, Kent's famous historian, born in London in 1732, was a highly-educated man who led a colourful life that landed him eventually in a debtor's prison in Canterbury. His *History and Topographical Survey of the county of Kent* was published in four folio volumes between 1778 and 1799, with a second amended edition in 1801. Hasted's account of Faversham obviously relies on Jacob, who he probably knew. For the Abbey, he relies on Lewis and Southouse – he even uses Southouses's 'tattered skeletons' phrase for the outbuildings in 1676.

On his own account, however, he describes Faversham at the end of the eighteenth century as follows: 'Many of the houses are large and handsome and the inhabitants of a good condition and wealthy in general'. Like Jacob he does not say much about the poor except as recipients of charities but Hasted does describe in some detail the effects of the horrific Ordnance Works explosion in 1781 in the Stonebridge pond area – 'perhaps was hardly ever before equalled in this kingdom' – and describes the statutory measures taken to compensate the widows and others whose properties had been destroyed, a rare example of human rights legislation at this period (Hasted 1798, 354–5).

Voices from 150 years ago: Crow, Giraud, Donne, Willement and an increasing chorus

At this stage, the voices begin to multiply. Edward Crow (1784–1867) was a great admirer of Jacob's achievement but never managed to sort out his mass of research data for publication. In 2009 a collection of Crow's work was published under the title *Historical and Various Gleanings Relative to the Town of Faversham and Parishes Adjoining*, edited by Peter Tann. Tann points out that Crow is especially good on the power of the Borough of Faversham – the Henry VIII charter of 1546, Crow says, had virtually turned Faversham into a self-governing state. Crow himself supported reforms in the 1830s that did away with most of these independent powers, such as the Company of Mercers founded in 1616.

Like the earlier writers, Crow is particularly useful when describing buildings that are now lost. For example, he describes the medieval ruins of Davington Manor at the top of Dark Hill, a building completely forgotten in recent times. Within the town, he describes many old properties that have since been demolished to make way for new roads or industries. What he does not do is to describe and comment upon the housing of the poor, the crowded streets that can be seen on, for example, the tithe maps of 1840 and the 50 inches to the mile Ordnance Survey of Faversham Town published in 1865.

Later in the nineteenth century, Francis Giraud, town clerk and member of a Faversham Huguenot descended family, and the Rev. Charles Donne, Vicar of Faversham, combined to produce a *Visitors Guide to Faversham and Brief Notes on Surrounding Villages*, published in 1876. Giraud explicitly wanted to cover the time since Jacob's much-admired book. This period covered the introduction of the railway, building of many new houses, the growth of the Kentish Stock Brick industry and the expansion of the Ordnance works into the marsh. For medieval material, Giraud and Donne relied heavily on earlier writings, adding to it from the account of Thomas Willement.

Willement was a celebrated expert on the Gothic renaissance, specialising particularly in stained glass window restoration and design. In 1845, he acquired Davington Priory as a home. Willement then restored Davington Church (the former church of the Poor Nuns) and the surviving Priory buildings. In 1862, he used documents to write and publish *Historical Sketch of the Parish of Davington in the County of Kent and of the Priory There*. Willement contributed to the creation of stained glass windows elsewhere in the town.

A new interest was emerging in the earlier history of the town, especially in the Saxon and Roman periods. The discovery of the rich Anglo-Saxon cemetery had greatly stimulated interest in the Saxons. The interest in all things Roman came from many antiquarian finds at various places in and around the town and was part of a nationwide eagerness to chart (and in many ways to identify with) the Roman Empire. Prehistory remained a romantic enigma.

Voices from the late nineteenth and early twentieth centuries

From the mid-nineteenth century onwards, an explosion took place of both opportunity for the publication of small, specialised research items, and the number of individuals able to use these opportunities because of improved education. From the later nineteenth and early twentieth century there are numerous historical publications about Faversham in journals such as *Antiquity*, the *Gentleman's Magazine*, and county archive type annual publications such as *Archaeologia Cantiana*. The numerous newspapers were ever willing to publicise exciting discoveries, especially if they were of gold (as they often were in Faversham).

Even in small Faversham, a significant monthly *Journal* had sprung up. In 1861, the Faversham Institute for the encouragement of Literature, Science and Art was founded. Within a year of founding, it had a brand-new luxury home in the town centre, complete with reading room, library, and lecture hall (Pl. 1b). Giraud and Donne describe it as 'one of the most successful of its kind in the whole country and free from debt'. The Institute ran classes, offered examinations, and organised lectures, concerts, and fund-raising activities. Its Journal published many articles on the history of the town, by a variety of people. The Institute lasted until 1979 when it was demolished.

Similarly, the Kent Archaeological Society (KAS) was founded in 1857, publishing *Archaeologia Cantiana* annually. In 1872, Faversham hosted the Annual General Meeting of the KAS over a weekend. Most of the time was spent touring the historic sites of Faversham. George Bedo, a young railway clerk who would die tragically in a swimming accident in 1876, presented a paper to the gathered intelligentsia on the Saxon finds in and around Faversham. Godfrey-Faucett spoke on his recent excavations at Stone Chapel (Anon. 1874, lxi–lxxxiii).

The late nineteenth century was a time of high prestige for Faversham's antiquities and well-preserved town records. Many Faversham articles were published in *Archaeologia Cantiana*. This died away in the twentieth century, however, with only Whiting's 1920s excavations of the Roman Cemetery at Ospringe gaining much mileage (see below). It appeared that Faversham's days of antiquarian glory were over.

Indirect voices from the past

So far this chapter has been concerned with the consciously constructed voice from the past – someone speaking to you via the written word. The stories told by the earliest writers such as Lambarde or Southouse are passed on almost unchanged. If they are the first 'tellers of tales' about Faversham, where did they get their information from? Was it mediated by earlier voices that we do not know about, maybe through an oral tradition? Here are some mostly anonymous but genuine voices.

With the coming of Roman Christianity to Britain in (tradition says) AD 597, literacy returned to Britain, though remaining largely a skill of monks and clerics. One of the very few historians' voices from the early medieval period is the Venerable Bede writing his *Ecclesiastical History of the English People* in AD 731. He was living at the monastery at Jarrow in Northumbria, a long way away from Kent, but it is the Bede who introduces the idea of the three different kinds of post-Roman invaders – the Saxon, Angles, and Jutes, with the Jutes getting Kent. Bede refers constantly to Canterbury, seat of the Archbishopric, and describes as accurately as he can the mission of St Augustine in AD 597, but there is no mention of anywhere that could be Faversham.

Another set of voices, nameless but distinctive, comes through the *Anglo-Saxon Chronicle* (ASC). There are several versions of the ASC written at different monasteries, similar but not identical. They generally start very early on in Roman times and the story of Hengist and Horsa being invited in by Vortigern in AD 449 comes from the ASC. In fact, however, the *Chronicles* were not actually written down until the end of the ninth century after which they were attended to every year, so the early years must be taken with caution. The *Chronicles* stop at AD 1154, 'the year the King Stephen dies and was buried where his wife and son are buried at Faversham, in the minster that they made': this is the sole mention of Faversham but very direct (*ASC*).

Monasteries produced hand written and often illuminated manuscripts. Although manuscript illustrations usually depict biblical scenes, they often give lots of interesting data on contemporary clothing, body language, scenes of pastoral life, and appearances of buildings (Solomon's temple can look very like the cathedral down the road) Sometimes

FIGURE 1.2. A contemporary portrait of King Stephen holding a model of his Abbey at Faversham (Matthew Paris (1200–1259))

illustrations do relate to current affairs: Figure 1.2 shows such a picture of King Stephen, taken from a page with three other Kings, and in Stephen's hand is Faversham Abbey.

Then there were institutional accounts – the lists of taxes, tithes, stores, court offences and so on, held by the monasteries, manors and, after the tenth century, the fast-growing towns. Faversham has Town Books dating back to AD 1251 and Port Books to AD 1650, as well as an exceptionally well-preserved series of town charters dating from AD 1252 to 1685 and including an AD 1300 engrossment of the Magna Carta. All the town charters remain in the possession of the town, a remarkable circumstance, with other medieval town documents in the Kent History and Library Centre. Many other documents relating to the religious institutions of the medieval period, such as the Abbey Leiger used by Southouse, are invaluable to the historian.

The Domesday Book, dating from AD 1080, is earlier than the town charters and is the most famous of English mid-medieval texts. Although it has its weaknesses, it remains an amazingly detailed list of places and their economies, right down to the number of pigs that can be pastured. (see Chapter 6). Then there are earlier charters which usually specify ownership of land and give then-current landmarks to make the boundaries clear. Charters go back to the mid-Saxon period and Faversham's earliest dates from AD 811, with a possible even earlier one from AD 699. Also from this early period are law codes such as that of King Wihtred of Kent that give us the flavour of life then, what was fair and acceptable and what was criminal, with all shades in between.

Few stories survive from the earlier medieval other than those from the Scriptures, but the later medieval period produced many romances, some of which have local relevance. Chaucer's pilgrims would have come through Ospringe and stayed at the Maison Dieu. Others like Fitzstephen's romantic account of London around AD 1170 are relevant – probably Faversham never had huge cooking stations by the Creek where you could get a ready meal, but it may well have had young men practising their archery in the shooting meadows and maidens dancing by the light of the moon (Fitzstephen 1598, section 20)

Using a multitude of sources, then, sense can be made of the medieval period once literacy arrives. It is significant that the sixteenth century 'perambulators' like Lambarde and Camden were very active collectors of material from the dissolved and often demolished religious institutions, building up collections that helped save the medieval world for scholars to come. Mid-medieval Faversham during the Viking invasion period culminating in the Norman conquest is covered in Chapter 6. High and Late Medieval Faversham are covered using historical sources in Chapters 7 and 8, with the archaeological contribution to understanding medieval Faversham in Chapter 9.

Sources for earlier periods: the rise of archaeology

Antiquarians have been around for a long time. They are collectors of ancient objects which are cherished and often displayed. There has long been status in owning such objects, perhaps as sacred objects e.g. part of the True Cross or the bones of a saint, or as symbols of power and conquest like the regalia of other nations or as objects of high aesthetic value, demonstrating the taste of the owner. For antiquarians, seeing antiquities as forensic clues to the past is irrelevant.

Antiquarianism is still very much with us, as the most cursory glance at auction sites will show. As a practice, it has very little to do with archaeology: indeed, the process by which these items of 'value' are obtained is often seen as looting by archaeologists. For archaeologists, the material world is something to be examined for meaning – for archaeologists, a context is the imprint of a past event on the ground. On any one site being investigated, there may well be thousands of contexts, each one contributing to the narrative through its unique character.

The limitations of The Venerable Bede and the ASC's accounts of early history have already been mentioned and for the pagan Jutes in the Faversham area between AD 450 and 650, archaeology is the only way to gain any understanding of their lives. This Germanic culture is not the easiest to investigate. They used organic materials such as timber, textiles, horn, and bone, which rarely survive in the ground, and turned their noses up at pottery. If it was not for their love of jewellery, weapons and prized objects, and their habit of burying their folk fully dressed and equipped for the afterlife, then the quest would be extremely difficult.

Chapter 5 will tell the story as far as it is known of the Jutes in the Faversham area, until the first documented mention of Faversham in AD 811. In this, the depressing and, by modern standards, scandalous story of the looting of the Kingsfield cemetery will be told. As Andrew Richardson, an expert on Kentish Anglo-Saxon burials, has said, although the finds purchased from the workmen by antiquarians are catalogued, we cannot even be sure that they came from Faversham itself. Andrew suspects that the town became the centre of a black market for antiquities stolen from other cemeteries in Kent. This is very like Defoe's smuggling suspicions (Richardson pers. comm.).

Chapter 4 is concerned with the period between the first invasions under Caesar in 55 BC until the final letter in AD 410 from the Emperor Honorius saying to the desperate Brits, you are on your own. Unlike the pagan Jutes, this culture had literate people. We even have a few voices – Caesar writing about Kent in *De Bello Gallico*, Tacitus writing about the Claudian invasion and the Iceni revolt. The third century *Antonine Itinerary* lists along Iter II (Watling Street) a settlement called *Durolevum* which could be in the Syndale area. There is, however, little written material that can shed light on what it was like in the Faversham area at that time. We are back to the efforts of archaeologists.

Some Romano-British archaeology is easy to spot, especially the remains of important buildings. After the abandonment by Rome, brick and tile went out of use in Britain for 800 years, so the Roman building materials stand out in landscapes as terracotta scatters in a ploughed field or inserts in a later church wall or distinctive layers under the surface. The characteristic shape of Roman brick and tiles makes positive identification easy. Given the fascination that Roman culture held for the Victorians, an almost obsessive prioritising of Roman remains, especially villas and planned towns, went on well into the twentieth century in Kent. Films, novels, school curricula were all part of this obsession and painted a vivid picture (often wildly misleading) of the Roman empire. Archaeology can set some of this to rights, although the humbler types of structures from that time are much more elusive.

Archaeology is indispensable with prehistoric times, covered at the end of Chapter 2 and in Chapter 3. The familiar three ages system of Stone Age/Bronze Age/Iron Age, based on the artefacts left behind by prehistoric peoples, was first devised by Christian J. Thomsen, Head of the National Museum in Denmark, in 1848. John Lubbock, author of the definitive *Prehistoric Times* (1865), refined the Stone Age definition by subdividing into Palaeolithic (Old Stone Age) and Neolithic (New Stone Age – farming introduced). More recently, the Mesolithic, or Middle Stone Age, has been defined. This system still serves us for prehistory, though much refined by increasingly accurate dating of material cultures.

Until very recently hardly anything was known about the prehistory of the Faversham area. A few stray finds of flints and a late Bronze Age hoard from the Isle of Harty had been notified to the Sites and Monuments Record

(KCC SMR) but that was it. The lack of interest in the pre-Roman was unsurprising – the area does not have any glamorous passage graves, stone henges or surviving barrows. Neither has local industry been kind to archaeological remains in the Faversham area. Brickearth extraction has removed the archaeology from great tracts in and around the town, recording only antiquarian valuables. In more recent times, gravel extraction has scooped out huge swathes of the land. Furthermore, this has been an area of intensive farming for a long time, with any mounds removed from the path of the plough and early material turned over and over until it has lost any obvious connections with other items. Yet, with care, discoveries are possible, as Chapter 3 will show.

None of the discoveries mentioned above, however, makes much sense without knowledge of the broad context in which it occurs – the climate, sea level, physical processes, vegetation, wildlife. Much of this comes under the heading of environmental archaeology and at the time of writing almost none has yet been done in the Faversham area. It is possible, however, to rely on palaeontologists, geologists, and historical geographers to give us a broad framework within which to situate our people and their lives. This is the main subject matter of Chapter 2

The earliest true archaeology done in the Faversham area was the investigation in 1872 of the Stone Chapel by Mr T. G. Godfrey-Fausett. Although much criticised for his methodology and conclusions by later archaeologists, Godfrey-Fausett was trying to answer questions about the origin of this building through inference from a careful study of the remains. This is archaeology.

In the 1920s William Whiting, of the local Cremer and Whiting brickworks, organised investigations of the Romano British cemetery alongside Watling Street at Ospringe. The finds were described carefully in a series of articles in *Arch. Cant.* (Whiting 1921; 1923; 1925; 1926; 1929) and Whiting was responsible for the setting

FIGURE 1.3: Roman pottery found during the excavation of the foundations for the Argosy cinema in Preston Street

up of the Faversham area's first museum in the Maison Dieu in Ospringe, where a fine display still exists. What is lacking, however, is chronological interpretation, the construction of a narrative: in the 1920s antiquarianism still dominated.

The last 50 years in Faversham's investigations: historians and archaeologists working together

In 1962, the Faversham Society came into being, originally founded to save Abbey Street from demolition as part of slum clearance. The Society soon expanded into historical research and education. The publication of the Faversham Papers began in 1964 with, to date, one hundred and thirty published on a wide variety of local topics. Since then the Society has gone from strength to strength, and now (2017) is run from the impressive Fleur de Lis Heritage Centre in Preston Street.

There are many rumours about informal archaeology going on in Faversham over the 1950s and '60s, but little was recorded apart from some brief notifications of finds to the SMR. In 1965, however, one of the first major rescue digs outside the bombed ruins of places like London and Canterbury took place. This was the excavation of Faversham Abbey by Brian Philp, prior to the clearing of the area for the playing fields of the new Queen Elizabeth Grammar School. The excavation was published in 1968 (Philp 1968) and the finds are currently curated by the Faversham Society. The full story is told in Chapter 9.

Since then, the most important change period has been the 1990s. In 1991, after an enormous row over the discovery and planned destruction of the remains of the Rose Theatre in London by developers, a new set of Planning Policy Guidelines (*PPG16*) was set up by Parliament to guard against the blind destruction of the material culture of the past. This went further than simply saying attention must be given: the work had to be carried out by a professional Archaeological Unit, according to set procedures with the developer carrying the costs.

PPG16 has had an enormous effect in the UK on the understanding of the past through its material remains. Wedded to another new phenomenon, the National Lottery funding of large scale research projects usually professionally organised, this was a golden age for archaeology: it became a career for young people, not just a hobby for elderly retirees. The technical side of the investigations improved enormously. Alongside this was the 'Time Team effect': no other so-called archaeology TV programme has ever conveyed the real nature of archaeological investigation so truthfully, where one small sherd of pottery can shift the interpretation of an entire culture, and where 'nothing' can be just as telling as 'something'.

This flowering of archaeology largely by-passed Faversham. The large-scale development of the Davington estates had taken place in the 1960s, with few developments of any size taking place in Faversham in the period 1990 until now. Where small scale development had taken place, as along the Creek on brownfield sites, *PPG16* interventions took place but in most cases, were rushed or the site declared to be of no interest due to industrial interventions.

Furthermore, the reports on these investigations, known as 'grey documents', were not officially published and were available only at the KCC headquarters at Maidstone, although happily in recent years an increasing number have been appearing online. It must be remembered that the actual Unit attending to a *PPG16* project is chosen by the developer after receiving tenders and can therefore come from anywhere in the country. This means that the records and finds are taken away to be stored, sometimes far away, and although records and finds should be returned to local depositories, this may take a very long time.

In the early twenty-first century, many Faversham people felt that archaeologically they were no better off than in the dark days of the antiquarians buying up the Saxon/Jutish grave goods, not one of which has remained in the town. Commercial units came and went usually without notifying anyone except the owner and the planning authorities. Matters are very different in a place like Canterbury where one Unit, the Canterbury Archaeological Trust, attends to all the archaeology within the city walls and has excellent community relations. For the rest of us, the situation had gone sour.

In Faversham, the situation was eased by the formation of a voluntary community archaeology group in 2004, under the umbrella of the Faversham Society and called the Faversham Society Archaeological Research Group (FSARG). The aim from the outset was to investigate only in those areas where there was unlikely to be any development and yet where there were important research questions to be addressed. The first project *Hunt the Saxons* 2005–6 was an investigation using the gardens of houses in the Tanners Street/Lower West Street part of Faversham which was, according to historians like Jacob, the location of the early town. Over the next 12 years, much of the rest of the town (where gardens had not suffered from brickearth removal) has been investigated, with 113 reports published online and lodged on the KCC HER. The group has also hunted down most of the 'grey documents' (Pl. 2).

FSARG's activities have yielded much information about the town (KCC Kent Heritage Conservation Group 2003), but the most important findings concern prehistory. A light touch keyhole approach used with meticulous sieving has yielded a staggering number of flint tools, along with prehistoric pottery fragments. Meanwhile, the historians have been busy. Alongside the Papers, the Society has published reprints of important past accounts such as Jacob's *History* and Giraud and Donne's *Visitors to Faversham*. The displays of the Fleur de Lis Museum give a vivid idea of what the town was like, from the post medieval period onwards. A family history service has been provided, based on the very detailed resources available through the Society's archives. Several local people have built up and published superb collections of historic photographs (Kennett 2009; Swain 1981).

In 1988, a Historians group with quarterly meetings was founded and is still running in 2017. Through being able to discuss their work with others at regular intervals members can help each other. Individuals have contributed invaluable accounts such as Duncan Harrington and Patricia Hyde's translation of the Town Books (2008) and account of the oyster trade over 11 centuries (Harrington and Hyde 2002), Arthur Percival's research into the Faversham gunpowder industry and John Owen's accounts of the history of the Shepherd Neame brewery (Owen 2012). Nevertheless, with all this high-quality research and publication about Faversham, it is a startling fact that Giraud and Donne's *Visitors Guide* (1876) remains the last overall summary work on Faversham and much of that is derived from Jacob's 1774 publication.

Final comments

The problem, as Jacob so rightly said when getting his book together in the early 1770s, is not too little information but so much that condensing it into a manageable book is very challenging. This outline given in Chapter 1 of the sources and information available nowadays shows that the problem of selection has become even more taxing than in Jacob's day. Add in the facility of access to knowledge via the internet, and the task becomes overwhelming. These considerations have led to the decision to confine this volume to the Faversham's early years up to AD 1550, with a glimpse of what lies ahead in the years AD 1550 to 1600 in Chapter 10.

There are bound to be aspects of the early history that have been omitted or accepted with great caution. New discoveries take place all the time – for example, at the time of writing, initial exploratory work on a proposed large building site at Perry Court has yielded evidence for yet more late Iron Age settlement. Nevertheless, let us hope that, like Jacob, for the moment we will succeed.

CHAPTER TWO

Ice, mammoths and the first people: 600,000–8000 BC

···

Introduction

This chapter outlines the physical setting for all that comes later. 'Later' includes what is happening as I write, looking out at Faversham Creek in late spring 2016. In a response to what is perceived as an ever-increasing threat of flood to Creekside residences, an earth bund is being built along the west side of Faversham Creek. It will run along the Front Brents as far as Crab Island and then curve inland, protecting Church Road from the incoming waters. Why is this risk considered to be now so serious that it needs this expensive solution? Is it to do with climate change or higher sea levels or sinking land? This chapter is intended to improve your understanding of the way in which the physical world has affected the Faversham area and its people and will continue to do so: the world waits for no-one.

The solid geology and human development in the Faversham area

The geology that Faversham people are familiar with is that of rolling chalk hills to the south and flat, low lying marshy muds to the north (Holmes 1981). Beyond the marsh and the Swale waterway to the north, the land rises again in the distance as the low clay hills of the Isle of Sheppey. How do these rocks fit together and how do they help or hinder human endeavours? Figure 2.1 sets out the situation, using a cross section through the Weald of Kent running from south-west to north-east. The town lies at the intersection of several different rock types – specifically, it lies where the thick chalk layer dips down northwards underneath a sandy layer, and then both layers dip down under the London clay. The map in Figure 2.2 shows the solid geology of the Faversham area.

The most striking result of this combination of rocks and the main reason for the settlement of this 'foothills' zone from earliest times involves water supply. Chalk is a soft rock and can be scratched with the fingernail so on first consideration it seems odd that it is associated with uplands. Chalk is, however, very porous. Rain water soaks into it rapidly with no chance to wear the chalk away, and then sinks down through the chalk until it meets a non-porous rock such as clay. There the water accumulates and saturates the deep chalk, forming a great underground sponge reservoir.

Figure 2.3 shows what happens where and when the chalk slopes down under the non-porous London clay, and the water emerges as powerful springs.

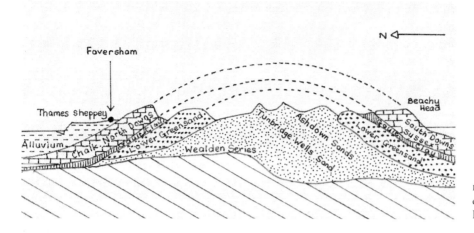

FIGURE 2.1. Section north-east to south-west across Kent and East Sussex

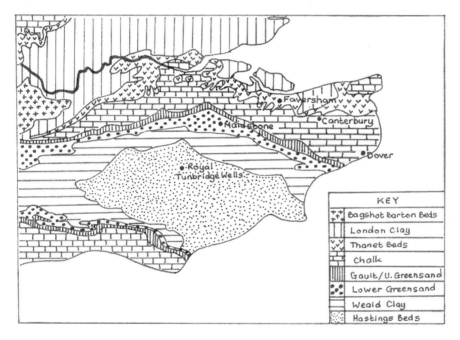

FIGURE 2.2. Solid geology map of Kent.

Even in these days of large scale water extraction by pumping stations in the Faversham area, many of these ancient springs continue to flow, such as the ones at Luddenham, Clapgate and Church Farm. From these springs, streams continue to flow down to the Swale, as they have done for eons. Further up on the North Downs, deep, steep sided, dry valleys running south to north slice into the chalk. Some of these valleys are deep enough to cut down to the saturated water level, creating springs with streams in the valley floor.

This kind of spring was the source of the Westbrook stream, so centrally important in the history of Faversham. The course of the Westbrook is shown in Figure 2.4, based on an early map. Since then, its lower course has been much modified by improvements such as the Faversham Navigation in 1842–3 that straightened out some of the meanders. The centre stretch has been used for mills of various kinds over the years and has been greatly altered. The most drastic change, however, has been in the upper, southerly stretch where twentieth century water extraction, particularly at the Ospringe pumping station (at TR 00106 60166), has caused the complete disappearance of surface water to the north of Chart Mills (at TR 01057 61332). The spring that was the source in living memory, just east of Painters Forstal (at TQ 99540 58767) and the powerful springs near Ospringe Church that fed the stream further have all dried up. Since 1965 any excess water in times of exceptionally heavy rainfall is carried in a culvert underneath Water Lane in Ospringe. In the lower central section, however, just west of Tanners Street in the town a reduced Westbrook still survives and feeds into Stonebridge Ponds. This indicates springs surviving along the lower course of this vital stream

Apart from the contribution to water supply, the basic rock types in the Faversham area are not particularly kind to human settlement. The chalk downs lack surface water and the London Clay is a sticky mess when wet and hard as stone when dry. The sandy layer between the chalk and London clay is mostly Thanet Sands in the Faversham area, a greenish sandy deposit with low fertility. Chalk has been quarried from medieval times in the Faversham area for use in creating lime for fertiliser and in mortar. The chalk itself has some use as a building material, and its flint nodules have been indispensable in many ways to people living in this area, but Thanet sands and London clay had no

FIGURE 2.3. Block diagram showing the reasons for lines of springs occurring naturally

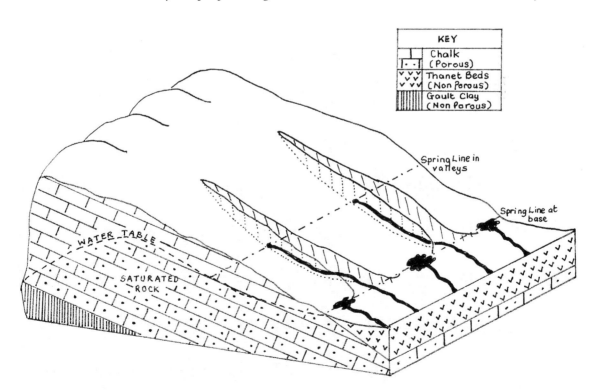

KEY

Chalk (Porous)	
Thanet Beds (Non Porous)	
Gault Clay (Non Porous)	

Spring Line in valleys

Spring Line at base

WATER TABLE

SATURATED ROCK

such uses. Yet this is the belt of land that comes to be known eventually as the 'garden of England', a rich and fertile stretch of orchard, horticulture and hop gardens (see Lambarde's praise for the Faversham area in Chapter 1). Clearly, however advantageous the geology has been for water supply, there is more to explaining Faversham's success than the solid geology and it is time to consider the effect of the Ice Ages.

Quaternary climate change and its effects on the Faversham area

Only 20,000 years ago, a mere yesterday in the story of our world, conditions around what would become the location of Faversham were bitterly cold, with the ground frozen to a depth of hundreds of metres. The sea was many miles away, much of the water in the world being locked up in huge ice sheets to the north and south of the planet. Go back 100,000 years, however, and in the Faversham area the climate was warm and well-watered with abundant vegetation and animal life such as monkeys and hippopotami, and the sea was just down the hill.

This constant shifting from freezing cold to warm has been going on for around 2 million years. Even when the Faversham area was warming up after that bitter Last Glacial Maximum 20,000 years ago, there was a relapse about 12,000 years ago, lasting for around 1500 years. After that the climate warmed

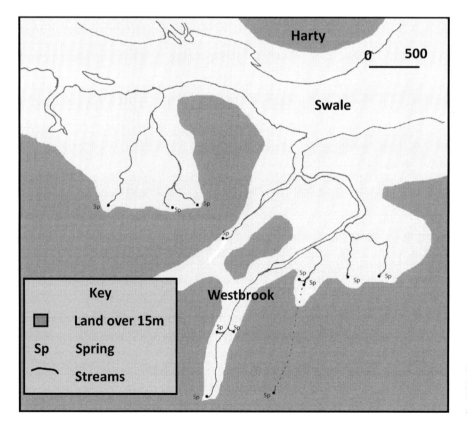

FIGURE 2.4. The basic physical geography of the immediate Faversham area

up rapidly, and people returned to live in lands that had formerly been frozen and uninhabitable. This re-settlement will be fully described in Chapter 3. The rest of this Chapter is devoted to what archaeologists call the Palaeolithic, known in the popular press as the Old Stone Age.

The drastic climate changes in what are geologically very recent times have left very clear signs in the landscapes of Northern Europe and other high latitude places. In Scotland, the great U-shaped valleys carved by huge glaciers are plain to see. Across the North European Plain lie vast ridges of moraine dumped by the ice sheets. Down here in Kent, the signs are not so obvious but are nevertheless profound, and crucial as a setting for the human story ever since.

We will now attend to the effects of the Ice Ages in the Faversham area on deposits, sea levels and river valleys such as the Westbrook. The changing animal and plant life of the area will also be covered. Section C will cover evidence for hominid activity in the Faversham area up until the relapse into cold around 12,000 years ago.

The superficial geology – puny deposits but big implications for people in the Faversham area

Earlier in this chapter, the rocks familiar to Faversham people digging their gardens were listed. Yet many local people reading this chapter will be thinking that the soil in their garden or allotment is not chalky or clayey but either a yellowy brown, loamy and easily worked soil or a gravelly deposit. If the reader is someone from up on the Downs, in a village such as Sheldwich or Throwley, then the soil may be a sticky brown clay loaded with lots of flints. These deposits are described in detail by Holmes (1981, chap 8 and 9) and can be seen in Plate 3a.

In the area to the west, east and south of Faversham these surface deposits are brickearth (the yellowy-brown deposit) and gravels. Up on the Downs, clay with flints predominates, although patches of brickearth are known. These deposits are comparatively thin layers, but their presence has been and still is vitally important to human activity. They were laid down during the last 1.5 million years, the later ones at a time when there were hominids in this area. Because in the Faversham area, the brickearth dates to that last main Glaciation about 40,000–20,000 years ago, long after the earliest hominids lived in this area, their remains can sometimes be found on former living surfaces underneath these deposits

These Ice Age deposits occur in layers around 2–3 m thick. At the base of the brickearth, resting on the underlying chalk, are often found sarsens (Holmes 1981, 75). These are large, rounded lumps of cemented sand. Sarsens were formed in a layer of Thanet sands that used to exist on top of the chalk and which has long been eroded away, leaving these bizarre boulders strewn around as lonely survivors; large sarsens were used for the trilithons of Stonehenge and other prehistoric monuments such as Kits Coty in the Medway Valley. Often the brickearth in the Faversham area overlies gravels, in which case the gravels contain the relic sarsens.

To understand the origins of these superficial deposits it must be recalled that although Kent itself was never actually covered by moving ice, during those intensely cold periods the ground was frozen to almost unbelievable depths, creating what is called permafrost. In the short warmer summers, the top metre melted, giving a slushy layer on top of the slippery frozen ground below. The melt water carried loose rock with it. Indeed, sometimes whole hillside sheets of thin, thawed surface material overlying permafrost slid downhill, a process known as solifluction (Holmes 1981, 66, 85). Gravels therefore accumulate in the floors of the valleys. Sometimes large sheets of melt water spread fine silts out over large areas – this is thought to be one way in which brickearth is deposited, another being when very fine silts are blown away by cold dry winds and accumulate in sheltered areas such as the sides of valleys. These features are easily observable in the Westbrook valley (see geological map with superficial deposits: Pl. 3a; Holmes 1981, 83–9).

Clay with flints is thought to be a residue produced from the weathering of chalk and former overlying rocks, accelerated by the cold conditions of much of the last 1.5 million years (Catt 1986, 151–9). The flints were originally formed by the accumulation of silica around the silicate skeletons of creatures in the Chalk Sea. Flints are not soluble in rainwater so remain in the clay residue at a much higher concentration than in the original chalk. The presence of a skim of water-retaining clay with flints on the North Downs partly explains why the North Downs has kept a relatively dense cover of woodland, unlike many other chalk regions.

To the north of Faversham is alluvium – river, lagoon, and sea mud deposits that in North Kent cover the marshlands as well as collecting in the stream valleys. This young alluvium itself covers brickearth and gravel deposits. Nearby at Shellness at the eastern tip of Sheppey and along the beach at Seasalter, there are sand and shingle build ups, full of shells. The continuing process of deposition of alluvium and beach materials can be seen happening every day in Faversham Creek and along the beach (Holmes 1986, 95–6).

In the Faversham area, brickearth and gravel have been very extensively quarried in modern times, the former for the brick making industry, the latter for road stone and other industries. The steep cuts in the ground lining for example, Stone Street in Faversham are clearly visible on the LIDAR map (Pl. 4) and are the product of 'digging off'. The gravel excavation areas are often allowed to fill with water and they form a chain of lakes to the west of the town, nowadays used for recreational fishing. When chalk quarries are added to the list of interventions, quarrying and 'digging off' have obviously drastically affected the landscape in and around Faversham in modern times.

What is sometimes overlooked, however, is the enormous advantage of brickearth for settlement and cultivation compared with waterless chalk/

clay with flint up on the Downs and sticky, hard to work, densely wooded London Clay stretching northwards. Here those words of early topographers about Faversham quoted in the first chapter should be recalled – 'This is a very fruitful area, the very garden of Kent' wrote Lambarde in 1576 and in 1586 Camden wrote 'Very commodiously situate for the most plentiful part of this country lieth round about it '. Chapter 3, on prehistoric settlement and life in the place that was to become Faversham, will demonstrate that this favourable perception of the area goes back thousands of years before Lambarde and Camden. The brickearth belt, giving light, easily worked soils, running along a medial line between the Chalk Downs and the alluvium or London clay, fed by constant springs, has long been favoured by man. Alan Everitt, the landscape historian, calls this foothill area the 'Original Lands' of Kentish settlement, and the truth of this is greater than even he realised back in the 1980s (Everitt 1986, 45–7).

Sea level change and the phenomenon of isostasy in the Faversham area

In the later history of Faversham, from the Romans onwards, the central importance of the Westbrook Stream and the tidal Creek is unarguable, as will be seen in Chapters 4–9. For 1000 years at least, the Westbrook has been harnessed for water power and its clear waters, fed reliably from chalk springs, have been highly attractive for much longer than that. The tidal Creek giving access to the sea is, however, a more recent phenomenon and to understand this, we return to the Ice Ages.

The British Isles are part of the Continental shelf of Europe. A continental shelf is an underwater landmass stretching out from a continent and is shallow compared with the true ocean. The shelf is heavily masked by deposits washed down from the main continental land mass. In northern Europe, the shelf extends far beyond what is now the British Isles: the North Sea is a Continental Shelf sea and very shallow indeed by oceanic standards. During the Ice Ages, at the heights of the many cold periods, a great deal of water was locked up as mile-thick ice on the land. Because of this world-wide shortage of liquid water, at the Last Glacial Maximum (only 20,000 years ago), sea level was around 120 m/400 ft, lower than it is now. Dry land stretched from west of what is now Ireland to the continental land masses to the east.

Every time the climate warmed up, the ice melted. Rushing debris-laden rivers sliced down into the solid geology underneath, empowered by the steepness of the slope down to sea level and with erosion maximised by the debris scraping the riverbed. Remnants of earlier gravel covered flood plains were left behind, stranded high on the valley sides. Meanwhile, however, sea level was rising rapidly as the water returned to the oceans. As the waters rose, the rivers eased back on their erosive powers and indeed ended up dumping a lot of the material that they were previously able to carry in their vigorous stage, thereby creating a new flood plain that filled up their previous steep sided valleys.

When you realise that these alternating freeze/thaw conditions happened not once but many times in the Quaternary, with sea level up and down, the complexity of the landscape that is being formed becomes daunting. The ever-changing character of the rivers has created gravel covered terraces, remnants of former flood plains, along the Thames, Medway, Darenth and Stour, each one corresponding to a different up and down phase. Underneath the Thames, deep down, are the buried courses of earlier Thames flood plains and valleys. All of this, in a miniature way, is true of the Westbrook valley.

For us here in North Kent, it gets worse. Not only does the melting ice change sea level, alter the behaviours of the rivers and deposit all kinds of different superficial deposits, but the simple removal of the colossal weight of the ice from the land has profound (though delayed) effects. Continental land masses are floating in a 'sea' of semi molten material below the crust. The landmass covered with a burden of thick ice is weighed down and nearby land that is not under the ice consequently rises up, in a see-saw effect. When the ice goes away, the depressed land rises in recovery. Meanwhile the land just beyond the ice – Kent, in other words – subsides to compensate. This tilting is a process known as isostasy.

In places like Scotland and Scandinavia, the land is bouncing up at, geologically, a very speedy rate. Around the coasts of North Europe are raised beaches and cliffs, now well beyond the reach of waves. Around the shores of the southern North Sea, however, we have lands that were just beyond the reach of the ice sheets and these are currently sinking and drowning. North Kent is one of these southern zones and is subsiding, it has been calculated, at a rate of 2.1 mm a year (Aldiss *et al.* 2009, fig. 4 map). If – and this is a big 'if'– this rate has been the same since Roman times, the land has sunk down by around 4 m, or in other words *relative* sea level has risen by 4 m. So, quite apart from the *absolute* rises in sea level due to more liquid water in the sea, in North Kent (and Romney Marsh, northern Germany and the Low Countries) there are ongoing rises in relative sea level as well due to isostatic subsidence (see Fig. 3.1).

Now we can see the reason for the flood-protection bund on Faversham Creek, and also the Thames Barrage, the Delta project in the Netherlands and other forward planning actions being currently taken by Government agencies. We can also see that the term 'British Isles' is misleading from a prehistoric point of view. Over the last million years, there have been many millennia during the cold times when 'Britain' was just a bump in the north-western corner of continental Europe. There have also been many warmer times when this corner of the continent was cut off, as it is now. During the last great Ice Age, Britain was just a corner of the land mass: neither the Channel nor the North Sea existed as water areas. About 9000 years ago (7500 BC), the melt waters gathering in the North Sea basin broke through southwards to the Atlantic once again and Britain reverted to island status.

When did the Faversham area become near to the coast again? When did the lower Westbrook valley become flooded by the ever rising sea, with the head of the tide moving inwards every year? That will be a major theme in Chapter 3 when looking at evidence for early settlement, but the Westbrook and other nearby rivers do deserve a little more attention.

The Ice Ages and the rivers in the Faversham area

Almost no work has been done studying the Westbrook in its own right. The long term use of it for mills has modified the character of the water way in many ways, with artificial ponds, straightened watercourses, and mill races. Reconstructing the lower parts of the original stream is made even more difficult by the large-scale removal of brickearth and gravel. The 'head of the tide' is nowadays an artificial construct and the Creek itself has had its course much altered to improve navigation. The Westbrook's upper and middle parts do, however, seem to be more straightforward, with classic accumulations of gravels in the floor of the valley and brickearth on the slopes and there is no reason to think that it changed its basic course by much over the whole of the Ice Age period.

Beyond its former source springs, the Westbrook valley winds up into the chalk Downs as a dry valley. These dry valleys, common in the Faversham area, are puzzling: how can a valley form when the porosity of the rock means that there can be no surface running water? Again, the reasons are thought to go back to the severe glacial conditions that came and went. During times of permafrost, the chalk was in effect no longer porous. The summer melt of the top layer and the rush down slope of melt waters and debris carved out these winding valleys. Once the chalk warmed up it became its old porous self. Any surface water soaked straight in except in unusually rainy times when temporary surface streams, known as nailbournes, flow briefly.

In the lower part of the Westbrook, however, seeing whether it originally flowed to the west of the Davington Plateau to Oare Creek or to the east of the Davington Plateau to Faversham Creek is difficult. The route to the west is where the gravels and brickearth are (or used to be) in abundance: perhaps at one stage the Westbrook joined a melt stream coming down the Syndale valley (where there is also plenty of gravel and brickearth) and between them they dropped this load of stones. The fact is that there are buried channels under the stony deposits, carved out when the sea level was much lower and later filled in, just as is the case with the larger rivers. It does seem, though, that by early medieval times, the lower Westbrook was flowing in its present valley, between the Davington Plateau and the town: greater understanding awaits further research.

In 2000 Tim Allen, a Whitstable archaeologist, advanced a carefully supported theory that up until around 6000 years ago, Sheppey was fully joined to the mainland at the western end of what is now the Swale (Allen 2000). The Swale was a small river flowing eastwards then north-east to join the Thames. As this was the Mesolithic period (see Chapter 3), sea level was still relatively low and the coast was, Allen estimates, around 50 km away. The river bed of this proto-Swale river and its tributaries (one of which is the Westbrook) were cut down to lower levels than they are nowadays.

As the ice melted and the land tilted, sea level rose and flooded the Swale more and more, creating firstly an estuary and eventually breaking through to link up with the Medway. At the same time, the lower Westbrook valley was flooded and become gradually tidal. This theory is supported by others who argue that the Swale was not a through route until after the Roman period when there were some quite severe transgressions (invasions) by the sea (Lawson and Killingray 2004, 5). The changes of these historic times must await the next chapters, and are clearly going to be very important in understanding Faversham's history.

Changes in flora and fauna in the Faversham area

Some of the evidence for Ice Age ecosystems in North Kent is easy to find. As long ago as 1754, Edward Jacob, the Faversham historian and naturalist, reported on the finding of fossil elephant bones from superficial deposits at Leysdown on the Isle of Sheppey (Hasted 1798, 263). Swalecliffe Cliffs have been very productive of animal bones dated to Middle to Late Palaeolithic (Holmes 1981, 86–7). In the Faversham area where superficial deposits are nearly all dated to the Late Palaeolithic the animal bone evidence is from this later period. Many enthusiasts collected these bones keenly in the late nineteenth century to early twentieth century along with shell and insect fossils, and they can be seen on display in the local museums such as the Fleur de Lis Heritage Centre in Faversham.

Finding out about the past vegetation, however, is more challenging. Over the last 30 years, great advances have been made in the collection and analysis of ancient pollens, seeds and plant fibres. The Middle Palaeolithic site at Ebbsfleet, Kent, was discovered and excavated in 2004 and for nine years, the finds were analysed in their entirety – plant and animal remains, flint tools – to give a sophisticated reconstruction of a site not far away from Faversham. The Ebbsfleet account is, however a rare example and nothing like that has yet been done in the immediate Faversham area: the following account is based on reported animal bone finds from the immediate area and otherwise on extension from findings elsewhere in North Kent like Ebbsfleet and nearby Swanscombe.

The Faversham area experienced constant change in its flora and fauna during the Ice Ages. The different vegetation zones, each adapted to a particular climate, would shift towards and away from the polar and high mountain ice cap regions as temperatures waxed and waned. Although Kent was never actually ice covered, at times it was so close to the Ice Sheet front that it would have been a lifeless, stony wasteland, only thawing on the surface during the short summer. Some think that at peak cold times, the very highest parts of the North Downs would have had permanent snow caps.

As the climate warmed up after an intensely cold climax, low growing plants would have been able to survive, flowering swiftly in the brief summer period. As the climate warmed further, trees would have returned, with first of all coniferous trees, dwarf willow, birch and rowan colonising the thawed landscape. During the warmest times, deciduous trees like oak or beech would have established themselves, with oak preferring the wetter clay soils and beech the drier chalky soils. Ash, elm, black poplar, hazel would have been part of this mature forest.

At all times, even the colder ones, there would have been a lot of marshy land, with wandering multi-channel rivers and shallow lagoons. We are so accustomed to tamed landscapes, controlled rivers and sea walls, that we can forget how in a rainy climate like ours, swampy landscapes are commonplace. In the warmer times, willow and alder woodland would flourish in the marshy areas with sedge, rushes and reeds around the water's edge. You will have noticed that the plant species are very similar to those we have today. The native plants are flowering, seed producing species which support an ecosystem with plenty of insects and bird life as well as the larger animal species. 500,000 years ago for the Hoxnian Interglacial is not long at all in the world of plants.

The situation with the animal population during the Ice Ages is different. Although there are many familiar species around, such as wolves, shrews, European beavers, hares, wild horses, red deer, bears, lynx and at colder times reindeer and musk ox, there were also animals living in the Faversham area that you would certainly not see on any country walks nowadays. The most striking of these is the Woolly Mammoth, whose teeth and tusks have been found in the Late Palaeolithic gravels at Oare. This was not the only elephant species around here – in the Middle Palaeolithic, the straight tusked elephant was common, though it became extinct as the last great Ice Age set in. Other large mammals whose remains have been found locally include the Woolly Rhinoceros; giant deer with vast antlers; hippopotami, some species very large; spotted Hyenas; aurochs (giant cattle). Locally we have not had evidence for sabre-toothed cats or the cave bears of Kent's Cavern, Torquay, all of which are too early in the Palaeolithic for our deposits (Holmes 1981, 89–91).

The coming of humans

So far this has been about the Pleistocene, going back 1.5 million years as if it were no time at all. Indeed, in geological terms, with an Earth now reckoned to be about 4.5 billion years old, it is a mere moment. From the point of view of our own species, *Homo sapiens* ('Wise Man'), however, a million years is a very long time indeed. *Homo sapiens* have only been around in Europe for around 40,000 years. Putting us in our place even more is the current estimate that the species of *Homo sapiens* has only been around for about 200,000 years. This is not the place to go through current theories of human evolution – there are many splendid books and websites on the topic – but it is important to remember that until around 14,000 years ago, the evidence we find for human activity in the Faversham area does not imply humans like us.

Plate 3 shows a photograph of evidence for the earliest known human activity in the Faversham area. The small pointed flint hand axe was found in 2011 in a

Years ago	Temperature	Name given to period	Hominids in Britain
10,000–present	Rapid warming	Flandrian ongoing interglacial	Mesolithic onwards
50,000–10,000	VERY COLD	Devensian glaciation	No hominids for most of period. *Homo Sapiens* from 40,000 years ago
100,000–50,000	Warm forested	Ipswichian interglacial	Neanderthals towards the end, but otherwise no hominids
	VERY COLD		NO-ONE
	Warmer		Levalloisian industry
360,000–100,000	VERY COLD	Wolstonian glaciation, has warmer periods	NO-ONE
	Warmer		Levalloisian industry
	VERY COLD		NO-ONE
400,000–360,000	Warm forested	Hoxnian interglacial	Acheulian and Clactonian industries. Swanscombe man (*Homo Heidelbergensis*)
450,000–400,000	COLDEST	Anglian glaciation	NO-ONE

TABLE 2.1: A climate timeline for the last 400,000 years in Britain

hundred year old garden at the top of the valley side in Ospringe. It lay around 40 cm down underneath a layer containing numerous late Bronze Age tools. The top 20 cm layer had obviously been dug over a lot, but the layer in which the hand axe was found was undisturbed brickearth (FGW, KP83).

Trying to date this hand axe illustrates only too well the difficulties. To date an artefact, archaeologists often rely on recognising its distinctive shape as similar to one of known age. This is more reliable when there is a group of artefacts – an assemblage – found in association in an undisturbed context. But for the comparison to work, the 'type' artefact must have been dated scientifically. Traditionally this is done by dating the layer in which it has been found using modern methods such as readiocarbon dating or thermoluminescence. Yet hand axes like this were made, it is thought, for at least 400,000 years (Wenban Smith 2007; Emery 2010, 37 for Wymer's classification). It is extremely difficult to date the deposits in which they are found – many of the modern methods cannot work so far back and anyway, the artefacts are found in or under superficial deposits which are fragmentary and varied and difficult even for experts to analyse. Moreover, they have often been re-deposited in the superficial deposits which are much younger than the actual worked flints.

There is some help from logic. Between about 150,000 and 60,000 years ago, no evidence exists for hominids living in these islands. This was not because it was too cold: much of this period was pleasantly warm, with rich wild life such as horses, rhinos, elephants and macaque monkeys. This particular interglacial period began with a very abrupt ending to a severe Ice Age. A rapid warm up followed and this corner of Europe swiftly became cut off by the sea. Hominids, who had left the area when it was too cold, simply did not get around to returning: after all, there was plenty of room on the mainland (Sutcliffe 1995). So, logically, our hand axe did not come from that time. Furthermore, it is not like the flint axes of those who did come back around 60,000 years ago. So, we have 400,000–250,000 years ago as the most likely date range (unless of course this is the one theory-smashing piece of evidence for hominids in Britain in that warm interglacial ... such is the problem of circularity in archaeological arguments).

The tip of the axe was broken off in antiquity, so this is probably why it was abandoned, but what was this person like who threw away his/her hand axe on the top of the hill in Ospringe? To answer this, we have to look outside the Faversham area but not far: the river terrace gravels of Swanscombe, Kent, have produced not only huge numbers of hand axes and other stone tools similar to our little hand axe but also an incredibly rare find, part of a hominid skull.

The thickness of the Swanscombe skull, its small brain capacity compared with modern man and the thickness of his/her eyebrow ridges are clues to the fact that this is not a skull of *Homo sapiens*. This is probably a remote ancestor of ours. What is fascinating though is he/she is probably also an ancestor of another kind of human being, the Neanderthals, named after the Neander Valley in Germany where bones of this type of human were first recognised. Neanderthals reached their peak, it is thought, much later on and we will return to them below. The 250,000 year old Swanscombe cranium is from a type of human named *Homo heidelbergensis* by the specialists, after the first find spot for this kind of human remain: it is this kind of human who probably made and/or used this little hand axe (Wenban Smith 2007, 50–1).

Hand axe usage lasted for a long time but towards the end of that period, just before this area became empty of humans for 130,000 years, a different kind of stone tool making culture developed. The lower flint hand axe in Plate 3a was found in a field near Shottenden. Rather than being made from a shaped nodule of flint, this one is made from a thick flake, removed from a specifically shaped core. This flake axe, of a type known as Levalloisian, would date from that 250,000 years ago stage, just before the severe Ice Age that would drive the humans away for millennia. A similar unifacial hand axe based on a large flake was found in a Middle Iron Age ditch during an excavation following the route of the Ashford to Canterbury Road water pipeline behind Macknades in 2007 (Allen 2007, 11).

Now let us jump that uninhabited-by-man interglacial gap and come to the time when the next and most recent major advance of the ice was beginning to happen, though with many comings and goings on the way. This takes us through to around 60,000 years ago. This is the time of the Neanderthals, people like us in many ways, though with larger brains, heavier brow ridges and stockier bodies. We are still, however, in what is defined as the 'Middle

Palaeolithic' or Middle Old Stone Age: that which is defined as the 'Upper Palaeolithic' does not begin until the arrival in Britain of Homo Sapiens, our direct ancestor.

There are two pieces of incontrovertible evidence for Neanderthal presence in the Faversham area, two *bout coupé* hand axes. One was found near Brenley Corner (KCC HER, TR 05 NW216) and the other more recently in a Luddenham field. *Bout coupé* hand axes are a distinctive type, bifacial-worked in the shape of a rounded triangle (Pl.3b, centre). They are only found in Britain in a brief warmer period between 60,000 and 40,000 years ago, and are therefore considered a unique diagnostic variant of this period. By around 35,000 years ago, however, Neanderthals had disappeared not just from Kent but from the world. What became of them, why they became extinct is not known though there are many theories (Stringer 2007).

Homo sapiens, humans like us, first make an appearance in this part of the world around 30,000 years ago in the period just before the peak of the last Ice Age. From Oare we have a couple of flints of characteristic Upper Palaeolithic shape (Wenban Smith 2007, 71). A fine crested blade was found in an allotment at Stonebridge ponds: crested blades were large distinctively shaped pieces created in the process of making of axes and were often trimmed for use themselves (Butler 2005, 72). There have been, however, no cave paintings or exquisite leaf shaped blades yet discovered around here: at that time, even during a short warmer period around 13,000 years ago, people had only just started moving away from south-west France and northern Spain where they had, very wisely, spent the coldest period. Upper Palaeolithic evidence from anywhere in Britain is scanty and speaks only of wandering hunting groups. Then, around 12,000 years ago came that sudden relapse into very cold conditions, which put off even those bold hunting nomads. This corner of Europe became empty again for 1500 years until it thawed out and then re-settlement started with a vengeance and has continued to this day.

Let us try and see what it might have been like in the Faversham area as the last Ice Age weakened, around 13,000 years ago. For the first time ever, we have a vivid idea as to what the animals looked like, for this is the time of the great cave paintings of south-west France and northern Spain. The drawings at Rouffignac, in the Dordogne, dated to around 15,000 years ago, portray 138 mammoths, for example, and in the caves of nearby Lascaux and Altamira in Spain are pictures of bulls, bison, giant deer and horses. At that time sea level was still much lower than it is nowadays and where the North Sea now lies was a vast plain. The Westbrook, already established in its course, would have cut much deeper down into the land – we are looking at a scene whose evidence lies buried amongst the deposits that backfilled the Westbrook valley as sea levels rose.

Our scene is down on the gravels of this little flood plain where the prehistoric Westbrook leaves the steep sided valley between the Davington Plateau and the chalk headland opposite (where the *Bull* pub is now). Here the stream has made a little flood plain and wanders around. Coniferous forest clothes the slopes behind and by the stream are willow and reeds. The permafrost has gone but winters are still cold and snowy.

By the stream is a clearing and our woolly mammoth is taking a drink. This is a bull mammoth, a gigantic animal 5 m tall at the shoulder and weighing around 10 tons. For all his intimidating size, he is a vegetarian, as is a woolly rhinoceros sharing the drinking spot. From a branch above, a young lynx is watching, its tail twitching: it is not large enough to tackle these animals. In the woodland behind, which is broken by clearings created by the grazing mammoths and rhinos, are red deer and here and there the huge antlers of a giant deer catch the light of the setting sun. The birdsong is familiar – robins settling down for the night – but as twilight comes a large shadow flits across: a giant tawny owl is on the prowl. Hidden further up the narrower part of valley, watching all this along with us are some very familiar small creatures with wooden, flint tipped spears ....

This may seem too fanciful – how can such huge animals have existed around here such a relatively short time ago and yet have utterly disappeared except for their bones? We have now come onto one of the most controversial and fascinating events from the unrecorded past – what is known to many as the 'Fifth extinction'. This was the extinction of the megafauna (huge animals) at the end of the Ice Age period, when, after the relapse, the world really started to warm up.

The extinction at first thought seems like a simple case of the effects of extreme climate change: the big beasts simply could not cope with the new conditions, for example a much higher density of forest and a rapidly advancing coastline. This is, however, complicated by the fact that the same phenomenon took place all over the world (except in Africa where megafauna survived, albeit not in 'woolly' form). In North and South America, not only the mammoth disappeared but also the giant armadillo and giant sloth. Yet the changes in climate are not the same or at the same rate in all of these places. Which brings us to the other major change in the world's ecosystem – the arrival in increasing numbers on the scene of *Homo sapiens*, our immediate ancestors with all of their cunning and clever ways.

There are endless arguments over what really happened and why (Todd and Erlandson 2013, for example). It seems possible that mammoths were hunted to extinction. We have mammoth killing sites from many places, and butchery marks on the bones. Hide, meat, bone and ivory would have been important. Human subsistence hunting seems less likely, however, as a reason for the extinction of giant sloths and armadillos in the Americas. Nowadays, many scientists go for a mixture of factors – rapidly changing ecosystems and man intervening in these changes in complex ways: the extinction of the mammoth by being hunted beyond its capacity to replace itself may have then affected the environment in unintentional ways such as vegetation levels no longer being kept down.

Final comment

Whatever the reasons for the extinction of the megafauna, we will leave our hunters in the Westbrook valley to choose their evening meal. We know that in a short time, the ice will come back and that after another short while the Ice Ages will be over (for now) and the age of the European megafauna with it. From then on, *Homo sapiens* will be in charge, building bunds against the encroaching sea.

CHAPTER THREE

The people of the great warm-up: 8000–55 BC

....

Introduction

In Chapter 2 we raced through a period of 600,000 years. The time span in this chapter is nowhere near so grand but still lengthy: we will travel through 8000 years of the human story in the Faversham area, journeying from the end of the last Ice Age through to the day when people on the cliffs of Dover saw the first Roman invaders approaching across the sea.

This period is prehistory – 'pre' because the story is based not on written material as with 'history' but on the material clues that people left in the landscape, their burials, forts, houses, their possessions and creations, the different layers in the ground that built up as activities stopped, started, changed. Sometimes the changes are not man made but natural – invasion by the sea creating new estuaries and islands and depositing mud, or retreat of the sea with a build-up of freshwater marsh. This is the province of archaeology.

Until the early nineteenth century and the great breakthrough in thinking that came about from geological observations, many people thought that the world had existed only for 4004 years, a figure arrived at by Archbishop Ussher in 1650. The Archbishop arrived at this figure from calculations on listed generation spans in the Bible. The antiquities in the landscape – the Pyramids, ancient Rome, Stonehenge – belonged within this time scale, with evidence for the devastation of the Great Flood to be found all around. Even the young Charles Darwin, during his seminal 5-year voyage in HMS *Beagle* starting in 1831, ponders the effects of the Deluge as he records the skeletons of extinct giant armadillos and sloths in the strata of far Patagonia (Darwin 1845, 165–6).

The growth of archaeological activity and increase in findings in Faversham in the later twentieth and early twenty-first centuries was described towards the end of Chapter 1. We all know how fascinating it is to discover and touch objects used and cherished by people who are long gone but before we move onto the findings of archaeologists about Faversham's early history, some words of caution are essential.

The axiom 'Absence of evidence is not necessarily evidence of absence' is drummed into every novice archaeologist and its truth is particularly well demonstrated here in Faversham. As mentioned in Chapter 1, until recently the evidence for prehistoric activity in this area was so scanty that it was assumed that people simply did not live around here in prehistoric times. Now we have from FSARG's work alone more than 1000 flint tools, 44 kg of heat stressed flints and 60 kg of struck flints including many cores. We also have 4.5 kg of prehistoric pottery. These flints and pot sherds date from different times in prehistory and everything has a provenance, i.e., we know exactly where every item was found and with what it was found: soon in this chapter some significant concentrations and scatters of prehistoric finds will be described and discussed. Nevertheless, even including investigations carried out by commercial archaeologists on development sites, only a tiny percentage of the local area has been investigated, though growing all the time. Who knows what remains to be found?

Further problems arise from burying on the one hand and destruction on the other. In the oldest parts of Faversham, such as Tanners Street and Lower West Street, the dumping of waste in the gardens has been going on for so long that the prehistoric layers are as much as 2.5 m down. Then there is destruction – archaeology swept away by the sea or rivers, and artefacts of organic material like textiles, leather and wooden objects decaying in the ground until nothing is left except maybe a stain in the soil. We must also accept that large tracts of land around Faversham have been 'dug off' by extractive industries with evidence for past activity lost forever.

Thirdly, there is the problem of interpretation. There are big arguments, for example, about the bronze hoards (large collections of bronze artefacts, ingots, broken items) found buried in the countryside – a famous one found at Harty will be described later in this chapter. Some archaeologists explain these burials as security precautions – hiding your trade goods whilst you go into town and through misfortune not returning for your secret stockpile. Other archaeologists, however, see the hoards as religious offerings. Without a time-machine and a translator, it is near impossible to know which is the right explanation – maybe both? Similar arguments go on in relation to all sorts of archaeological features and finds.

Then there is the practical problem of the treasure hunters, the descendants of the mud-larks who supplied the antiquarians in London in the eighteenth and nineteenth centuries. Many metal detectorists are very conscientious people who report their finds diligently to the Lottery-sponsored Portable Antiquities Scheme (PAS) and sometimes very interesting discoveries come from a detector's initial find. Near Faversham, for example, a large previously unknown Roman villa was discovered in 2004 because a detectorist finding a small Roman coin hoard reported it to the PAS Liaison Officer: archaeologists went in and uncovered a hypocaust system straight away (see Chapter 4). Detectorists are, however, by their nature highly selective in what they collect – they inevitably leave behind a field that has been picked over and no longer yields a truly representative assemblage of evidence for past activities.

Finally, there is an ongoing problem of archaeologists not taking flint tools seriously, especially in Kent where flint is such a commonly occurring natural item. Because the man-altered flint has been in the ground for so long – hundreds of thousands of years for the early hand axes – they have, in the opinion of busy archaeologists, lost touch with their original context and are therefore of little use in interpreting the past. It is surprising how often an assemblage from, say, a Roman villa site, has a collection of worked flint which is not described and discussed in the published account. Only where worked flints occur in a deposit otherwise mostly lacking in flint (e.g. brickearth) and relate to what is an ancient living surface do they attract full attention.

Despite all these cautions, it is remarkable what can be found when you start looking: prehistoric Faversham is becoming inhabited.

Faversham in the Mesolithic (Middle Stone Age)

The story begins 11,000 years ago, around 9000 BC. The most recent Ice Age was just finishing, as discussed in Chapter 2.

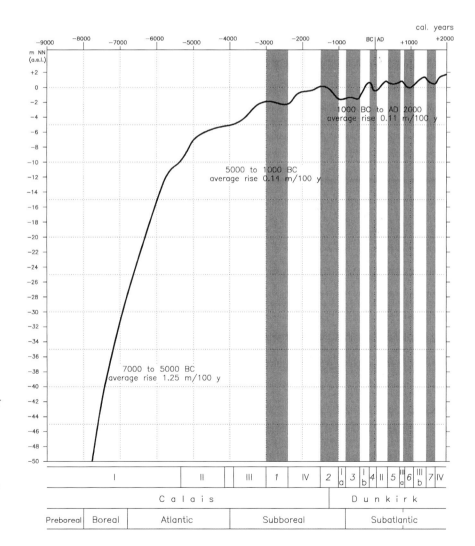

FIGURE 3.1. Sea level change in the southern North Sea, as charted by Karl-Ernst Behre (2007, fig. 7). This shows not only the phenomenal rise in the earlier post-glacial times but also the fluctuations in more modern times

During the Ice Age sea levels had been much lower and rapidly melting ice caused a swift and spectacular rise in sea level. Figure 3.1 shows the rise in sea levels in the southern North Sea over the last 10,000 years. This graph was constructed from data coming from around the southern North Sea, based on charting alternating layers of peaty deposits and muddy marine deposits in coastal areas, such as the Thames estuary. In Chapter 2 we heard that in 8000 BC (10,000 years ago), dry land stretched from what is now Britain across to Eurasia: the Baltic Sea was a lake (Coles 1998; Gaffney *et al.* 2009). The name 'Doggerland' is given to the dry North Sea basin, after the Dogger Bank which is a particularly shallow part of the present sea. For some time, fishermen in the Dogger Bank area have brought the remains of vegetation and evidence for human occupation up from the sea bed in their trawls. As sea level rose, the Dogger Bank became an island, around 7200 BC, and around the same time the waters broke through to re-form the Channel connection to the Atlantic. Around 5000 BC, the sea finally overwhelmed the Dogger Bank island. To keep a sense of proportion for these dates, by 7000 BC agriculture, towns and temples already existed in the Middle East (Pollock 2004).

The rapid warming meant that the vegetation cover and wild life changed rapidly. In 8000 BC Kent would have been a frozen tundra wasteland with migratory reindeer in the short summer. As the temperature rose, dense forests of conifers replaced the tundra then mixed woodland with extensive marshes near the ever-encroaching sea. There would have been abundant wild life – deer, bear, and beaver, and wolf, wild cattle such as aurochs, lynx, and otter. The seas and rivers would have been full of fish, with shellfish in the shallower waters. Of course, humans would be attracted back to such a rich environment – the Great Wild Wood – for hunting, fishing, and gathering food.

At the height of the last Ice Age, European humans had withdrawn to three main south European areas to survive. Because there is a distinct difference even today between the DNA format of people in eastern and western Britain, some geneticists argue that this corner of the continent was re-occupied from two very different directions (Oppenheimer 2006). Some groups worked their way up the coast of Europe from the south-west France–north Spain redoubt (the home of the cave paintings of Lascaux and Altamira) and ended up settling the west coast of future Britain. Another wave of migrants came in from the east, working their way up the Rhine Valley and colonising across the North Sea Basin: as the sea levels rose, some of their descendants ended up in eastern Britain. It has even been suggested by Oppenheimer that the languages spoken on either side of what eventually became the British Isles, were different from the outset, with Celtic ancestor languages on the west coast and a form of ancestral German on the east side. This is another one of those arguments that is difficult to judge, but what is certain is that some of those early migrants found a home in what is now Faversham.

In the broadest terms, of the 113 small scale 'keyhole' excavations carried out by FSARG between 2005 and 2015, 83 produced at least one Mesolithic finished flint tool. The excavations took place in Ospringe, Faversham, Preston and Davington. The Davington Plateau produced by far the most Mesolithic flints. At the time of writing, there are 479 finished flint tools or cores dated to the Mesolithic in the FSARG Lithics Database, along with a great many waste struck flakes and heat stressed flints (Pl. 4a). Alongside the findings of FSARG, commercial investigations at Abbey Fields (Allen and Scott 2000) and a voluntary research excavation in Perry Woods in 1965 (Woodcock 1975) shed additional light on the Faversham area in the Mesolithic.

The Mesolithic people were skilful flint workers. Throughout the whole Mesolithic period, their flint work remains elegant and streamlined, with elongated blades, dainty scrapers for cleaning hides, micro-burins to bore holes in wood, leather, and bone. Larger core-based tools known as tranchet adzes were used to work wood. In the earlier part of the period, 8000–6000 BC, an important flint product was a very small and thin section of a blade known as a microlith. Rows of these would have been mounted into wooden or bone bases to produce a harpoon or a saw (Pl. 4b).

Microliths are so small that only very careful archaeological methods find them. With the FSARG pits, those richest in microliths were on the Davington Plateau such at Ravenscourt and the Lawn high on Brent Hill. Keyhole 87 at Ravenscourt also yielded six other Mesolithic flint tools, four of them from the same context. This same context also yielded the greatest quantity of struck flakes and heat stressed flint for K87 (FGW, Brent Hill report).

A. J. Woodcock, writing about discoveries in Perry Woods in 1964, gives a careful description of a large quantity of Mesolithic flints gathered from two sites near Shottenden Camp (Woodcock 1975, 169–77). One site was excavated in 6 inch (15 cm) spits and at the other, surface finds were picked up. He comments on the fresh and sharp condition of the flint tools, their colour being a pale grey and mostly without any cortex (skin) left on the flint. So far, this is very much like the Mesolithic flints found by FSARG in Davington, Preston and Ospringe. Some of the types of tool he describes are very like the ones from Davington, such as micro-burins and retouched blades.

Nevertheless, the types of microlith are not the same. Up in Perry Wood, the microliths were rod-like whereas from Davington there were no rods, rather a complex of retouched forms ranging from a trapezoidal shape to a triangular one. Furthermore, 15 of the FSARG excavations produced at least one small artefact of a type called a Horsham point. In the Davington area, eight tranchet adzes, the wood working tool typical of the later Mesolithic, have been found. The Perry Wood assemblage has no Horsham points and only a few dubious adze fragments.

Woodcock dates his Perry Woods assemblage provisionally to around 6500 BC, in the Middle Mesolithic period. For Davington, presence of signifiers such as Horsham points and tranchet adzes points to links with what Jacobi has called the Wealden culture, a Middle Mesolithic culture beginning to go its own way after the Channel breakthrough (Gibbard 2007). This gives a provisional date for the Davington Plateau finds as around 5000 BC, running through perhaps to the Late Mesolithic when the sea level rise had begun to ease off and the coast was much closer.

Down by Clapgate spring (Pl. 4d) in these Late Mesolithic times, around 5000–4000 BC, there were yet more people around. During September 2000, an archaeological evaluation was undertaken by the Canterbury Archaeological Trust (CAT) on the site of a proposed housing development between Graveney Road and Abbey Fields, about 1 km north-east of Faversham. The site lay either side of the main London to Ramsgate railway line. Fifty-four trenches were excavated in Area 2 to the north where Clapgate spring is situated. The work revealed rare and regionally important evidence for Late Mesolithic activity and later periods to which we will return in this chapter.

Near Clapgate spring was found a highly concentrated pattern of flint discard together with flint debitage (waste pieces from flint working), re-worked tools, blades (some re-touched) and numerous finished scrapers. The extremely fresh condition of most of the assemblage, along with the presence of multiple re-fits, suggests that this was an occupation site on which intensive or protracted flint tool production took place. The finds lay upon an ancient land surface, nowadays 0.3 m down, and covered by washed-in brickearth (Allen and Scott 2000).

Chris Butler, an expert on the British Mesolithic, reminds us in his invaluable book *Prehistoric Flintwork* (2005) how difficult it is to reconstruct the lifestyles of people living so far back in time when the clues are so scanty. According to Butler, however, logic says that where you have an assemblage with tranchet adzes, picks and a wide variety of flake and blade tools, this is more likely to be a base camp for these semi-nomadic people. Where the assemblage is more microliths with bladelet cores, micro-burins, and lots of improvised tools such as roughly made thumbnail scrapers, then this is more likely to be a short stay hunting camp (Butler 2005, 114–16). Using this argument, the Perry Wood collection looks like a short stay camp (though often returned to) whereas the Davington Plateau and Clapgate look more like base camps. The fact that the Perry Woods site is much further from a good water supply than Davington and the Clapgate site could well be significant.

What is true of all our Mesolithic sites, including the ones in Preston and Ospringe is that they were found on light soils, Head Brickearth for the Preston/Ospringe/Clapgate ones and Head Gravel and patchy brickearth deposits for the Davington Plateau. A similar close link between superficial deposits and prehistoric settlement is commented on in the Abbey Fields/Clapgate Spring report. The Perry Woods report is not so specific about the soil types of the two sites but does say that this is a Thanet Beds area 'infilled with brickearth'. These hunters and gatherers do seem to prefer the light soils near to the spring line with easy access to nearby flinty areas uphill. The high and dry chalk downs with their sticky clay-with-flints overlay and the London clay, even stickier and not even with any flints apart from pebbles seem much less attractive except for hunting expeditions.

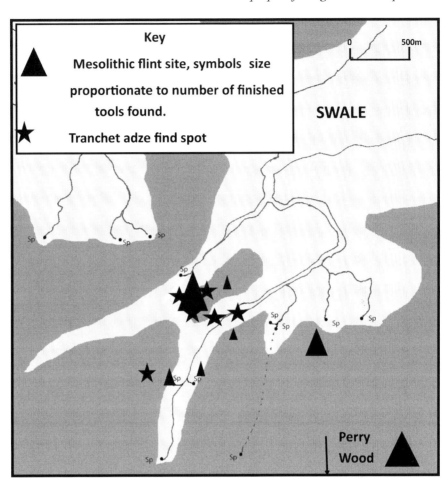

Key

Mesolithic flint site, symbols size

proportionate to number of finished

tools found.

Tranchet adze find spot

SWALE

0   500m

Perry
Wood

FIGURE 3.2. Known
Mesolithic sites in the
Faversham area

Underlying these observations, however, we must never forget that Mesolithic times, even after huge inroads of the sea, had more dry land than now. In the only Creekside borehole that we have in central Faversham, the Pumping Station shaft drilled in 1965 (Philp 2003), there is a peat layer lying on flints and gravel at a depth of 3.35 m below present OD sea level. Who knows what lies under the alluvium of the marshes and the Swale, down on the buried banks of that ancient river, flowing quietly down through its wooded valley 8000 years ago to join the ancestral Thames many miles away?

The arrival of farming: the Neolithic (New Stone Age)

The Neolithic, running from around 4000 BC to 2200 BC in south-east Britain, is the era of the building of some of the most glamorous and enigmatic prehistoric monuments in Britain. This is the time of the original setting up of Stonehenge, of building great passage graves, long barrows, and avenues of stone, orientated to solar events. It is a time of courtyards where corpses lay for discarnation (rotting away of flesh), for creation of clay statuettes of women, decorated handmade pottery and beautiful highly polished hand axes, often made of stone from distant places.

The earliest known organised production of food and other useful materials through domestication of animals and plants dates from the Middle East in around 9000 BC. Knowledge of farming spread across Europe from the Middle East, with changes from hunting and gathering taking place first in what is now Greece around 7000 BC but taking another two and a half thousand years to reach Northern Europe. The earliest farming known in Britain took place around 4000 BC. Whether the ideas about farming were brought to this country by migrants from the continental mainland or whether the ideas were picked up by travelling traders and fishermen who brought the new notions back home and converted their neighbours is another one of those ongoing arguments. What is certain is that nearly all the types of domestic animals and plants used in Britain by those earliest farmers were not native European in origin but lived their wild existence in the Middle East. The exception is the pig, descended in modern northern Europe from native wild boar. Even with pigs, however, a southern European type was found at the beginning of the northern Neolithic, although soon to be displaced by the domestication of heftier local wild pigs (Caliebe *et al.* 2017).

What was happening in the Faversham area at that time? Until recently the answer would be, we don't know. Except for a few 'stray finds' handed in by keen eyed locals to the former Sites and Monuments Register, nothing seemed to be known. In fact, this was true for most of Kent which, it seemed, had mostly been by passed by the new ways of life. Apart from the famous megaliths of the Medway Valley and the earth barrows of the Stour valley (Ashbee 2005, 101–12) there seemed to be very little of significance – no henges, long barrows, pottery, and flint assemblages. Most seriously, there were no known causewayed enclosures in the Faversham area.

The first farmers built causewayed enclosures. On hill tops, structures were created that are as enigmatic to us as are henges and cursuses. They consist of large concentric circles, each made up of short lengths of ditches with causeways in between them. The ditches were U-shaped or V-shaped in cross-section. When excavated, the ditches often contain pottery and lots of animal bones, mostly cattle. Quite how these enclosures were used is unknown. The best-known is Windmill Hill in Wiltshire near Avebury, after which a whole Neolithic culture was originally named (Oswald 2011).

Until recently, no causewayed enclosures were known in Kent. Now, however, we have four that have been at least partially excavated and are not far from Faversham. Two separate ones were discovered in 1998 and 2004 on the Isle of Sheppey during a building programme at Kingsborough Manor. These enclosures were at the highest point of the Isle of Sheppey, with uninterrupted views across the Swale to where Faversham now stands (KCC HER, TQ97 SE52). Another was excavated in Ramsgate in 1997–8 (KCC HER, TR36 SE24) and the most recently uncovered was at Burham, investigated in 2012 as part of the Medway 'Valley of Visions' Project (KCC HER, TQ76 SW389).

It has been argued that the enclosures on Sheppey and Thanet represent bridgeheads, where the new way of life first took hold: whether through immigration of continental farmers or by Mesolithic traders getting new ideas overseas is another of those ongoing archaeological arguments. From these bridgeheads, the theory goes, the new ideas and practice spread from Thanet along the Stour valley and from Sheppey along the Medway valley. Distinct differences are seen between the causewayed camps and associated river valley Neolithic archaeological cultures. This theory also says that for the area in between the two river valleys, the barrier of the forested North Downs was so impenetrable that early farmers avoided it (Hammond 2007, 376–80).

Although classic Neolithic structures have not been found in the Faversham area (yet) there is, however, a fair amount of evidence for the presence of people in this area throughout the Neolithic. With the FSARG keyhole excavations alone, 67% of the pits have yielded at least one Neolithic flint tool, and some, such as several pits on the Davington Plateau, a lot more than one. Arrowheads are particularly subject to changes in fashion over time so these small items are particularly useful for sorting Early Neolithic finds from Late Neolithic ones. There have also been some interesting stray finds, for example of a part of a polished stone gouge found in Green Way, Davington and handed in to Maidstone Museum in 1966. Polished gouges of this type are rare in Britain.

More evidence has been found by other investigations in this area. At Clapgate Spring, Tim Allen found evidence for early Neolithic activity, possibly continuous from the Late Mesolithic (Allen 2000, 6). From the excavation of Faversham Abbey and an adjoining Late Iron Age ditch system in the grounds of the about to be built Queen Elizabeth Grammar School in 1965 (see Chapters 4 and 9) many very characteristic Neolithic stone tools were found. These flints were found boxed in amongst the more conspicuously impressive finds from the Abbey and nearby Roman Villa and are not mentioned in the otherwise excellent 1968 publication on the Abbey and Villa (Philp 1968) so their exact provenance is unknown.

As an overall pattern, it seems that Early Neolithic finds are found more in the lower Westbrook valley, such as at Clapgate, in the QE playing fields and on the Davington Plateau, with the later Neolithic finds being more common in the middle part of the valley, in what is now the Ospringe area. In the garden of the former *Anchor* pub on Ospringe Street, FSARG found a small assemblage of two beautifully made Late Neolithic scrapers, accompanied by eight sherds of Late Neolithic Grooved Ware pottery, four sherds of Impressed Ware and nine flint tempered sherds of Late Neolithic type. In association with these in a gravel covered valley floor context were animal bones that included the bones of red deer and two teeth from aurochs, the huge native oxen who became extinct in this country probably by the end of the Bronze Age. Apparently, our early farmers were having a little hunting trip, camping beside the prehistoric Westbrook (Pl. 4b) (FGW, KP44).

Finally, in 2010 FSARG carried out a detailed georesistivity survey accompanied by highly organised metal-detecting in the Paddock that forms part of the grounds of Davington Priory (FGW, Davington Priory). The Priory shares the high part of the Davington Plateau with the cricket ground and some 1960s' housing. The Davington Plateau has been mentioned several times already in this chapter and it is time to look at it more closely.

Plate 3a shows the geological map of the plateau and Plate 5c the LIDAR map for the area shown by the box on the geological map. LIDAR is a new kind of aerial survey carried out using laser and is extremely good at picking out the bones of the land regardless of any tree or building cover. The correspondence between the two maps is very strong. The Westbrook valley passes to the east of the plateau and at one point the eastern and western sides of the valley approach quite closely. This is the location of the Stonebridge Crossing, either side of which lie keyhole excavations that yielded greater than usual numbers of Neolithic flints.

The Priory Paddock was not excavated although at one point a Neolithic scraper was found on the surface. What is significant, though, is the pattern of resistivity markings found in the north-western corner of the field, shown encircled in Plate 5b. Note that in one case a light ring (drier ground) cuts across the radiating darker line (wetter ground) and is therefore later in construction than the lines. Elsewhere in this pattern, the opposite is true – the dark line cuts the ring feature. This pattern hints at several prehistoric possibilities: much too small for a causewayed camp but possible for a henge bank and ditch with later overlay. What does seem clear is that there is evidence for a very interesting sequence of activities here: investigation awaits another day.

The Early and Middle Bronze Age (*c.* 2200-1200 BC)

So far, the people whose possessions we have found in the Faversham area have been managing without the use of any metals. Flint, found in abundance around here, has been the main material for tools. Although the Neolithic people were adept in the use of other materials such as bone, wood, antler, and presumably smoke-tanned skins for leather, these do not survive in the ground under normal conditions, so it is not surprising that we do not have finds made from these organic materials in the Faversham neighbourhood. Unlike their Mesolithic ancestors, however, Neolithic people had learned skills in making and decorating pottery, such as the Grooved and Impressed ware found in Ospringe, and this gives important clues to their whereabouts 6000 years ago.

Around 2200 BC a new material culture appears in Europe. The name given to these people, the Bell Beaker people, comes from the distinctively shaped and decorated pottery vessels that accompanied them, often in their graves. These are the people thought to have been responsible for introducing the Neolithic people in Britain to the glories of bronze. Copper and tin, the metals that go to make bronze (in the later Bronze Age lead was also added) are not difficult to work. Bronze artefact making does not require great skill or elaborate smelting equipment. The melting points are relatively low and the fluid mixture easy to manage. The trouble with copper and tin, however, is that their ores are not very commonly found and not at all in south-east England with its young sedimentary rocks. So straight away we are into trade routes that move ores and bronze goods around Europe, and the Beaker folk are seen as the pioneers of this continent-wide trade (Larsson and Parker Pearson 2007).

Beaker people had a very distinctive material culture and, unlike the indigenous Neolithic people who buried their dead in collective tombs, they buried their dead individually under round barrows. There is plenty of evidence for Late Bronze Age settlement in the Faversham area, as we shall shortly see, but for this Early Bronze Age period and the following Middle Bronze Age we have very little. In this we are not alone in Kent: the absence of round barrows in the landscape is striking when compared, for example, with distributions of similar features in the chalk down lands of Wiltshire and Sussex.

The problem with spotting prehistoric features such as round barrows (or *tumuli* as they are called on Ordnance Survey maps) in the landscape in Kent is twofold. Except in Thanet and on the open downland towards Dover, the North Downs are nowadays thickly wooded. Seeing what is there from the air has been nearly impossible around Faversham: the arrival of LIDAR techniques is going to be revolutionary in this respect, and the next few years could well see major new discoveries of evidence for prehistoric activity on the hills south of Faversham.

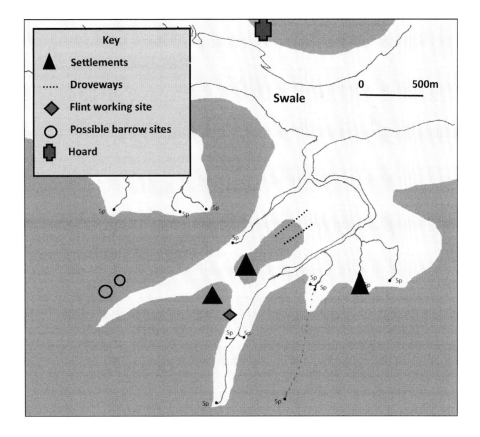

FIGURE 3.3. Late Bronze Age–Early Iron Age sites

Secondly, the lighter soils of the brickearth and other drift deposits along the northern edge of the Downs and up the valleys have been so valuable for farming over the years that barrows on such land have long since been levelled. In many cases the brickearth has been subsequently removed. There is rumour of two barrows being present on the ridge at Beacon Hill, across the valley west from Syndale (KCC HER: TQ96 SE65/66) and historic aerial photographs of the spot hint at a couple of ring ditches. To the west in Norton there are hints at a rectangular enclosure identified on an air photograph, dated on uncertain grounds to the Bronze Age (KCC HER TQ96 SE36). In Ospringe, just south of the church, excavations for the laying of a gas pipeline in 1994 revealed a ditch and a flint working surface dated generally to the Bronze Age (Priestley Bell 1994). Also of interest are a tanged bronze dagger and a halberd said to be from Faversham, now in the Ashmolean Museum, Oxford (Ashbee 2005, 123). These were donated in 1927, but the precise find spot is not known.

Chapter 3: Intermission: Weather forecast

At this point, 7000 years into this chapter's time span and only 3000 years away from our present era, a weather check is needed. When we last looked at what was happening, at the beginning of this chapter, temperatures were increasing rapidly, sea level rising at an almost unimaginably swift rate and huge areas of land being flooded. Have things settled down to become more as they are now?

Yes and no. The sea level rise graph in Figure 3.1 shows that, by 1500 BC, which is where we are, absolute sea level is similar to today. Temperatures are warmer in north-west Europe and rainfall less. Change, however, is on the way. Over the next millennium, temperatures will cool and rainfall increase. Glaciers will increase their length somewhat. The sea level graph shows, in fact, that sea level will drop a little during the last millennium BC. Land that has been under the sea at high tide will now become salt marsh, and the earlier salt marsh become low lying dry land. Inspection of the graph shows this reversal of sea level rise – to use the technical terms, this regression rather than transgression of the sea – has happened several times over the last 2000–3000 years: there is the Medieval Warm Period and the Little Ice Age (see Chapter 10), for instance.

Another factor, though, that must never be forgotten in thinking about sea level (and sea levels are extremely important for places like Faversham on the north Kent coast) is the subtle sinking of this part of Britain called *isostatic subsidence*. The sinking rate nowadays for our area is estimated at 2.1 mm a year, one of the highest in Britain. If that has been the rate for the last 3000 years, taking us back to 1000 BC, the land around Faversham in the Late Bronze Age would have been, in absolute terms, 6.3 m higher up above sea level than it is now. Looking at this the proper way round, since the Late Bronze Age the land around north Kent has subsided by 6.3 m. Of course, the assumption that 2.1 mm p.a. was the constant rate is very dubious – the rate of subsidence is affected by all sorts of factors – but it is still a startling thought and very relevant in following the rest of this chapter and chapters to come.

As elsewhere in Kent, Early Bronze Age finds by FSARG are minimal compared with other periods in prehistory. Four tanged arrowheads have been found in Davington pits and barbed and tanged ones at the south end of the Mall and in a Davington garden. One small sherd of Beaker pottery was found on the Davington plateau, along with a few other, possibly Middle Bronze Age, sherds. The Clapgate Spring excavations yielded mostly Late Bronze Age flints and pottery. Still, there are enough scraps, bits, and hints to invoke the mantra about 'absence of evidence ...' and very recent work (in 2017) is revealing tantalising circular field markings and a possible surviving barrow mound upslope near Sheldwich and Badlesmere.

The Late Bronze Age–Early Iron Age (*c.* 1200–600 BC)

This period, around 1200–600 BC is particularly intriguing because the original nineteenth century division of prehistory into Stone/Bronze/Iron Ages becomes misleading. The changes in human activity in southern Britain around 1200 BC are so great that the culture – beliefs, ideas of right and wrong, traditions – must have changed drastically, even though bronze remains the only metal in use. The dead are no longer buried in round barrows, however, and, in fact, we do not know what people of this time did with their dead as skeletons are rarely found. The thousand-year-old tradition of henges ends. Farming becomes much more settled and organised, and the landscape becomes 'managed' for the first time with forest clearance, field boundaries, ditches and droveways. Permanent settlements appear (Champion 2007, 100).

Down south in Europe the spectacular Bronze Age civilisations, such as the Minoan in Crete and the Mycenaean in Aegean Greece were in ruins, barbarians such as the Dorians were moving west and south. The term 'Dark Ages' has often been used for this time in the eastern Mediterranean.

The great north to south trade routes with tin, amber and other valuable materials moving down to the Mediterranean and sophisticated, finished goods coming north, were abandoned. It has been argued that the cause of this downfall was a shortage of tin and, as we shall soon see, the recycling of bronze scrap became very significant in Northern Europe at this stage. Down in the Mediterranean, however, the techniques of smelting and working iron ore were being mastered. Iron ore is easy to find but processing the ore to produce a usable metal is far trickier than processing copper, tin, or lead ores. Mastery must have taken long trial and error.

What was life in the Faversham area and in north Kent generally like during these hard times down south? The answer, based on current evidence, is that it was a lively place to be. Tim Allen has counted 22 coastal settlements of this Late Bronze Age–Early Iron Age period between Seasalter and the Wantsum channel, on land that became quite empty in the following Late Iron Age–Roman times (Allen 2009, 189–207). In the Faversham area, we have at least three settlements to add to that figure. Allen himself found one of these areas of activity near the Clapgate Spring. Field boundaries and ditches associated with Late Bronze Age and Early Iron Age pottery and the rather crude types of flint tools that they still used for everyday work were found, along with part of a curvilinear ditch that could be the drip trench for a round house (Allen 2000, 7–8). This would be the first evidence for a round house found in the Faversham area.

Up on the Davington Plateau, FSARG investigations took place along a curving line shown on the geo resistivity survey of the Davington Priory Cricket Pitch (Pl. 5a). This well-marked feature runs from north-west to south-east. These investigations culminated in a larger trench in 2012, small compared with the huge areas that commercial units tackle but big enough for us to get most of the answers needed (FGW, OA86).

The resistivity mapped curving feature was interpreted as a hollow way rather than a ditch. It was flanked to the east by a marked step in the gravels, the upper level of which corresponded to the top of the infill of the hollow way. The infill contained more than half of the Late Bronze Age/Early Iron Age pottery and flints from this period, although there were also many Mesolithic flints, residual in all contexts. Into the surface of the infill/gravel level was sunk a straight sided circular hole, probably a large post-hole, dating to a later stage when the hollow way had filled up.

The Late Bronze Age–Early Iron Age flint from this pit was, as would be expected (due to competition from bronze and iron for tool making), crude, mostly piercing tools of varying size, small basic scrapers, and simple utilised flakes. There were, however, several unusual and exceptionally well made multipurpose tools, which look as if they could have been made by the same maker (Pl. 4c). The pottery was much more varied and sophisticated than the earlier Bronze Age pots or indeed the subsequent Middle Iron Age ones. It included sherds of rusticated ware; thin walled sherds with oxidised finish; bases dense with very finely ground flint; flint tempered wares with very fine flint pieces. None of the sherds was large but they were larger and less abraded than midden scatter sherds therefore not associated with the composting of fields using the household middens. Perhaps they had been trodden into the infill of the sunken way?

Although the excavated area was too small to reveal any large features such as a round house drip trench, the sheer quantity and variety of the finds suggests a definite settlement up here on the plateau, very much in contact with an outside world from which new techniques were being learned. The absence of animal bone or shell in all the Davington Cricket Pitch pits points away from this being a temporary feasting site of some kind. This is a site worth further investigation. Similar, smaller assemblages were found at OA67/67X and on the other side of the Westbrook Valley on the spur overlooking the Stonebridge Crossing from the east (FGW, KPs 9A, 67/67X).

Another site where Late Bronze Age–Early Iron Age pottery has been found is Syndale, a spur of higher ground that links geographically with the Davington Plateau with the marshy ground of the lower Westbrook separating the two uplands. We will be hearing a great deal more about Syndale in Chapter 4 on Roman Faversham. Roman Syndale has been of interest to antiquarians and archaeologists for around 150 years and has been dug and picked over incessantly. Earlier in this chapter, the problem of archaeologists setting aside or even ignoring archaeology that does not fit with their main interest was mentioned and that has certainly been the case with Syndale where searching for Roman period archaeology has overwhelmingly dominated research. One of the more thorough reports on Syndale from 2008, however, has a useful analysis of all the pottery found and amongst the considerable amounts of Roman material are 74 sherds of Early Iron Age pottery, most of which were *in situ* in a single trench. There are even some of those rusticated ware sherds that have been seen at Davington and the Stonebridge Crossing. In this case occupation (probably a single home stead) seems to go on continuously through to the Late Iron Age (Wessex Archaeology 2003, 16).

Other evidence for Late Bronze Age/Early Iron Age activity in the Faversham area continues to turn up. Upstream from the Plateau, in Water Lane, FSARG found a late Bronze Age flint working site which was excavated using 3-dimensional coordinates for every piece of man-affected flint that came out. The flints were classified into categories – heat stressed flints/waste struck flakes/finished tools and so on – and the results plotted using a software programme designed for astronomical plotting. The large quantity and distribution of the uniformly small heat-stressed flints is very noticeable and this may be a small 'burnt mound' of a type found elsewhere in prehistoric Britain, although the pit was too small to make any decisions. Anyway, the amount of struck flake, 11 cores and finished tools implies something more definite. The pipeline discoveries south of Ospringe Church have already been mentioned, giving at least two flint working sites in the middle Westbrook valley, close to where good quality raw flint can easily be found.

To the north of Faversham, at the lowest level of the superficial deposits just as they begin to disappear under the more recent alluvium of the marshes, work in advance of gravel extraction by Brett's Aggregates took place in 2011. Archaeology South-East, Brett's archaeological consultants, cleared a large area revealing Late Bronze Age droveways going down towards the Swale. The droveways were probably used for sheep, though no actual animal bone was found. This site yielded bone pins and small amounts of pottery (Priestley Bell pers. comm.). At this time, the Swale was not yet a through channel to the Medway and still a river, and it was possibly not yet fully tidal (Allen 2000, 169–82)

Continuing down one of these droveways to the river – maybe a drinking place for the animals – and crossing the river, you would come to what nowadays is the Isle of Harty. Although now politically part of the Isle of Sheppey, until quite recently Harty was much more closely associated with Faversham (see Chapter 6) with a ferry connection. In 1872 at Harty, a Late Bronze Age hoard was found, with 32 items including three moulds with an axe cast from one of them. The hoard included hammers, a whetstone, a gouge for working wood (handles, presumably) and bronze scrap fragments. This very fine assemblage is now in the Ashmolean Museum, Oxford and, as the museum description says, it gives a unique glimpse into the metalworker's craft.

Hoards like this are quite common around the shores of the Wantsum (the former channel between the Isle of Thanet and the mainland) and along the Swale shore (Perkins 1999). Some archaeologists see them as ritual deposits linked to the presence of water and there are Late Bronze Age sites like Flag Fen in Cambridgeshire and indeed the River Thames itself in London where Late Bronze Age artefacts seem to have been deliberately cast into the waters (Pryor and Bamforth 2007). Other Late Bronze Age 'deposits', however, do seem to be stores of scrap and tools of the trade, i.e. the capital and working equipment of a travelling bronze smith. Whichever theory you prefer, these hoards are highly personal collections buried in what was a specially selected spot, whether for security or ritual or elements of both.

We can imagine our travelling bronze smith working his way along the coast from Thanet, perhaps in a small boat with companions, then turning up the Swale and landing on the right side to see what was what. He looks across at the droveways and fields on the lower slopes, at the wisps of smoke from cooking fires rising from the village on the Davington Plateau and, to his left, the Clapgate Spring settlement. He then finds a good place to hide his bronze stock while he goes across the river and walks up a drove way to find some food and business in the village. Sadly, he does not return and his hidden stock remains as a reminder of the uncertainties of the world.

The Middle Iron Age, 400–100 BC

Tim Allen, whose work in the Faversham area has been so useful, has suggested that the north Kent coast settlements at this time were badly affected by even more changes happening in the Mediterranean lands, causing yet more shifts in trade routes. This was brought to a head, he argues, by the displacement of bronze as the most important metal by iron. By around 800 BC around the Aegean, the finer points of working iron had been sorted, although it is wrought rather than cast iron that will dominate European culture up until the fourteenth century.

The 22 Late Bronze Age–Early Iron Age settlements listed by Allen, to which we can add the Clapgate settlement, the Davington Plateau village and Syndale, became, he argues, deserted by around 400 BC (Allen 2009, 199). Many were re-occupied in the Late Iron Age. Up until around 1000 BC, the Kent coast had been on the trading route between Cornwall and Europe. By around 500 BC, in the south, Etruscan and Classical Greek civilisations were flourishing, early Rome was flexing its muscles and they all wanted iron. The routes from the Mediterranean now led to the rich haematite fields of the Eifel in the Rhineland: North-West Europe had become a backwater.

Quite what happened to the people who lived on the Davington Plateau during this time is uncertain. It is possible that through using scrap bronze, the Late Bronze Age in effect lasted longer in this corner of the world. There were definite links with north-west France at this stage but not with further places (Adams 2017, 41–3). Maybe the villagers went on living a scaled down version of the Late Bronze Age culture? Yet – and this comes from work carried out by Tim Allen himself working along the route of a water pipeline being installed just south of Macknades in 2007 –considerable evidence for Middle Iron Age activity has been found to the east of Faversham (Allen 2007)

This Middle Iron Age settlement lasted through to the Late Iron Age and the coming of the Romans. The pipeline trench revealed evidence for V-shaped ditches and pottery kilns, lots of large pottery sherds and lumps of daub from the hut walls. Most important in this context, there was evidence for iron working, using local ironstone from the Thanet Sands. Perhaps the people from Davington moved down here where it was easier to work the iron? Or perhaps these iron working people were incomers from the continent, yet again bringing a different way of life? Whatever the reality of the so-called Middle Iron Age in the Faversham area, the Macknades settlement and the Syndale homestead were flourishing when the Roman fleet was sighted sailing along the east Kent coast and with this, prehistory ends, and history takes over.

Final comments

This chapter is, as far as I know, the first published attempt at summarising the prehistory of the Faversham area. It has drawn upon a range of unpublished material such as the 'grey documents' of the commercial archaeological sector, articles in *Archaeologia Cantiana* and other magazines and journals, unpublished theses by students, reports of stray finds to the KCC SMR (now the HER), the archives of the Fleur De Lis Museum in Faversham and other Museums such as the British and Ashmolean, as well as 12 years of work by FSARG.

Considering that 20 years ago almost nothing was known about the local prehistory, great progress has been made but, as was pointed out at the beginning of this chapter, only a minute fraction of the local area has been explored. In 2017 there are, however, several sites designated for housing development over the next few years. These will be closely examined and will surely add to the prehistory narrative. The areas that are extremely unlikely to be developed will, however, remain a mystery: the marshlands, the woodlands, the grade 1 agricultural lands will continue to keep their secrets for many years to come. Finally, this chapter owes an enormous debt to Tim Allen, a local professional archaeologist who has taken the prehistory seriously.

CHAPTER FOUR

The coming of Rome: 55 BC–AD 410

Introduction

> By far the most civilised inhabitants [of Britain] are those living in Kent, a purely maritime district, whose way of life differs little from that of the Gauls. Most of the tribes in the interior do not grow corn but live on meat and milk and wear skins. All the Britons dye their bodies with woad which produces a blue colour, and this gives them a more terrifying appearance in battle. They wear their hair long and shave the whole of their bodies except the head and upper lip.
>
> (Caesar: De Bello Gallico)

You have just read the words of Julius Caesar. This is the first eyewitness account we have of Britain, let alone Kent, and it is a very detailed description indeed. Books four and five of Caesar's *De Bello Gallico (The War in Gaul)* give an account of two invasions of Britain, a tentative and exploratory one in 55 BC and a much larger scale and serious one in 54 BC. *De Bello Gallico* makes fascinating reading but here we are concerned with insights into the Faversham area.

The first invasion, which was mainly to scout for good harbours, friendly natives and to learn something about the local fighting methods, did not last long and the Roman troops ventured only into the immediate countryside around what is now Deal. They learned, however, some major lessons the hard way. For one thing, their ships (of which there were about 100 transports for infantry and cavalry and several faster moving warships) had difficulty beaching on pebbly banks with problems of large tides and bad weather. For another, the natives were very war-like and their fighting methods were unfamiliar and disturbing to the Roman troops. For example, they used chariots: on the mainland, the war chariot had gone out of use 200 years before and a Roman soldier would only have seen one on a racing circuit.

The second invasion was, for the times, gigantic. Eight hundred specially built ships, with low sides to cope with the tidal changes, carried five legions (25,000 men) and 2000 cavalry to Britain and the period of stay was much longer. They aimed to land at the same place as the year before, succeeded and this time fought their way inland. After besieging and defeating locals at a large fortification about 12 miles (19 km) inland (thought to be Bigbury Hill Fort, near Canterbury) storm damage to the ships caused Caesar to rush back to the coast and see that repairs were organised. Then he returned to the Bigbury area where the Romans had set up a camp. The locals had by now got themselves organised, under the leadership of Cassivelaunus, a man from north of the Thames and the battle was long and hard. The Romans won, and the local warriors scattered, leaving many dead. After this, it was off to the lowest crossing point of the Thames to deal with the powerful tribes up there and meet Cassivelaunus and his forces on their home ground.

The rest of the story mostly takes place in what is now Essex, but Caesar's army would have passed along the line of what later became Watling Street, following the foothills of the Downs along the spring line. In doing so, he must have come through the Faversham area, and past the iron working village and the Syndale homestead that we met at the end of the last chapter. The sight of 20,000 armoured infantry soldiers (allowing for some left guarding the boats) and 2000 horsemen passing is almost unimaginable. Crops and stores would have been looted, of course, and maybe houses set on fire but hopefully those early Faversham folks ran off to the woods when they heard the massive force coming.

More trouble was to come, though. Cassivelaunus was having a rough time north of the Thames, so he sent word to the chiefs of the four tribes living in what is now Kent, urging them to attack the Roman naval base and ships. This they did but were soundly beaten. Cassivelaunus then sued for peace which Caesar granted with appropriate conditions – the year was passing, and Caesar wanted to be back in Gaul by the time of the Autumn equinox.

This campaign was not a serious attempt to conquer a new territory for Rome: Caesar had quite enough on his hands with tempestuous Gaul. It was instead a piece of showing off, to impress the Senate back in Rome with his skill and daring as a commander. Ten years after that second invasion he would be assassinated, and it would then be 87 more years before Roman armies returned to Britain's shores.

Late Iron Age Faversham

De Bello Gallico tells us more about the people of *Britannia* – or, rather, about south-east Britons as the Romans did not, on this occasion, go far north of the Thames. These people of the south-east coast came, according to Caesar, from across the Channel not long ago and were closely related to the Belgae tribe from the Low Countries. We are told that the population is 'exceedingly large, the ground thickly studded with homesteads and the cattle very numerous'. The people used coins for exchange, small lead potins between themselves and imported gold Gallo Belgic staters for business with overseas. We are told that eating hares, fowl and geese was forbidden and that:

> 'wives are shared between groups of ten or twelve men especially between brothers and between fathers and sons, but the offspring of these unions are counted as the children of the man with whom a particular woman cohabited first'.

These customs are hard to check out archaeologically to put it mildly, but the density of population, use of coins and pottery copied from Gallic prototypes can be investigated

Figure 4.1 shows the distribution and character of Late Iron Age finds in the Faversham area. None of these data is from a fully excavated site – we have not yet seen, for example, a fully excavated round house, let alone an *oppidum* (fortified Late Iron Age settlement). Yet the quantity of distinctive 'Belgic' (Gallic-style) pottery is impressive and unarguable. If each of these pottery assemblages corresponds to a homestead or group of homesteads, then this area was indeed 'thickly studded'.

The best described and published Late Iron Age archaeology in the Faversham area came from the investigations at the Queen Elizabeth playing field in 1965. Archaeologist Brian Philp fought for access and funding to carry out a major rescue operation for the remains of the former Faversham Abbey, burial place of a King. The Abbey site, at that time under orchard, was to be bulldozed flat to provide playing fields for the new Queen Elizabeth Grammar School. This project certainly 'unhoodwinked' Faversham people (to use Southouse's memorable phrase, Chapter 1) about the Abbey which will be described along with the rest of Faversham's medieval archaeology in Chapter 9. A completely unexpected bonus, however, was a Roman villa that turned up during the actual

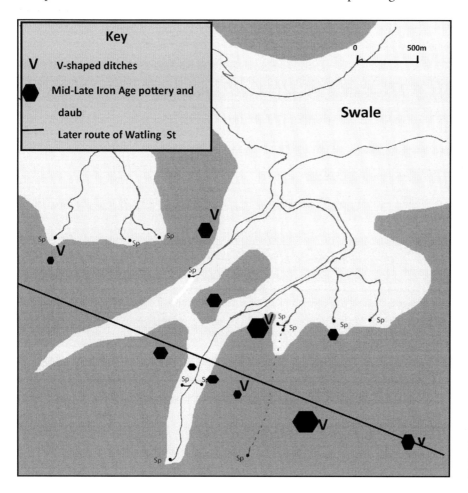

FIG 4.1. Mid–Late Iron Age settlement in the Faversham area

levelling and underneath this villa were the remains of 'Belgic' occupation – indeed, the villa evolved from the 'Belgic' farmstead in a continuous development through the next couple of centuries.

The excavation of the villa was an emergency operation and the investigation of the underlying farmstead, revealed only at the end of the access time, was just a token excavation, to use Philp's words (1968, 65). For a 'token' it is remarkably accomplished and informative and makes a major contribution to the Late Iron Age story of Faversham. The most significant features were two large V-shaped ditches that seem to form part of a sub-rectangular enclosure. There was not time to investigate these further, but such a ditch arrangement usually encloses a round house with associated outbuildings. Under the villa ran three other shallower ditches, also V-shaped in section (see Fig 4.2): Philp saw these as field boundary markers rather than defensive in nature. Still more field boundary ditches were spotted (though not dug) as the levelling of the playing field continued.

All the ditches contained Late Iron Age pottery which is very well illustrated in the 1968 publication (Pl. 6b). The illustrator, Gerald Clewley, apologised for having 'only' a thousand sherds, representing about 100 vessels, to describe. At the base of the two large ditches was pottery dating from the end of the first century BC, but the upper fill of the big ditches and the main fill of the smaller ones could all be dated later to around AD 10–50, i.e. overlapping the Conquest in AD 43. These later assemblages were, in Clewley's words 'thoroughly Belgic' and contained copies of Gallo-Belgic butt beakers and imported Gallo-Belgic platters. The pottery was both handmade and wheel thrown, with characteristic combing, rouletting and cordon decoration. This does appear to be a classier

FIG 4.2. 'V'-shaped 'Belgic' ditch in the Queen Elizabeth playing fields site, under the foundations of the later vill.

assemblage than that found in the iron working village or at Syndale. This spot must have been a fine location with a view out towards the Creek and the sea beyond and up into the hills behind. Water flowed northwards to both the east (Cooks Ditch) and the west (the Creek). What with the overseas trade contacts and the comparatively luxurious life style, perhaps this was the local chief's house?

About 10 miles (16 km) to the east beyond the great Blean forest, what we know as Canterbury was beginning to develop between the invasions. Bigbury, the fortified stronghold that still exists just south of Harbledown, had been besieged by Caesar. It was not a hill fort in the same way as those of Dorset or Wiltshire – in fact, it dates back only to the first century BC. After Caesar departed, however, people moved down to the crossing point of the Stour and began to set up what is known as an *oppidum* – a fortified town. From this has come the Canterbury we know. So far there are no signs of an *oppidum* development in the Faversham area. Although at one point we thought that the Davington Plateau was showing signs of embankments that had been levelled away and historic references to embankments around Davington were found, investigations have not supported this theory. Syndale has not, as far as I know, even been considered as an *oppidum* site.

What about the site of early Faversham itself, seen by all historians as the part of the town next to the Stonebridge Crossing? Certainly, further up Dark Hill, Belgic pottery has been found. The trouble, however, with looking for the prehistoric in Tanners Street and Lower West Street gardens is the depth of the archaeology, underlying 2000 years of continuous occupation. Further complications come from the gradual rise in relative sea level so that early prehistoric settlement in the little flood plain of the Westbrook would by now be below the water table. Finally, there are the major disturbances caused by the post-medieval gunpowder industry. Nevertheless, we can imagine small ships coming and going and maybe a beach market near the landing place for locals to sell produce such as iron, hides, hunting dogs, and slaves (Strabo, Bk IV, chap. 5) and buy exotic goods such as jewellery, quality pottery and amphora containing wine (a sherd of a Dressel 1B amphora was found in the iron working village south of Macknades: Allen 2007, app. 1).

At this moment in time, on the brink of conquest, the Faversham area was clearly well populated. That combination of reliable springs, light fertile soils, nearby woodland for timber and firewood, sheltered valleys, excellent access to the sea and thence to mainland Europe or across the Thames estuary to the prosperous Trinovantes in Essex, sailing from and to a sheltered harbour in what is a notoriously harbourless coast seems to have worked as well then as it has done throughout Faversham's long history.

The population of the whole of Britain at that time has been estimated at several million (Fowler 1983, 33). In the Faversham locality, allowing ten people, including children and slaves, to each of the 11 places mentioned, gives 110 inhabitants. There must surely be many sites not yet discovered so it is fair to at least treble this to 330. In the 1801 census, only just over 200 years ago, the population of the whole of Davington parish, including children, was only 146, that of the large Ospringe parish 645 with 220 in Preston next Faversham. Obviously, in 1801 Faversham town itself had many more people at 3488, but even so the comparison of the estimated Late Iron Age population with the rural parishes, nearly 2000 years later, is startling. 'Thickly studded with farmsteads' sums up Late Iron Age Faversham very well.

The Imperial Conquest and the early years (AD 43–240)

> To [the emperor Claudius] ... the Senate and the Roman People [dedicate this arch] because he received the surrender of 11 British kings, defeated without any reverse and was the first to bring barbarian tribes beyond the Ocean under Roman sway
> (Inscription on triumphal arch in Rome)

The Faversham area is awash with Romano-British remains. The distance from Deerton Street, west of Faversham, to Brenley Corner to the east is around 10 km (6.2 miles). In that stretch, there are at least seven villas, a major Roman road and cemeteries yielding between them hundreds of burials. At Brenley considerable evidence for iron working has been found, along with other buildings and a small shrine. At Syndale there was a sprawling settlement along Watling Street and connections down to the Creek. All of this was up and running by the end of the first century AD and developed further during the second as will be demonstrated shortly. Figure 4.3 shows the second century situation, as known in 2017.

In AD 43, the invasion of the island of *Britannia* took place, with a mass landing in Kent. By this time, the southern parts of Britain were already well in touch with the Roman way of life, and the Romans were welcomed by tribes such as the Atrebates in what is now Hampshire. The landing itself and the setting up of a fortified naval base at Richborough happened without trouble from the natives but the journey inland through Kent was more eventful and culminated in a large-scale attack at the Medway crossing. The victorious Roman forces then continued to the Thames crossing.

The further details of the Conquest, though fascinating, are not relevant here – for us the question is what was the impact on the Faversham area? Again, the passing through of the troops must have been witnessed by the 'Belgic' farmsteaders around Faversham. It has even been hypothesised that some invading ships came up the Creek but there is no evidence for this. What is very likely is that the train of the Emperor Claudius passed through the Faversham area during his short visit to make his mark on the victory in AD 43. Along with the general splendour of a travelling Emperor, he was accompanied by 12 elephants which must have made quite an impression on the local people. (Dio Cassius, *Roman History*).

For a long time, local antiquarians thought that a rectangular ditched enclosure on Syndale hill was a Roman marching camp, laid out during the initial AD 43 Conquest. Indeed, it is marked on the earlier Ordnance Survey

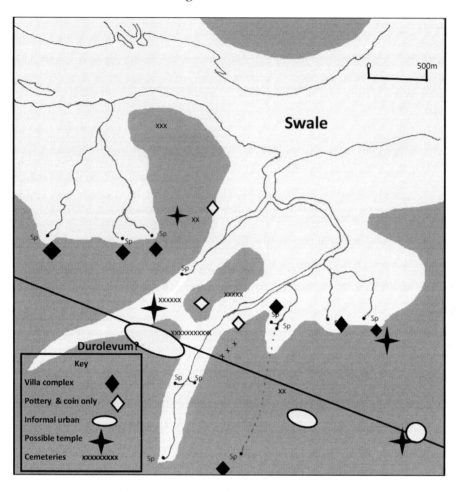

FIGURE 4.3. Roman
settlement in the
Faversham area in the
second century AD

maps, e.g. in 1865, as a Roman Camp. In 1872, the Kent Archaeological Society
held its Annual General Meeting in Faversham and was lectured inside the
bounds of the 'Roman Camp'. Wessex Archaeology, however, reporting in 2003,
on a project for the *Time Team* television series designed to test the idea of a
Claudian marching camp on Syndale, was dismissive mainly because of the
lack of any military type finds. They interpreted embankments and ditches as
being created either by Late Iron Age inhabitants or by seventeenth–eighteenth
century landscape gardeners (Wessex Archaeology 2003, 24). A later, large scale
investigation of the archaeology of Syndale, carried out in advance of proposals
for a hotel on the site, also produced a negative on a marching fort, seeing the
earlier features as indicative of a Late Iron Age farmstead at Conquest time
(SWAT Archaeology 2008, 21).

Much discussion has also taken place on the likelihood of Syndale being the
location of the small Roman town *Durolevum* ('enclosure by the flowing stream')
mentioned in the Antonine Itinerary of the early third century (Codrington
1901, chap. 1). Faversham lies between the two main cities of Roman Kent,

Durobrivae ('the enclosure next to the bridge' i.e. Rochester) and *Durovernum Cantiacorum* ('enclosure by the alder grove' i.e. Canterbury). Both are on Watling Street, at crossing points of major rivers and *Durolevum* lay between them. The distances quoted in the Antonine Itinerary from *Durobrivae* and *Durovernum Cantiacorum* to the minor settlement of *Durolevum* do match the location of Syndale, with only minimal fiddling (Roach Smith 1842; Rivet 1970).

The existence of clustered settlement of some kind along both sides of Watling Street at Syndale has been confirmed by numerous excavations, some published and some still hearsay at the time of writing. In fact, Syndale and the field opposite that contains the Stone Chapel (about which more in Chapter 5) have been subject to around 200 excavation trenches and pits over the last 160 years. In the 1920s, William Whiting, the owner of local brickworks, carried out many excavations just to the north of Syndale and found nearly 400 Romano-British burials, both cremations and inhumations, accompanied by pottery and accessories in immaculate condition, a further strong piece of evidence for a nearby urban settlement. (Whiting 1921; 1923; 1925; 1926; 1929; Hayter and Whiting 1929), (Pl. 7).

Many of the trenches yielded abundant Roman finds (glass, pottery, iron work, evidence for iron working), some have shown cobbled surfaces, mausoleums, and part of Watling Street itself. Not a single brick, stone or flint house wall, however, or even a robbed foundation has been found, instead there is an abundance of post-holes. People lived in timber framed houses and there is yet not a trace of public buildings of the kind found in the likes of Canterbury and London. Only a limited scatter of tiny, worn tile fragments and a few higher-quality finds in a well hint at maybe a higher status building, perhaps a *mansio* (a kind of Roman roadhouse; Siburn 2001, 171–96). If so, it must lie well away from Watling Street: overall *Durolevum* is looking very much like a small working town of humble folk, serving the passing trade and the local hinterland. The only wall found is possibly a precinct wall for the Stone Chapel, but even that has uncertain dating – Roman or medieval? (Ward 2008).

To east and west of *Durolevum* stretches the line of villas. Most of these lie to the north of Watling Street but some to the south, uphill. The pattern that the northern ones make is so regular, each villa so similar in distance from Watling Street and from their nearest neighbours that it is unlike anywhere else in Kent. Indeed, Paul Wilkinson suggests (Wilkinson 2009, 24) that this is an organised Roman landscape, laid out in measured portions. Such organisation, known as *centuriation*, usually involves allocations to colonists, especially veterans from the army (Peterson 2006, 153–6). Centuriation is an appealing idea, but does not seem to fit with the fact that all the sites investigated so far seem to have been a development from an original 'Belgic' homestead site. The regularity is perhaps related to the spring line location of these villa estates, with water emerging at frequent, regular intervals at the foot of the chalk (see Fig 2.3). Each of these villas, shown in Figure 4.1, is on a major spring, essential for the water-rich Roman-style domestic life. Nevertheless, the idea of legal boundary setting for these villas is very interesting, especially as we will see in the next chapter that these boundaries are thought to survive into the Anglo-Saxon era (Everitt 1986, 192–3).

The locations of most of these villas have been known since the eighteenth or nineteenth century: the alien, easily recognised nature of the architecture, pottery and building materials makes their remains conspicuous in the landscape. Few, however, have been investigated in any depth and none has been the subject of a long term thorough investigation. Table 4.1 summarises the story so far.

These villas have much in common but have interesting differences in detail. The well published Queen Elizabeth Playing Fields villa (hereafter QE villa) excavated by Brian Philp in 1965 can form the model (see Fig 4.4). Philp (1968) traces the growth of the villa from a small rectangle with a veranda to a bigger building with corridors running down the longer (east and west) sides of the house. The villa reaches an apogee with the addition of a southern wing with a hypocaust and apse, probably housing a principal dining room: coloured mosaic pieces were found in the ruins of the hypocaust. The north end of the villa was not excavated as it lay beyond the playing field boundary, but auguring suggested a wing at the northern end as well. In the last stage, the eastern and western walls were renewed, one section cutting through the apse and giving a flat front to the southern wing.

Philp estimates that, including the unexcavated northern section, the villa was about 40 m (about 130 ft) long and 21 m (69 ft) at its widest, with an area of 743 m². It faced south-east across the Cooks Ditch. At the time of writing (2017) excavations by the Kent Archaeological Field School (KAFS) are ongoing in the neighbouring Abbey Fields, across the Cooks Ditch and rumours have circulated about a bath house, a possible large aisled barn, and other outbuildings: we look forward to the full publication of the findings.

The other local villas asterisked in Table 4.1 have had very different investigation histories. Blacklands and Deerton Street have been excavated to some extent by KAFS and have had interim publications (Wilkinson 1997; 2005; 2007; Philp 1997). Sheldwich villa up on the higher slopes south of Watling Street was discovered in 2004 and is known only from georesistivity and

TABLE 4.1: Comparison between excavated villas of the Faversham area (Luddenham, Clapgate and Buckland unexcavated)

Site	Start(century)	Finish(century)	Bath-house?	Hypocaust type?	Painted plaster?	Mosaic/ tesserae	High quality finds?	Spring?
Blacklands	late 1st–early 2nd	early 4th	yes	Channelled with chalk blocks	yes	yes	Tweezers, brooches, stylus	yes
Faversham	late 1st	late 3rd	yes	Channelled passages	yes	yes	Rhenish ware, window glass	yes
Deerton St	late 1st	mid-4th?	?	Yes, but no detail	yes	yes	[all very ordinary]	yes
Sheldwich	late 1st/ early 2nd	late 3rd/ early 4th?	?	Tile *pilae*	yes	yes	Rhenish ware	yes

FIGURE 4.4. The excavated Roman villa in the Queen Elizabeth School's new playing field in 1965. In the background are the two Abbey Barns (see Chapter 9)

gradiometric surveys and small-scale excavation (Reid 2013; Wessex Archaeology 2013) (Pl. 6c). The Clapgate villa is even more scantily known, with a nineteenth century report of walls, a floor and associated finds near the spring. Luddenham villa, known from the fact that the nearby church is built almost entirely from re-used Roman building materials, has never been excavated at all so any inferences come from the re-cycled material (FGW, KP82).

Interesting differences emerge when hypocaust remains are found. With Luddenham, box flue tiles used in the foundation of the former tower of the church show that the villa must have had a second century hypocaust system. Box flue tiles are also said to have been found on the Clapgate spring site. The Blacklands, Deerton Street and Sheldwich villas, as well as the QE villa had hypocausts: central heating was obviously a Roman innovation admired by the local bigwigs. Yet it is intriguing that there were at least three very different types of hypocaust used in these villas. Sheldwich and Deerton Street had the pillars of tiles that are usually shown in drawings of Roman villas. At the QE villa, however, the arrangement was entirely different with lined channels for the hot air to flow through. Blacklands had pillars but these were made of large rectangular chalk blocks rather than tile stacks, an arrangement somewhere in between pillars (*pilae*) and channels. Whether these differences are because of cost or fashion is hard to tell, but it does show differences in taste.

The very frequency of these villas brings home the fact that this was a quietly prosperous and settled area, at least for the first 200 years of the Roman occupation. As well as these villas, there are an increasing number of scatters of Romano British pottery and other finds being identified locally without an associated villa. These were probably associated with much more ephemeral buildings, maybe round houses, maybe square houses. Examples of non-villa-based sites have been found at Syndale, down near the Stonebridge crossing, up on the Davington Plateau, at Oare (Gidlow 1969) and in the iron working villages south of Watling Street.

One such iron working site has already been identified as existing from the Middle Iron Age onwards (Allen 2007). In 1961, archaeologists working during the construction of the M2 on the site of the Brenley Corner roundabout found a total of 16 hearths with lots of iron slag, clinker and nodules of the local ironstone, associated with large quantities of Romano British pottery, brooch pins, querns and coins and several stretches of a flint cobbled road with a side ditch One small building, with a cobbled floor and post holes showing a timber construction, contained an image of a fertility goddess and is thought to be a shrine (Anon. 1961; KCC HER: TRo5 NW5). The two sites are so close they may have formed a straggling community, where the locals got on with their manufacturing and trading.

Temples were a common feature of Roman settlements. Inside the cities there would be formal Roman style temples to the Roman Emperor and classical divinities but in rural areas the style of the temple is usually very Romano-British. Typically, this would be a square chamber (*cella*) with a walkway around it and an altar within, with the walkway covered by a roof as well as the higher ceilinged *cella*. In Kent, the best-known examples of this come from *Vagniacae* (Springhead), a small town on the Rochester to London stretch of Watling Street. At Springhead, there were at least seven of these Romano- British temples (Andrews *et al,* 2011, 13–134).

In the Faversham area, there is very little solid evidence for temples, although they must have existed. The shrine at Brenley, where a small statuette of Dea Nutrix was found, has already been mentioned and is probably the most certain religious spot. A tentative identification has been made of a temple site near Broomfield Farm in Oare, based on Roman foundations spotted in 1844. Even earlier, in 1755, after the demolition of the central tower of St Mary of Charity, a Roman altar and many Roman bricks were found, we are told in a 1930s Archaeological Journal article describing Roman Faversham (Editor *Archaeological Journal* 1929). This suggested a temple on this site, although see Chapter 9 for reservations.

There are other interesting suggestions. Wilkinson has suggested that the Stone Chapel was a Saxon conversion from an earlier Romano British temple rather than from a Roman mausoleum as is usually thought. He does, however, date this temple as fourth century, so it would not have been standing during this earlier period under discussion. Wilkinson also proposes that the Blacklands villa site should be considered as part of a major Roman religious sanctuary, including a temple and a cockpit theatre seating twelve thousand (Wilkinson 2012). This theory has only been circulated informally (Wilkinson pers. comm., 2017), and much more evidence is needed to validate what would be a very unusual site. Blacklands will come up again in the next chapter.

Finally, there are the cemeteries. Hundreds of burials have been excavated around Faversham, 389 from near Syndale alone (Fig. 4.3). Most of the burials were cremations but some inhumations were found in the Ospringe/ Syndale cemetery and at Preston Mill where five skeletons were excavated in 1860. (KCC HER: TR06 SW21). The usual finding is of a pot containing calcined bones with a tile flat on top to seal it, or a grave with a supine skeleton. Generally, cremation is thought to be the custom during the first two centuries of Roman rule, with inhumation preferred from the late third century onwards, although there are exceptions to this. Earlier archaeologists thought that the practice of inhumation came along with early Christianity but in fact it comes in earlier than the spread of the new religion.

Grave goods accompany both cremations and inhumations, accompanying the dead person in the afterlife. Sometimes pots or glass ware are used but occasionally gaming counters or jewellery or grooming equipment like tweezers are found. Unlike household goods which are used until broken then dumped, archaeologically recovered grave goods are complete and usually perfect. The very impressive collection from the Ospringe/Syndale cemetery is housed at the Maison Dieu Museum, Ospringe, with some examples shown in Plate 7.

Because cemeteries were located outside towns, along roadsides, they are very useful for reconstructing the boundary between town and countryside and the locations of roads in Roman times. Thus, the nineteenth century finds of burials on Davington Hill, at Oare and out towards Uplees (Fig. 4.3) suggest a road running out towards the Swale, which would link with a connection over to Harty where there was Roman activity (KCC HER: TR06 NW2 and others).

Let us finish this section with a walk through this new landscape, arriving along Watling Street from *Durovernum Cantiacorum* in the east. The year is around AD 240, the Emperor Gordian III rules the Roman Empire, and first you must get past the great Blean forest that crowns the hills and runs off to left and right as far as the eye can see. Once through the forest and looking downhill, the countryside spread before you has been thoroughly tamed in the nearly 200 years since the Conquest. There are plenty of other people on the road – merchants, tradesmen, women going to the market in *Durolevum*, or down to the waterside to buy fish and oysters, craftsmen looking for work. At the foot of the hill, you come to the iron working village, which is full of blasts of hot air and smoke, the acrid smell of red hot iron, the pounding of hammers and the hiss of the hot iron being quenched in water. A small shrine invites you to make a thank you offering for a safe journey through the woods.

Further on, you can see on the slope down to the sea a couple of red-roofed villas showing up brightly in the sunshine. The fields around are ploughed and down on the lowlands you can see sheep and cattle. Up to the left, the forest edge curves around and continues along the Downs. As you approach *Durolevum*, you pass tombstones and grave markers and then the first simple houses appear alongside the road, and a hill comes in sight with houses around its flanks and some small pottery kilns on its outskirts. Then come shops, inns, small shrines and, again, iron workshops though not the actual smelting of the ore. A cobbled road runs down to the right towards the water. It too is lined with grave markers and in the distance, you can see a small temple and beyond it a huddle of villa buildings, beyond that the sea.

Everything is so peaceful and quietly prosperous that you think this could go on for ever. But it is not to be - trouble is coming and there will be no more Roman style villas built in this part of the country.

Chapter 4: Intermission: Weather forecast

Time for another look at what is happening with the weather and sea level. This is now 1800 years ago, and we are in what many authorities have called the Roman Warm Period.

This means that glaciers are melting faster. On Figure 3.1 in Chapter 3, it can be seen that, in about AD 240, sea level is rising. For whatever complex reasons (and there is a lot of argument about this) the soil, peat and mud levels that tell the story say that this was a time of advancing sea, formally known as a marine transgression. This advance may not be by much but it is enough for lands on low lying coasts to become uninhabitable.

Insurrections and barbarian invasions AD 240–296

> In this war Carausius, a Menapian, distinguished himself by his effective actions .... He was put in charge of fitting out a fleet and repelling the Germans who infested the sea. Carried away by this promotion, he failed to restore the whole of the booty to the treasury, though he intercepted many of the barbarians ... when he discovered that the Emperor had ordered his death, he assumed the title of Emperor and seized control of Britain
>
> Aurelius Victor (4th century AD) *Liber de Caesaribus* 39, 20–1

This period is a very stormy one for the Roman Empire, with many rebellions, usurpations of power and, in north-west Europe, invasions by Germanic tribes such as the Franks and Saxons and, in the far north and west, Picts and Scots. The North Sea, Irish Sea and the Channel became crowded with pirates. In AD 286, Britain was taken over by a self-declared Emperor of Britain and Northern Gaul, Carausius. Carausius had risen from humble origins and served in the Roman navy, the *Classis Britannica*. He appears to have been both popular and competent, and he was left alone to rule Britain. In 293, he was assassinated by his finance minister Allectus, who took over the Imperial role but was defeated in an invasion by the junior Roman Emperor Constantius in 297 (Faulkner 2000, 80–96).

Durolevum must have seen a lot of movement along Watling Street in these times, with troop movements and refugees, and seems to have remained active into the fourth century, although by far the greatest amount of pottery and other finds date to the first–third centuries. For the villas and the iron working villages, it is another matter, on present evidence. It appears that the QE villa went out of use some time not long after AD 270 (Philp 1968). Wilkinson dates the end of full occupation at Deerton Street and Blacklands to the early fourth century, around 320 (Wilkinson 2005; 2007; 2012). Sheldwich villa has not been excavated on a full scale, but in the pit showing the demolished bases of the hypocaust *pilae* and wall foundations, the infill/debris layer above contained fourth century pottery such as Oxford ware and a coin of 364–378, hinting at an early fourth century demise date for the villa itself (Reid 2013). With the Brenley iron working village, records of which are limited, all the finds except the coins mentioned are dated to the first and second century AD, not even the third (Brenley: KCC HER entry TR05 NW3, Maidstone).

This was a time of change, a period in which the *Classis Britannica*, ceased to exist in the record. It is the time of the building of the so-called Saxon Shore forts at Reculver, Richborough, Dover, Lympne and other places in East Anglia, Sussex and Hampshire. For the first time, Canterbury, Rochester and London were walled (Millett 2007, 175–83). Other villas, even the large luxury ones at Folkestone and Minster in Thanet, went out of use around this time, though some were briefly re-occupied later. What survives belongs in the next post-Constantius period.

The later period AD 296–410

> Constantius died at Eboracum [York] in Britain in the 13th year of his reign [AD 306] and was deified ... On the death of Constantius, Constantine, his son by a somewhat undistinguished marriage, was made emperor in Britain and succeeded to his father's position as a very popular ruler.
>
> Europius (4th century AD) X, 1, 2, 3 and 2.2

Constantine, one of the best known of Roman Emperors, after whom Constantinople was named and who was the first emperor to make Christianity an officially accepted religion (Edict of Milan AD 313), might well have passed through Durolevum along Watling Street on his way to Dover to return to Rome in 306. He was 34 years old at the time and would live another 31 years as Emperor. He ruled with a strong hand but, after his death, the internal ructions started up again, with constant rebellions, usurpers, barbarian invasions. Gradually over the next hundred years, troops would be withdrawn from Britain to attend to troubles elsewhere.

During this time, the province of Britain was divided up into four parts, each ruled by a separate military governor. Taxes were strictly enforced, and large quantities of grain sent to the Roman frontier on the Rhine. In western and central Britain, towns like Cirencester and Wroxeter were still occupied and functioning, in some cases into the fifth century, but town life was no longer fashionable for the rich – in the west and centre of *Britannia* this was the century of some spectacular villa building with glorious mosaics and palatial buildings but out in the countryside and away from civic responsibilities (De La Bedoyere 1993, 55–71).

Even in vulnerable Kent, exposed to attack from the sea on three sides, the villas survived in the west, beyond the Medway. Lullingstone lasted until about 410, when it burnt down. Eccles, a very early large villa on the Medway, was having major modifications in the early fourth century. But Canterbury, London and Dover were in decline towards the second half of the fourth century, with an ever-increasing amount of land within the walls being given over to gardens (horticulture) and former living rooms to workshops and squatters (Millett 2007, 183–4). Two large village type settlements, Springhead (with the temples) and one uncovered at Westhawk Farm near Ashford that had thrived up to the mid-third century had fizzled out by the fourth century (Biddulph 2011, 248; Booth *et al.* 2008, 388–94).

In the *Durolevum* area, we have already seen that many of the villas appear to have fallen on hard times: the lights, you could say, are going out. What has not been found, however, is any evidence for burning or other forms of deliberate destruction of the villas. None of the exhumed skeletons from Syndale and Preston Mill shows signs of violent death. In Syndale itself, life goes on but, it seems, in a very restricted way. In Nigel Macpherson Grant's masterly and comprehensive catalogue of pottery from the large scale Syndale intervention in 2008, only 0.4% of the pottery dated to 350–400, with another 0.3% being of types that are dated 250–400 (SWAT Archaeology 2008, app. 2). All the rest is from the first–third centuries, and the same is true of finds from other investigations at Syndale, including the graves. Macpherson Grant (2008) and Malcolm Lyne (2001) both draw attention to the fact that, by around AD 370, whoever is left here is using coarse locally-made grog tempered ware that is very like that of the local Late Iron Age people 300 years earlier.

There is at present, however, one major exception to the view of this part of Kent as a landscape of ruined villas and people who are reverting to the lives of their ancestors, increasingly cut off from the great trade routes and manufacturing networks of the Empire. At Bax Farm, between Bapchild and Teynham and north of Watling Street was a villa to which was attached, in the mid-fourth century, a quite extraordinary structure, very different from anything else in east Kent (Wilkinson 2010). This is a large, elaborate, octagonal building with a central pool, built of high quality materials. Wilkinson identifies it as a bathhouse although it could be a grand reception room with a central ornamental fountain. It is, Wilkinson points out, very like a couple of fourth century examples from the West Country where luxury villa building was still going strong in the mid-fourth century. It is tempting to speculate about a local magnate who has monopolised agriculture and the Rhineland trade, and continues to parade Roman identity in a landscape that is mainly reverting to indigenous ways: until the rest of the Bax farm villa is fully excavated and dated any such speculation is premature.

We will leave Zosimus to have the last word: although organised Roman-type lifestyles continued in the west to a limited extent, this is the first stage of failure for Britannia.

> Honorius [Emperor in 410] wrote letters to the cities in Britain bidding them to take precautions on their own behalf
>
> (Zosimus, *c.* AD 420, *Nova Historia* Vi, chap. x)

Population across the whole Romano-British period

At the time of the Roman Conquest in AD 43, the estimate of population in the immediate area around Faversham was about 300 people. If we include the Brenley iron working village to the east and the Deerton Street villa complex to the west, reach northwards to include the Harty villa and southwards to the Sheldwich villa, and consider the archaeological evidence for settlement in the mid-third century, the population estimate is much higher.

Normally, a fair assumption would be that there is much evidence for past settlement at a specified time that has not yet been spotted. In Faversham's case, because of the distinctiveness of the Roman building material and cremation burials, combined with the great interest taken in local Roman remains from the eighteenth century onwards (Bedo's list of local Roman sites in a lecture presented to the 1872 KAS Annual General Meeting in Faversham is impressively comprehensive (ANON 1974)) most of the main villa and cemetery sites have been charted. The Sheldwich villa, however, was discovered in 2004, showing that new discoveries can still be made. There are indeed rumours of Romanised settlements in the Elverton and Buckland Church areas which have not been tested in modern times. Also, the 'homesteads' figure is likely to be on the low side. So, it would not be unreasonable to bring the population figure up to between 1500 and 2000 people for around AD 240 for the wider area.

Whether this was still the case by AD 400 is another matter. The tiny proportion of pottery at Syndale which can be dated comfortably to the later fourth century has already been mentioned. The burials at Ospringe are similarly biased – out of 114 burials with available dating based on the grave goods, only two are around mid-fourth century or later, i.e. about 2%. The graves of both later inhabitants contained coffin nails, and the coffin of one of them was outlined with flints. The Preston Mill skeletons are undated.

The only archaeological finding that seems to contradict this apparent decay is the large number of fourth century coins found in a variety of sites in this area: many writers (e.g. Millett 2007, 183–18) use this frequency as evidence of continued trade activity and vitality and perhaps it is in a modest way. Taking the total of coins from the three Syndale excavations that had reliable recording and dating (1991; 2003; 2008) the following distribution was found for the Roman coins (Table 4.2)

The comparison confirms the apparent contradiction very strongly. What is not obvious from Table 4.2, however, is that these late coins are very thin and low value. Fourth century coins have been found in other parts of Faversham

TABLE 4.2: Numbers of coins found at Syndale from the Roman occupation period

Date of intervention [by]	1st century	2nd century	3rd century	4th century	Total
1991 [Sibun]	0	0	3	21	24
2003 [Wessex Arch.]	0	0	1	4	5
2008 [SWAT Arch.]	1	4	9	34	48
Total for century	1 (1%)	4 (6%)	13 (16%)	59 (76%)	77 (100%)

and even in the deserted villas. Perhaps the key to the abundance of these late coins is the fact that Watling Street itself continued in use right up to the end. There is good evidence that Richborough fort was the last fortified garrison in Britain, with a depleted version of the Legio 2nd Augusta literally holding the fort. The largest amount ever of very late fourth century and early fifth century coins was found at Richborough, coming from its dying days: Watling Street was carrying traffic into the fifth century (Millett 2007, 181). Whether these late coins were dropped by travellers sheltering in the semi-ruined huts and villas of a now near deserted settlement or whether the local people were still trading low cost goods such as food and drink cannot be decided until a proper, careful, open-area excavation is carried out for Syndale, this modest but significant site.

Final comments

Much investigation remains to be done to help reconstruct the dynamic Romano-British landscape in the Faversham area. So far, despite all the local interest in the Roman occupation period, not one villa complex has been completely investigated, the closest to comprehensive being the two-week excavations of the QE villa in 1965. Some villas, such as the one at Luddenham, have not been investigated at all. There are many other partial investigations.

Whiting's splendid collection of grave goods with some skeletons, excavated in the 1920s, remains largely an antiquarian display rather than an informative contribution to reconstructing the changing landscapes of the time. The KAFS has, however, carried out many investigations of local Roman sites using students. Although publication of findings has so far been mainly informal, there is hope that, in the near future, there will be attempts to look at the whole landscape, integrating the findings with those of non-villa contemporary Romano British settlements.

CHAPTER FIVE

Faversham and the Kingdom of Kent:
AD 410–825

....

Introduction

> The Romans, therefore, declare to our country that they could not be troubled too
> frequently by arduous expeditions of that kind, nor could the marks of Roman
> power, that is an army of such size and character, be harassed by land and sea on
> account of un-warlike, roving, thieving fellows. They urge the Britons, rather, to
> accustom themselves to arms, and fight bravely, so as to save with all their might
> their land, property, wives, children. They then bid them farewell, as men who
> never intended to return. [Then]the terrible hordes of Scots and Picts eagerly come
> forth out of the tiny craft in which they sailed across the sea-valley, dark swarms of
> worms emerg(ing) from the narrow crevices of their holes, differing partly in their
> habits, yet alike in one and the same thirst for bloodshed and in a preference also
> for covering their villainous faces with hair rather than their nakedness of body with
> decent clothing.
>
>   Gildas, sixth century British monk: De Excidio Britiannae (The Ruin of Britain)

The last chapter ended with the sun going down on Roman Britain. It had set
early in east Kent, so that in most places by AD 400 the Roman infrastructure
had broken down and the Roman style villas and their associated buildings were
ruins. Only Watling Street, Richborough and faded versions of Canterbury and
Dover remained active. Even so, it should not be thought that everyone had run
away or been taken as slaves by pirates (ever a threat on the north Kent coast).
In 1962, in Longmarket, Canterbury, a hoard of silver and gold items and a coin
of Honorius dated to after AD 402, was found. It seems to have been buried
for security and never reclaimed. The silverware, beautiful but poignant if you
know the historical context, can be seen in the Canterbury Roman Museum
(Johns and Potter 1991).

The Kentish origin myth carries on the story as follow: by the 440s, the
British were becoming desperate, attacked on all sides by Scots, Picts, Germans.
Vortigern, the King of Britain, decided to do what the Roman Imperium had
been doing for a long time: employ mercenaries to fight off the enemies. In
449 two Germanic warriors, Hengist and Horsa were invited to join in, and
a company of men arrived in Thanet. Battles ensued, Horsa was killed and
Hengist eventually became the first King of Kent. The Venerable Bede tells
us that Horsa's grave and monument still survives in east Kent in 731 (Bede,

Ecclesiastical History, 63). This story is seen by many as the beginning of the conquest of Britain by Germanic tribes.

The two warriors feature in many versions of the story up to the modern day, and some authorities (such as J. R. R. Tolkien) believe that Hengist was a historical person. Whatever the truth, the Germans were here to stay. Bede tells us that Kent, *Vectis* (the Isle of Wight) and south Hampshire were occupied by Jutes, with other parts of Britain being taken over by the Saxons e.g. Essex by the East Saxons, or by the Angles in East Anglia. With the original landing place in Thanet, it is very likely that the Jutes came up Faversham Creek soon afterwards. They were certainly, on archaeological evidence based on grave goods, taking over in east Kent by the late fifth century (Riddler 2004, 25–6).

This chapter will follow the role of Faversham during this period of the creation and the end of the Kingdom of Kent: Kent was eventually taken over in the mid-eighth century by King Offa of Mercia, Mercia being a powerful Anglian-origin kingdom occupying the Midlands. Kent was finally absorbed into the Kingdom of Wessex in 825. The first part of this chapter will look at Faversham in the time of the heathen Jutes, as the Venerable Bede called them. The second describes the arrival and spread of Roman Christianity, with a chronological overlap between the first two parts. The third part deals with the eighth century, often looked upon as a golden time for the Anglo-Saxons, and ends with a statement in 811 from King Coenwulf of Mercia who, by 807, had taken over the direct rule of Kent, and an announcement of conquest by Wessex in 825. Although there are hints in various earlier documents that we will hear about, Coenwulf's announcement about the 'King's little town of Fefresham' is the earliest known time the name of Faversham can be found in a document. It is also the first time we are told that Faversham is a Royal Manor, a high note on which to end Chapter 5.

Chapter 5: First Intermission: Weather forecast, plus other warnings

Temperatures are falling again, and the weather is drier. This is leading to a slight fall in sea level up to around AD 700. This is the good news.

The bad news is that, in AD 536, the whole world will be affected by an event that causes the atmosphere to become dusty, the sun to be veiled and crops to fail, leading to famine. Arguments still go on as to whether this is caused by a huge volcanic eruption or by a meteor impact.

Then, in AD 541, the Old World will be devastated by a major outbreak of bubonic plague, called at the time the Plague of Justinian after the current Byzantine Emperor. The impact of this plague, and the outbreaks that follow the main one, is comparable to the Black Death in the fourteenth century.

How dark were the Dark Ages?

In Scandinavia, Germany and other parts of Europe never conquered by the Romans, the period defined in Britain as the 'Dark Ages' is seen as a continuation of the Iron Age, called by them the Long Iron Age. Although pre-literate (except for runic inscriptions) and still pagan (apart from Ireland where Christianity survived) the people are far from primitive, as we will shortly see: it is from across the North Sea (known in the UK until the nineteenth century as the German Ocean) that invaders will come for the next 600 years. What was happening in the Faversham area during the first four hundred years of that period?

Who were the Jutes?

The Angles, Saxons and Jutes were Germanic-Scandinavian tribes who had not lived under direct Roman rule, except as mercenary soldiers, or *laeti*. They arrived in Britain mainly through Kent, having worked their way southwards along the mainland coast from what is now Denmark (Jutland) and northern Germany. This was a time when many of these so-called barbarian tribes were on the move and some, like the Vandals and Visigoths, ended up in Mediterranean lands, leading to the end of the western Roman empire: the Visigoths under Alaric plundered Rome itself in AD 410. The Germanic Franks had already taken over Gaul by the mid-fifth century, creating a powerful kingdom under the Merovingian dynasty and they also had an eye on Kent.

In Bede's words, the Jutes, Angles and Saxons 'worshipped according to the custom of the heathen', following the Teutonic pantheon of gods which survives to this day in our names for days of the week (Tiy/Woden/Thor/Freya). They lived in timber houses, most commonly in large thatched timber halls, surrounded by small, square, sunken-floored buildings (SFBs or *Grübenhause*) of varied purpose, and their material culture was mostly organic – wool, flax, wood, leather, bone, horn and willow withies. Pottery they did not bother with much, except in some parts of the country, e.g. East Anglia, where cremation was the preferred way of dealing with the dead: there, cremation urns were crude handmade vessels but had highly distinctive individualistic stamped patterning. In east Kent, cremation burials of this period are rare, although six were recently found in the Ringlemere cemetery excavated by the British Museum in 2005 (Parfitt and Needham 2007, 51). Domestic pottery, however, was very simple and primitive, often grass tempered.

These people were, however, great lovers and creators of fine metalwork and the metal worker was a highly-respected person. People were buried fully dressed, with their equipment for life around them, warriors with their shield and spear, women with their weaving battens, spindle whorls and keys. The richer folk would be resplendent in their jewellery – buckles, brooches, necklaces, headdresses for the women, helmets, shields and swords for the men. They also loved glassware and highly distinctive glass vessels such as 'claw beakers' and 'palm pots' are often found in graves. The beads of necklaces were often multi-coloured glass, although they might also be amber, amethyst, painted baked clay or metal. Everyone, even the poor and children, could be buried with a knife, although a wealthier or higher status boy child might be buried accompanied by shield and sword as well.

Then there are more mysterious grave goods, found in the graves of some of the older women. These are crystal balls, enclosed in a silver cage with a hook for suspension from a belt. Sometimes these women also had perforated silver spoons and large sword-like weaving battens for use in the warp weighted loom (of which more later). Audrey Meaney, an expert on Anglo-Saxon burials, sees this kind of assemblage as indicating a woman of magical powers, a 'cunning woman', wise in the ways of this and other worlds (Meaney 1981). These items are found in burials on the Isle of Wight as well as in Kent, but not in the burials of the Saxon and Anglian peoples.

Kent is very rich in early Jutish burials. Around 300 Jutish cemeteries and burial sites have been recorded in Kent, with around 4000 burials recorded and thousands of artefacts recovered. The earliest (fifth–sixth century) burials are mostly in east Kent, east of the Stour. The most recently investigated at the time of writing has been a cemetery at the Meads, Sittingbourne, immaculately excavated in 2008 by the Canterbury Archaeological Trust, and subsequently conserved through an inspired community project (Richardson 2017) . This was the first Jutish cemetery to be excavated in Swale to modern standards. The story of the finding of splendid Jutish graves in Faversham and what happened to the finds is a much sadder tale, from many viewpoints.

The Jutes in the Faversham area

First, let us look at evidence for lifestyle. From the description above, most of the materials that made up the Jutish lifestyle were the kind that rot away quickly in the ground unless buried in waterlogged conditions. Their great halls have gone, leaving only post-holes, beaten earth floors and sometimes horizontal beam slots for the timber framework. Their high-quality textiles have rotted away, only visible occasionally when a fragment of clothing in the grave has stuck to a metal object and become mineralised. Their wooden furniture and platters for dining have disintegrated. All that can normally survive archaeologically is the metalwork, glass, the not-very-interesting pottery, animal bone debris (including human bone) and shells.

The metalwork and glass are only very rarely found outside of graves – they were too valuable to lose and could be recycled if broken – so as settlement evidence we are left with clay objects, such as pottery or clay loom weights. The loom weights were ring doughnuts of clay that were tied onto the bottom end of the warp threads in a vertical loom to hold the thread taut. At the foot of the loom there would be a row of these roughly made clay doughnuts. Although women were often buried with their spindle whorls which were decorated and much more personal, they were never buried with loom weights which were obviously far too crude and every-day. A lone loom weight was salvaged in 1954 from the ruins of the bombed site on the corner of Newton Road and East Street in Faversham, when the site was being bulldozed for the building of the Post Office. The Faversham bun shaped weight can be dated roughly to the seventh–eighth century.

Paul Wilkinson's excavation of local Roman villa complexes, described in the last chapter, has yielded some interesting evidence for what may indicate the first local incomers in the late fifth–early sixth century (470–550). At the large octagonal decorated structure built at Bax Farm, Teynham, in the fourth century, a series of Jutish kilns were built in the former hypocaust furnace. These furnaces re-used Roman materials – their floors were made from *tegulae* (tray shaped roof tiles). A few pottery sherds associated with the kilns suggest the date of 450–600 (Wilkinson 2010, 39).

A similar continued use of Roman ruins was observed at the Hog Brook site, the large aisled building associated with the Deerton Street villa, between Teynham and Faversham. This villa went out of use early in the fourth century. Here sherds of similar age to the Bax Farm ones were found associated with a crude repair job on a collapsed wall. Even more intriguing was a collapsed pier of the building that, in falling, seemed to have trapped not only a small domestic animal, but also a cruciform brooch, dated to around AD 550 (Wilkinson 2005, 35). Most dramatic of all has been the finding of large post-holes on

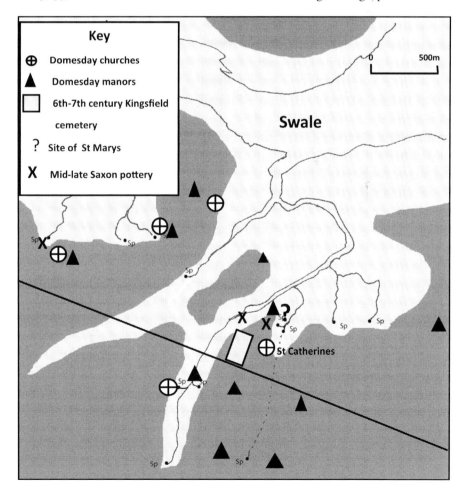

FIGURE 5.1. Early–Late
Saxon Faversham

the remains of the Roman villa at Blacklands. Wilkinson suggests that these represent a large timber hall, and claims that sherds in the packing material of the post-holes were again datable to 450–600. (Wilkinson 2012, 33).

Some early grass tempered pottery was found by FSARG in Preston Street along with a possible early to mid-Saxon iron knife. This find spot was very close to the Kings Field Jutish cemetery site, of which more below. The spur of land behind the Bull Inn at the corner of Tanners Street and West Street has yielded small amounts of pottery dated to the eighth–ninth centuries, as have pits on Dark Hill. This later period, the 700–800s, will feature towards the end of this chapter and is even harder to spot archaeologically than this early pagan stage that at least had eye-catching dressed burials.

What about the cemetery?

Until recent re-design, the Sutton Hoo gallery at the British Museum housed not only the glorious artefacts from the famous ship burial at Sutton Hoo in Suffolk (dating from around AD 625) but also many items labelled as coming from Faversham. This included a large display case filled with coloured glass vessels. In the literature on Kent's Jutish burials, it is common to find the Faversham Kingsfield cemetery named as the richest of them all, possibly associated with early Kings of Kent. Yet Andrew Richardson's' comprehensive text on the Anglo-Saxon cemeteries of Kent (Richardson 2005) does not include Faversham in its database of cemeteries, except for a couple of burials recorded by John Brent in 1874. Why?

The answer, by modern standards, is scandalous. During the building of the London, Chatham and Dover railway line through Faversham in 1858–9 a series of graves was exposed. Later, up to 1874, brickearth removal in the area to the immediate north and south of the railway line revealed yet more burials. The grave contents were remarkable – gold and garnet brooches, swords, golden headdresses, necklaces. What happened is that the workers grabbed the grave goods, sometimes fighting over them. They were then sold to the highest bidder. It has also been suggested that, at that time, Faversham become something of a black market for Jutish grave goods stolen from elsewhere in Kent (Richardson pers. comm.).

Fortunately, in this dire situation certain antiquarians made a point of buying as much as possible. William Gibbs was the main purchaser and offered such a good price that workmen saved finds for him. Later, William Gibbs left his collections to the South Kensington Museum and, after museum reorganisation, they ended up in the British Museum. Kings Field grave goods can, however, also be found in the Ashmolean Museum, Oxford, and Liverpool Museum with a few items in Canterbury, Maidstone and elsewhere. Where they are not to be seen is in Faversham itself, although the Maison Dieu Museum at Ospringe does display two fine examples of Saxon glassware.

The William Gibbs collection is the largest. In 1871, C. Roach Smith, a celebrated antiquarian, published a catalogue of the Gibbs bequest and lists 641 articles (Roach Smith 1871). This is not counting necklace beads separately: with 42 necklaces listed, some with over 90 beads, this would have made the number of items overwhelming. Here is the full range of items listed, with numbers for the commonest: swords, spear shafts, axes, whetstone, chapes, knives, javelin heads, shield studs, spear heads, arrowheads, shield buttons, shield bosses, studs, fibulae (brooch = 61), buckles (72), armilla (bracelet), pins, pendants, girdle studs, plates, hangers and pendants, rings, earrings, necklaces (42), decorative band, ornaments, tags, cases, bodkin, chain, hooks, badge, crystal balls, garnets, horse harness equipment, plates, purse frames, styli, spoons, tweezers, nail cleaners, locks, keys, draughtsmen (for a board game), bowls, glass bottles, cups and bowls and three crude ceramic pots.

The quality of much of this is outstanding (see Pl. 8). Most of it can be dated, by comparison with finds from places which have been excavated properly, to the mid-sixth to seventh centuries, i.e. from around 550 to 700. This matches with the brooch found at Hog Brook, and the sherds found on the deserted Roman sites. The Kings Field collection is particularly famous for its glass vessels – there are more glass vessel finds from Faversham than from all other Anglo-Saxon glass vessel finds in the county (74 vessels, all but eight from the period 550–700). The earlier types are clearly imported from nearby Merovingian Francia, just across the Channel, but later the types become so distinctive in colour and in decoration, e.g. bag beakers, that they are thought to have been made locally (see below).

So fine are these items that it is depressing to think how much was overlooked in the rush, what was trampled on or smuggled out for private sale or ignored as valueless. Evison suggests on convincing evidence that glass vessels were deliberately broken before sale: more money could be gained for three large glass fragments than one whole vessel (Evison 2008, 6). We have no idea as to whether these graves had mounds or other markers, neither will we ever know how these artefacts were arranged on and around the body and be able to empathise with the mourners. All we can do is guess, using information from better recorded sites.

Finally, and possibly the most serious loss of all, we do not have any knowledge at all about the people themselves. Nowadays, a great deal can be learned from the study of skeletal remains, not just age, sex, and pathology but illness patterns in childhood, DNA characteristics and whether the person is a local or an incomer. Perhaps the skeletons did not survive – the survival of the bones at the 2008 Meads excavation at Sittingbourne was poor. Perhaps they were collected and reburied by someone who respected their dignity. Perhaps they were thrown out with the rubbish. Whatever the answer, it is a sorry tale.

Faversham in the late AD 600s–Dark Ages?

From the evidence described above, a picture can begin to be painted of Faversham at that time. One clear deduction is that this was a definite settlement. Alan Everitt, in his influential book on *Continuity and Colonization in Kent*, would agree. Alan describes the long strip of fertile land running between the Downland and the marshes, stretching from Blean to Rochester, as the Foothills and labels them as the 'Original Lands' of settlement in Kent. He argues for continuity from Late Iron Age to Roman villa estate to Jutish estate, a continuity that can be evaluated from what you have read so far. Alan even suggests that St Mary of Charity was founded as a Minster church in the early seventh century. This would have to be reconciled with the dressed burial practice so colourfully present nearby until the late seventh to early eighth centuries.

However the continuity is expressed, what does seem very likely is there was much more to early Faversham than an agricultural estate centre. In the words of Vera Evison, an expert on Anglo-Saxon glass in the UK '... Faversham is an obvious candidate for the location of the glass house' (Evison 2000, 7). In a recent book, Martin Welch and Sue Harrington identify Faversham as the most likely central place for high status metal manufactures, both of iron and copper alloy (Harrington and Welch 2014, 32, 145, 208). If this includes items such as swords, then the level of iron working skills must have been exceptional. If it also includes those exquisite circular brooches with garnets set into a tracery of silver gilt, then the skill goes beyond good craftsmanship into art. No wonder the town is called Faversham, a combination of the Latin for 'makers' and Anglo-Saxon for 'town'.

Then there is the sheer wealth of the burials. The multiplicity of the items (42 necklaces, 71 buckles) implies that this is not a matter of one or two people having princely burials, as with the early seventh century burials at Sutton Hoo and Taplow, Buckinghamshire. Instead, this seems to represent numerous middling-wealthy burials. Socially that would fit with a highly skilled craft settlement, with the artisans (artists?) doing very well from their positions. Royal patronage is very likely and perhaps Faversham being a 'king's town' goes back to this time?

The burial goods supply strong evidence for export and import. In the early sixth century stages, most of the glassware and some of the metalwork is clearly imported from the powerful Merovingian (Frankish) people across the Channel: indeed, the Franks themselves claimed over-lordship of south-east England in this early stage. Items such as five strips of gold braid that are thought to have been part of a woman's head dress are clearly Frankish in style. In the late sixth–seventh centuries, however, designs became much more local and distinctively 'Kentish'. At this stage Faversham must have been importing all the raw materials except for iron which could be produced from the Blean ironstone, as in Roman times, or by recycling iron from the Roman ruins (Freestone *et al.* 2008, 36–46).

The imports would include gold, silver, garnets, amethyst, copper alloy and the raw materials for glass making. Although Roman *Britannia* in the early days had a working gold mine in Wales, it had long since shut down. The gold was probably from bullion, melted down gold coins known as *solidi* or gold plate seized as plunder. Silver almost certainly came from German silver mines. Copper alloy could also be in the form of bullion ingots, as bronze is relatively easily melted down and re-cycled. The origins of the garnets, amethysts and other gems are more uncertain, but they came from far off places, probably Central Europe, although India has been suggested as a source of the rarest garnets (Farges 1998).

The imported raw material for glass is particularly interesting. Chemical analysis of the Faversham glass shows that in the period of manufacture, AD 550–700, the main ingredient, as in Roman times, was a sodium based compound. This did not usually come from re-cycling Roman glass (although this was done to some extent), but from a kind of half processed material known as cullet. Cullet, was made in Egypt at that time, using natron (a naturally occurring mineral) from lakes and exported as rough chunks of glassy material. Thus, it would have travelled to Faversham all the way from the eastern end of the Mediterranean, probably up the great trade route running north from the port of Marseille. Towards the end of the sixth century, however, Faversham glass started to incorporate a new raw ingredient into the cullet: potash ash from plant material. This is thought to be because of disruptions in European trade routes in the later sixth century, due to the continued episodes of bubonic plague that were sweeping the Byzantine Empire (see *weather report*) (Freestone *et al.* 2008, 40–2).

All this makes it fair to assume that Faversham Creek was as important then as in later years. Faversham's convenient location, at the convergence point of Thames river trade and sea trade to the mainland, must have been the key factor. The higher, dry ground so handy for the waterside completed the attraction. So here we have, towards the end of the seventh century, a lively, busy settlement of workshops, smithies and glass houses with small ships coming and going and different languages being spoken, mostly Germanic dialects. These vessels would hop along the coast from one little port to another, with Faversham (or Cilling?) on the route along the north Kent coast.

The trading was almost certainly linked to Quentovic, a Merovingian trading emporium, that was founded by a Frankish king in the early sixth century. Merchants were drawn to this place because the number of trading posts at the time was limited. The town no longer exists, but it is thought to have been situated near the mouth of the Canche River, in what is today the French commune of Étaples. It was an important trading place for the Franks and its port linked specifically to Kent but it was abandoned, probably in the eleventh century (Hill *et al.* 1990).

Up the hill, between the waterside village and Watling Street, was the cemetery where the local artisanal elite were buried, suitably attired and probably with mounds or other markers for their graves. Somewhere there must have been rectangular timber thatched halls for people to live in, with lots of smaller workshops scattered around. Maybe some kind of proto-guild or confraternity emerged in this craft dominated settlement, with a wealthy lord, or even the King of Kent as patron: very likely the main Hall was on the spur overlooking the water way and, if Alan Everitt is right, close by would be a new little wooden church, the shape of things to come (Everitt 1986, 113).

Quite invisible archaeologically, however, are the original Romano-British inhabitants of this place – the folk who lingered on at Syndale, for example, in the last days of Empire. Syndale, it appears, became deserted through this early medieval period. According to Gildas, the monk who wrote a passionate diatribe against the British for their cowardice and corruption which had brought on the invasion and takeover, the British were either slaughtered, enslaved or ran away to the west. Some of the British took to the hills or crossed the sea to a new land they called Brittany. What happened to them around Faversham is, as yet, a mystery.

The Cross comes north

> Tell Augustine that he should be no means destroy the temples of the gods but rather the idols within those temples. Let him, after he has purified them with holy water, place altars and relics of the saints in them. For, if those temples are well built, they should be converted from the worship of demons to the service of the true God. Thus, seeing that their places of worship are not destroyed, the people will banish error from their hearts and come to places familiar and dear to them in acknowledgement and worship of the true God.
>
> Pope Gregory I, Letter to Abbot Mellitus, (Bede, *Eccleiastical History* i, xxx)

The return of Roman Christianity: the background

The story of St Augustine landing on Thanet in 597 and making his way to Canterbury to convert King Ethelbert of Kent is very well known, and it is fascinating to think that these events took place only 10 miles/16 km) away from Faversham. It is perhaps less commonly known that Christianity had already taken firm root in Britain in the third–fourth centuries. Some of the silver spoons in the early fifth century hoard found in Canterbury had the Christian symbol of the *Chi Rho* on them. Lullingstone, the villa on the Darenth that survived in use until the early fifth century had a cellar which had been converted into a Christian chapel. Further north, St Alban was martyred in AD 304 at *Verulanium* (St Albans) and around 430, a Romano-British Christian boy called Patricius was kidnapped in Cumbria and taken to Ireland as a slave.

In AD 380, the emperor Theodosius I issued the Edict of Thessalonica in which a form of Christianity became the sole official religion of the Roman Empire. After the abandonment of 410, the British Christians survived in the west, the Irish ones converted by St Patrick and the Scots and Picts converted by St Columba and others crossing from Ireland. They all held to a form of Christianity that differed in many ways from the 'official' Roman version brought over by St Augustine in 597. These differences led to the famous Synod of Whitby in 663, reported by the Venerable Bede in 731, which was supposedly about reaching a compromise between the two systems but really about asserting the dominance of the Roman church. The very speed by which the new form of Christianity had reached the Anglo-Saxon kingdom of Northumbria, only 66 years after the arrival of Augustine at Canterbury, and the ability to draw together such diverse interest groups at Whitby is astonishing. The power behind the Augustine mission is palpable. So how did it affect Faversham?

The conversion of the Faversham people.

So far, with one possible exception, evidence for the earlier Roman Empire version of Christianity has not yet been found in the Faversham area. The exception takes us back to that unusual late Roman octagonal structure at Bax Farm, Teynham. Although accepting a probable original bathhouse interpretation, Wilkinson argues for its possible later use as a baptismal pool, on the lines of similarity to Byzantine baptistries (Wilkinson 2010, 4). The lack of any evidence for a church nearby could be explained by the limited size of the excavation site. Whether or not this is a correct interpretation of the remains, there has been no suggestion of continuity of this role into the Anglo-Saxon period.

Alan Everitt, in his detailed discussion of the early church in Kent, takes it for granted that 'within one or two generations of Augustine's arrival a Minster church based on the new Christianity was built in Faversham (Everitt 1986, 124). He assumes this is the original St Mary of Charity (or Our Lady of Faversham, to give its early name), long since the parish church of Faversham. Minster churches served areas much larger than a modern-day parish, with priests travelling out from the central base to preach and pray in the open. Often Minster churches had nuns and/or monks attached to them. Later, as the population grew and Christianity caught on, Minster churches would found daughter churches in areas of new settlement, in cleared woodland for example, or on reclaimed marsh. These new churches would become centres for new, smaller parishes still linked in some way to the mother church.

A problem with this assumption about St Mary's being an early Minster, however, comes from one of the very few documents that survive from this period. This document records a meeting – a *witanagemot* – called by King Wihtred of Kent in 699 to pronounce upon the tax status of monasteries and minsters. These religious institutions were to be tax-free but had to promise to say special masses on behalf of the Royal Family, and especially for Wihtred's soul. Wihtred's document, dated and witnessed by the Archbishop of Canterbury and other dignitaries, contains two important clues about what is going on in Faversham itself (Ward 1947).

First, it lists the important religious establishments of Kent at that point: Canterbury Christchurch, St Andrew's Rochester, St Augustine's monastery at Canterbury and another monastery at Reculver. There were four nunneries; Minster in Thanet, Folkestone, Lyminge and Minster in Sheppey. These are well known from other documents, and founded in the early to mid- seventh century. Faversham is not mentioned.

A second problem is that this *witanagemot* took place at a place called 'Cilling'. In a later Saxon charter, dated to the early ninth century, Cilling is mentioned again, and is clearly a port near Faversham (Ward 1934, 125). The location of Cilling is another mystery, but the commonest agreement is that it was somewhere on Faversham Creek downstream from Fefresham, just upstream from Nagden and near what would later become Thorne Quay, the harbour for larger ships during the medieval period. Is this implying that Faversham-Cilling must have been an important, even royal place? Wihtred, however, soon after held *witanagemots* at Bapchild and Cliff at Hoo, and had held one a year before at Bearsted (Ward 1947, 6–7). None of these places was particularly associated with a religious establishment at that time.

Alan Everitt also says St Mary's is on the site of a Roman temple. This is to emphasise the continuity of the early foundations with the immediate past. Unfortunately, there is no solid archaeological evidence for the early existence of St Mary's. Neither is there for a Roman temple as the so-called Roman ruins north of the nave, reported in the late eighteenth century, have been shown from recent flood drainage work in the churchyard to be twelfth century in date, in keeping with the Norman character of the post- Conquest building (see Chapter 9). Other evidence is equally questionable (a Roman altar said to have been found during demolition of the central tower in 1755, urns and coins found in 1794 when the west tower was rebuilt). No record of these long-vanished items has been found so the jury must remain out on correct identification. Pope Gregory, in his letter quoted at the beginning of this section, was talking about using sites currently sacred to the local peoples, not ancient, ruined Roman ones.

The final snag with this idea of a very early conversion to Christianity of those prosperous Faversham merchant artificers and their families is that, in Faversham, rich dressed burial continues up to the end of the seventh century and into the early eighth. None of the many finds from what has been called the most prolific of Anglo-Saxon cemeteries bears any indications of Christian symbolism. Good Christians were buried in a shroud and took none of their possessions with them. The locals, it seems, were reluctant to drop their old customary ways.

Yet consider the words of Pope Gregory. They show a great sensitivity to the situation of the mission in this 'barbarous, fierce and unbelieving nation' (Bede, *Ecclesiastical History*, 73). Gregory makes it clear that the English were to be coaxed and persuaded and that a blind eye could be turned to ways that did not directly affect the precepts of the Roman Christian faith – a blind eye, maybe, to those rich dressed burials. Across the channel the Christian Franks also continued to practice dressed burial – perhaps we are seeing here another example of Frankish tradition in Kent?

Other early churches in and around Faversham

There are two other churches in the immediate Faversham area which, unlike St Mary of Charity, have demonstrable links to the Anglo-Saxon period.

One is St Catherine's, the parish church of Preston next Faversham until the parish boundary reforms of 1935, and still very much in use in 2016 as part of Faversham parish. The other is a fascinating ruin near Syndale: the Stone Chapel of Our Lady of Elwarton.

St Catherine's is a small church that was rural until the sixteenth century, accompanied only by its vicarage, and the farm across the lane where there is archaeological evidence for a stone built medieval farmhouse/barn (see Chapter 9). St Catherine's was the manorial church of several of those typically modest Kentish manors, of which more at the end of Chapter 6. Nineteenth century updating has blurred the earlier character of this ancient church, but one thing that came to light in the building works was a fragment of later Anglo-Saxon interlace stonework which has been identified as part of a Saxon Cross (Tatton Brown 1994) (Pl. 9c). Even when Christianity was firmly established, the field cemetery would have survived until the seventh–eighth century, with a cross at which the minster priest preached. Often the first local church building would be a some distance from the field cemetery, perhaps across a valley or river, and burials would henceforth be in the churchyard. In the case of St Catherine's, the very early (822) gift of this parish by King Coenwulf of Mercia to the Archbishop of Canterbury in perpetuity seems to have given rise to a church on the site of the cross.

The Stone Chapel (Pl. 9a) is a much more contentious site. It was a small church that became disused around AD 1530. One of the unarguable facts about it is that the lower parts of the walls of the chancel are made of Roman tufa blocks and brick and the floor is made of *opus signinum* (a Roman building material made of tiles broken up into very small pieces, mixed with mortar, and then beaten down with a rammer). Generally, there is agreement that this part of the church is a Romano-British structure converted to Christian use, but there the agreement ends. Considering the amount of archaeological investigation that has taken place in and around the Stone Chapel: in 1872 (KAS), 1926 (Hawley and Livett unpublished information), 1968 and 1971 (Meates and Fletcher 1969; 1977), 2005 and 2011 (KAFS); it is astonishing that arguments still rage.

In the published accounts listed above, some think that the structure is a converted Romano-British mausoleum: the ruin is close to a large Roman cemetery that was in use mainly from the first to the third century (see Chapter 4). This cemetery was associated with a Syndale settlement that ran along Watling Street 50 m (about 160 ft) to the south of the Stone Chapel site. Others argue that it is a converted Romano-British temple or shrine and claim to have found a precinct wall around it. Some say that it was near a spring, others that it is in a dry valley and at least 200 m (over 650 ft) from the nearest spring.

The most thorough of the excavations, those of Lt Colonel Meates and Lord Fletcher in 1968 and 1971, found evidence for Saxon presence. This consisted of the chalk and flint foundations for the wooden walls of the early church, and two *sceatta* (silver coins, see below) dating from around 730. They were firm on the idea of Augustinian continuity, as recommended by Pope Gregory (Meates and Fletcher 1969; 1977) . Yet, as Alan Ward points out in a fierce deconstruction of these interpretations (Ward 2009), the simple two-cell layout of this church is quite unlike the Augustinian early churches of St Peter and Paul and St Pancras on the St Augustine's Abbey site at Canterbury which had apses at the east end and porticae on either side. Ward also has many reservations about the stratification shown in Fletcher and Meates's records.

Again, the interpretation seems to miss the point that Gregory was talking of continued use of active pagan sites, meaningful to the locals, not deserted Roman ones. Whatever the answer, this remains a highly intriguing site where there are clear and obvious Romano-British and Christian usages, although the jury is still out on the continuity between the two.

There are some other churches in the area suspected of having an early-mid Saxon origin. These include Oare church, high on the terrace of Oare Creek and visible to shipping for miles, and Luddenham Church which is built almost entirely of material from a nearby Roman villa. These churches are certainly mentioned in the Domesday book, as we will see in Chapter 6: the possible origins of these and other local Domesday listed churches will be discussed then.

The accumulation of wealth

The Venerable Bede describing events in 709 writes:

> Wilfred's successor as Bishop ... was Acca, a man of great energy... he greatly beautified and enlarged the church... he devoted much care to obtaining relics of the blessed Apostles and martyrs of Christ and builds altars for their veneration... he has also collected accounts of their sufferings and other books on religious subjects and he has been diligent in providing sacred vessels and lights ... he invited a famous singer named Maban trained in vocal music by Pope Gregory's disciples in Kent to come and instruct him and his clergy.. and in all these activities he remains unflagging
>
> Bede, taken from Jane 1903: Vol. V chap. xx

Alcuin (former Bishop of York and at the time of writing Abbot of Tours at Charlemagne's court) writes in 790, 60 years after Bede, about monks and the clergy:

> [they] are vain, extravagant in dress, and haughty in bearing, utterly worldly in fact. They listen to plays rather than to the Scriptures; they prefer the 'cithara' to the sweet music of the Psalms. Too ignorant to write their own sermons, they have recourse to homiliaries. They share the worst superstitions of the people, believing in auguries and incantations.
>
> Alcuin 1909, 55

The eighth century was a rich and productive period for the Kingdom of Kent. As Christianity spread rapidly across Britain, Kent had the earliest and already most historic sacred buildings – Canterbury and Rochester Cathedrals, the monasteries of St Peter and Paul (later re-named St Augustine's) Canterbury, and Reculver, and the nunneries of Lyminge, Folkestone, Minster in Thanet and Minster in Sheppey. The nunneries were founded by aristocratic ladies, who were subsequently canonised.

The earliest charters began to appear at the end of the seventh century. Charters are legal documents that set out land ownership details and descriptions of estate boundaries. The implication is that the 'Original Lands', in which Faversham was an important centre, were becoming more crowded and competitive as the population grew. Making the situation more acute was the onset of a major transgression of the sea, with consequent loss of land. Low lying grazing land was becoming saltmarsh, and it would be some time before the creation of 'innings', which were areas protected from the sea by bunds and drained by ditches. This is perhaps the time when settlement starts to move upslope in the Downs, with increasing forest clearance

Elsewhere in the country, this was the time of growth of trading 'emporia ' – busy, well laid out beach market ports – such as *Lundunwic* (London), *Hamwic* (Southampton) and *Gipsewic* (Ipswich) (Clarke and Ambrosiani 1995, 31–45). Highly significant was the revival of relatively mass produced grey sandy pottery, made at Ipswich using a slow wheel. Ipswich ware is found all over East Anglia and north Kent and has been found in Faversham and on Sheppey (FGW: KP160). The Ebbsfleet (Gravesend) watermill, dated to *c.* 700 and located in west Kent, also reflects a new mastery of the landscape (Welch 2007, 206–7).

By this time, a distinctive coinage had emerged. During the earlier period, coins were in circulation but are not thought to have been used as currency. The gold Frankish *Tremisses* and their Kentish versions minted at Canterbury, the gold 'shilling', were used, it is thought, as prestige items for gifts such as from Kings to servants and followers, for dowry payments and burial adornment. The Kings Field cemetery yielded three *Tremisses*. By around 690 the supply of gold for coinage has dried up and the gold coins are replaced entirely by silver pennies known as *sceatta*.

During the first half of the eighth century, an enormous number of *sceatta* were minted, not just in Kent but in Frisia and the Rhineland as well – it is thought that a lot of the continental coins were re-cycled to make English versions (Sawyer 2013, 58). Figure 5.2 shows a *sceatta* found in the Ospringe

FIGURE 5.2. A 'porcupine' *sceatta* found in Ospringe allotments

allotments. It is of a 'porcupine' type, made in the Lower Rhine area, dated from 695–740. These tiny silver coins were by far the most convenient and reliable means of payment across north-west Europe, and could be used in trading across the newly emerging national boundaries, a kind of proto-Euro.

How is Faversham faring at this point? What has become of those glass workers, metal smiths and traders? The answer for this period is, infuriatingly, that we do not know. In other words, we know more about the people of the Dark Ages than of this time. During this period, wealth went not into graves for archaeologists to find but into the churches. Records of the time show that gifts of gold and jewels for crucifixes and other regalia, silk raiment, church furniture, relics brought from Rome, replaced the use of high status goods in burials, as in the quote from Bede that opened this section. These treasures were, of course, the magnet for the Viking towards the end of this century, as we will see in Chapter 6.

There are a few hints, archaeologically. The loom weight of mid-eighth century date (Pl. 10b) has already been mentioned and is our sole piece of reliable evidence at present for textile production in the settlement. In 2012 in Abbey Street close to the location of St Mary of Charity, at the very lowest level of a development site excavation, there appeared to be a Saxon sunken floored building (SWAT Archaeology 2009). There is also, possibly, a Saxon ditch in the churchyard of St Mary of Charity (SWAT Archaeology 2006) and rumour of a sunken floored building east of the church, dates not specified. Then, as mentioned earlier, there were pottery sherds in the Stonebridge crossing location that suggest a settlement in this location in the mid-Anglo-Saxon period (Fig. 5.3). This hints at two clusters of settlement, one around the St Mary of Charity site and one around what is now the Stonebridge Crossing. The cluster around St Mary's is probably associated with the Royal Manor, the

FIGURE 5.3. A handful of low quality eighth century pottery sherds from the Stonebridge Crossing area

Stonebridge one associated with the merchant craftsmen, with the east–west road that is still the main axis of the town passing through them both. The main port probably lay downstream.

Document-wise, we are no luckier. Except for the survival of the 'Town of Makers' name, i.e. Febresham, implying a continuation of the craft manufacture, there is nothing to give us a view of the town at this time. Not until 811 and 812 do mentions of the 'Kings little town' come up. The flurry of charters of which these are part are to do with the parcelling out of what must have been a large estate based on Faversham (Ward 1933). Thus, the Mercian King Coenwulf between 812 and 825 donates some sections of land around Faversham to Wilfred, Archbishop of Canterbury and sells other parts to him. The charter details enable identification of the areas being talked about. We also hear that in 825, Kent becomes part of Wessex (and will never again be a separate kingdom).

This is almost the last we hear of Faversham for 118 years.

Chapter 5: Second Intermission: Weather forecast

The weather continues cold and dry but, by AD 800, is warming up somewhat, glaciers are on the retreat, sea level is beginning to rise.

Will this last? See Chapter 6.

Final comments

Apart from the spectacular grave goods found in Faversham itself, the evidence from both archaeology and history is undeniably scanty for this period. The arguments for metal workers and glass makers in the town at this time are circumstantial. Although there is the possible mid-Saxon timber hall at Blacklands, within the town itself there have been no such finds, and even the sunken floored buildings are provisional identifications. Yet the presence of Germanic immigrants in the immediate area from as early as 500 is undeniable.

The archaeological problem arises from the absolute continuity of this settlement. Two clusters of activity have been suggested, one around the Royal Manor at the top of the upland and another industrial/trading cluster around the crossing point of the Westbrook. Both lie along that early routeway coming down from the Blean and running along to ford other streams at the lowest crossing point along the spring line. This zone, however, has remained the heart of Faversham ever since, and there are very few areas of open ground for investigations. Moreover, there is not likely to be any development in this central zone in the near future as many of the properties are medieval in date and passionately protected. In gardens, the depth of deposits since the early to mid-Saxon period is considerable. So only continuing, patient and meticulous small scale work can give some answers about this fascinating period in Faversham's past.

Invasion: AD 825–1100

Patricia Reid and Michael Frohnsdorff

Introduction

> Here terrible portents came about over the land ... and miserably frightened the people: these were immense flashes of lightning and fiery dragons were seen flying in the air: and there immediately followed a great famine and after that in the same year the raiding of the heathen miserably devastated God's church in Lindisfarne island by looting and slaughter
>
> AD 793: *ASC* Canterbury Manuscript

This chapter starts with invasions that continue on and off for over 200 years: the excerpts from the *Anglo-Saxon Chronicle* (*ASC*) throughout this chapter are selected from hundreds of descriptions of the terrible troubles of the time. By the end of this chapter, however, we will be on the brink of one of the most prosperous and creative periods in English and indeed in European history, since the height of the Roman Empire: Faversham shared in those happy times. The story of that remarkable twelfth to thirteenth century era, however, is for Chapter 7. For now, we must face up to hardship.

These difficult times were not just happening to the Anglo-Saxons of England. In AD 711, the whole Iberian Peninsula (future Spain and Portugal) fell under Muslim rule, and was re-named Al-Andalus. In 732, invading Muslim forces were soundly defeated at the battle of Poitiers, France by Charles Martel (Charles the Hammer), grandfather of Charlemagne. This is generally reckoned as a turning point for Muslim invasion into Western Europe, but Al-Andalus was not finally re-claimed by Christians until the fall of Granada in 1492. In Eastern Europe, constant invasions by Slavic tribes and Magyars from the steppes of Asia started up around 860 and continued until the Holy Roman Emperor Otto finally subjugated the Slavs and halted the Magyars (who then founded Hungary) in 955.

The marauding Norse, known as Vikings to the British, who we will hear much about shortly, did not simply attack England and France. The Swedish Vikings, known as 'Varangians', went south-east down the river Volga and founded the state of Kievan Rus on the Volga. Some Varangians went further south and founded the Varangian Guard for the Emperor of Byzantium. Harald Hardrada, King of Norway, who we will meet later in this chapter at the battle of

> ## Chapter 6: Intermission: Weather forecast
>
> The good news first. You may have noticed temperatures rising – warmer winters and summers. This warm period is going to last for about 300 years, well into the next millennium. This is a great time if you are planning colonising expeditions to the north – the ice is melting at quite a rate. Even Greenland is looking good!
> *Warning to people living in low lying coastal areas around the southern North Sea*
> Because of that melting ice, sea level is beginning to rise again, quite swiftly. Expect severe flooding, soon.

Stamford Bridge in 1066, was Commander of the Varangian Guard in Byzantium between 1034 and 1042, before he returned to make trouble around the North Sea.

Around the time of the Conquest of England by William the Conqueror (himself a child of a Viking dynasty who spoke French but dressed Scandinavian-style and lived by the Danish law), other Normans (Norsemen) were away conquering Sicily and southern Italy, and attacking western Greece to get to Byzantium. In 1095, Norman knights were in the forefront of the First Crusade to take Jerusalem from the Muslims. Then there were the great westerly journeys. Around 650, the Norse settled the Faroe Islands. By 874 (according to the Icelandic Sagas) they begin colonising Iceland. By the 980s, the Norse were exploring and settling in Greenland, where they stayed for nearly 500 years. They also reached eastern Canada where their sojourn was less successful.

All this is described to show that this middle medieval period is a very different world from that of the so-called Dark Ages. For whatever reasons – conquest, flight, exploring, colonising new land or being taken as a slave – many people were on the move and as they travelled around they kept in touch with homelands through trade, commerce and, as Christianity spread to the people of the north, pilgrimages and correspondence. Christianity and Islam carried literacy, so that we have at last plenty of first hand eye-witness accounts of events and lifestyle. In short, the world was opening up, becoming a smaller place and we will see the benefits of this in Chapter 7. These movements are colourfully summarised in the *Times World Atlas* (1993, 238–45).

For Faversham, however, this is a period when, until after the Norman Conquest, we have very little documentary or archaeological evidence for what happened. We must rely largely on evidence from nearby places such as Canterbury, Sheppey and Milton. Even in these places, where contact with Viking/Danish invaders is reliably recorded (Lawson 2004, 32) no archaeological evidence has been found for Viking presence: no graves or fortified camps such as the one at Repton, Derbyshire, that dates from the itinerary of the Great Viking Army in 873. A rectangular mound at Milton Regis, known as Castle Rough and traditionally seen as a fortress for Viking marauders in 893, has been shown, disappointingly, to be a thirteenth–fourteenth century moated manor house (SSARG 1973, 15–1). Only in Dover have there been found remains of a large timber hall burned to the ground in the late tenth century, and in Rochester and Canterbury evidence for the rebuilding of the Roman walls at this time (Brookes and Harrington 2010, 132, 126).

Nor do place names help. Kent was never part of the *Danelaw*, the part of England that was separated off by the Treaty of Alfred and Guthrum in 878 and given over to rule by the Vikings/Danes. Places like Yorkshire and Lincolnshire abound in Danish names, ending in *by* or *thorpe,* but there is no sign of these in north Kent, with one interesting exception. Nagden's Bump was a small streamlined hill of London Clay lying out on the marsh beside Faversham Creek north-west of Nagden Farm. The term Nagden's Bump means in Norse 'a small pointed stone on a hill', and Brookes and Harrington suggest that this could have been a seamark for ships entering the Faversham harbour (Brookes and Harrington 2010, 123). There have been other suggestions that Nagden was a burial mound (Wilkinson and Mussett 1998), but as the Bump was dismantled in 1954 to rebuild the sea walls after the disastrous floods of 1953, this hypothesis is beyond testing.

In a way, however, the absences themselves are significant. In the mid-tenth and mid-eleventh centuries, times were more settled, according to the documentary records, and local mints had started turning out coins again. From the mid-eleventh century peaceful phase, we find some pottery in Faversham, but it is handmade shelly ware (Pl.10d). It was almost certainly made locally using mud and shells from one of the coastal lagoons, although no kiln clamp site has ever been found. These shelly ware pots are almost prehistoric in technology, and do not compare well with the more sophisticated wares being turned out in the Danelaw up north. Maybe it is not surprising that a little town dependant on trade, industry, commerce, and fishing should suffer more than most from these turbulent times that disturbed and closed land and sea routes.

At the end of this chapter, we will take a close look at the Domesday Book entries for the Faversham Hundred. A hundred is a collection of embryonic parishes, led by one centre. Usually the churches for each parish are linked in some formal way to the main church in the central place, through payment of tithes for example. During the time span of this chapter, hundreds develop

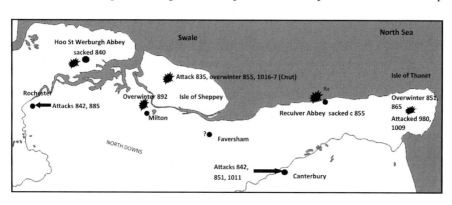

FIGURE 6.1. Documented invasions in the Faversham area, 835–1017

out of the much larger units called 'lathes' that Kent was divided into in the mid-Anglo-Saxon period. The Domesday Book is the most remarkable taxation document of early years, with detailed and systematic listings of types of people and economic assets. Some other local manors and hundreds will be included for comparison, notably Middleton (Milton Regis). This will give us a vivid picture of what it was like in the Faversham area towards the end of the eleventh century.

The Vikings arrive

The early phase

> ... for the first time the heathen men stayed over the winter on Sheppey and in the same year three and a half hundred ships came into the mouth of the Thames and stormed Canterbury and London and put to flight Beorhtwulf, King of Mercia
>   AD 851: *ASC* Canterbury Manuscript

The first recorded appearance of these Norse raiders was in Dorset at Portland, in 789, and then on 8 January 793 the monastery and church of Lindisfarne, in Northumberland, were pillaged and destroyed and the monks slaughtered. Thus began one of the most terrifying episodes in the history of this country and indeed of much of Europe. The Northmen and Danes used two main routes; the northern and direct one was also the most dangerous, straight across from Norway to Shetland, Orkney, Caithness, the Hebrides, and thence to Dublin and the Isle of Man, where they established kingdoms and a passageway into York and Northumbria. The safer route for their shallow-bottomed ships was to hug the coast from Denmark until they reached the narrowest point for crossing to England. Many of the earliest raiders thus made landfall at Sandwich and Thanet. Their ships would fan out along the coasts or probe up the estuary.

At first, they sought islands to fortify as bases, with large safe anchorages for their fleets, so the raiding parties could set off into the interior to rob, sack, burn, rape and pillage, with the security of a safe retreat. Thanet, with the anchorage of Sandwich Bay, and the river Stour, navigable up to Canterbury, was an immediate attraction, but in 832 they attacked Sheppey (*ASC*, 62) and in 841 (according to the *ASC*) attacked Romney Marsh, slaughtering or enslaving its inhabitants, moving on in 842 to London and Rochester where great slaughter took place.

For the next 60 years, they were rarely far away. In the winter of 851 they wintered on Thanet for the first time and the following spring a fleet of 350 ships appeared in the Thames. Canterbury and Rochester were sacked (*ASC*, 65), and no doubt other settlements such as Faversham were raided and plundered. It must be significant that this is the end of Faversham's recorded history for 200 years. To make matters worse in 854 they wintered on Sheppey for the first time, which inevitably meant that the Swale was used to shelter their ships. They would then use all the neighbouring creeks to put their raiding parties ashore.

It is not clear how long this incursion lasted but, in 865, the heathen force was encamped on Thanet. The practice of local authorities agreeing ransoms for them to go away had now begun, a desperate measure as they only went away for a brief period and the news spread of rich pickings. In 865 the promise of money did not stop them stealing away by night to ravage most of Eastern Kent (*ASC*).

During the next few years the fortunes of the Anglo-Saxons reached their lowest ebb. Various armies were now on the loose across East Anglia, Mercia, Northumbria and Wessex. King Alfred of Wessex eventually turned the tables at Edington, Wiltshire in 878 and his immediate enemy, Guthrum, agreed on peace, became a Christian and settled his forces in the Danelaw. Two of Alfred's strategies were now bearing fruit. He was settling Vikings as co-foederati (much as the Romano-Britons had done with the Saxons) whose interests now lay in preserving their property against other marauders. He was also developing a navy. He was also not above paying attackers a ransom or tribute to win himself time. In 885 he drove off a force that was besieging Rochester, which had surrounded itself with a fort, and sent off a naval force into East Anglia which defeated and captured 16 ships. (*ASC* 79, 81)

Then finally came the Norse warlord Haestan, sailing from Boulogne with a mighty host. He set up a base at Appledore and a second stronghold at Milton Creek with 80 ships in 892. Alfred blockaded him there with another fort and managed to dislodge him. In 893 Haestan and his host crossed over into East Anglia, probably induced to do so by the paying of tribute (*ASC*, 88). There they took possession of another fort at Benfleet, sheltered by Canvey Island, and here Haestan may have met his end under attack from the men of Essex and London. The war continued in many other parts of England until 896 but then the remaining armies dispersed and left the country at peace at long last. The occupation of Milton Creek and the fort at Benfleet may well serve us as a model for what may have happened at Faversham. Such Viking forts are likely to leave very little trace.

The recovery of Faversham

In 896 it might have seemed another short respite for the south-east was in prospect, just enough time for the area to recover sufficiently to make another marauding attack worthwhile. But while the region lived in constant fear, it was 84 years before the Viking fleets returned. The fight had turned to the north where Alfred's children, King Edward the Elder (899–924) and his sister Aethelflaed, Lady of the Mercians and her husband, the earldorman, Aethelred, slowly and painstakingly fought to recover the Danelaw, that half of England that their father had been forced to surrender to the Danes in 878. The fight went on under Athelstan, king from 925 to 939, who won a victory over an alliance of Viking and Celtic rulers at Brunanburh in 937 and became virtually King of Britain (*ASC*, 106–9). With the accession of Edgar (959–975) the land seemed at last to be at peace.

How did this affect Faversham? First, King Athelstan held his *Witan* here in 930 (Camden 1610). Perhaps the *Witan* also met at Milton in 932. These two strategic royal manors were at either end of the Swale, which was the important seaway route to London. No other manors in Kent were accorded the honour of hosting a *Witan* by the King, and their importance probably induced William the Conqueror later to retain them as two of only four royal manors in Kent. Both had become the seat of hundreds, probably about this time, as it became necessary to re-organise the administration of Kent which had been so brutally undermined and destroyed for 60 years.

We know that Athelstan's *Witan* enacted laws and may have been responsible for the legislation that later appeared at the preface to the Domesday Book with penalties prescribed for all who threatened the land routes to Faversham. We know also that Archbishops Odda and Dunstan began the re-construction and re-furbishment of all the north Kent churches which had been destroyed by the heathen Viking. We do not know whether Faversham church was included in that number.

Three other developments may well indicate that Faversham had arisen from the ashes. Markets were within the prerogative of the king's grant, and in Kent only two such are indicated in the Domesday Book, one of which is Faversham. Also, part of the strategy to strengthen communities against the Danes was the establishment of *hagae*. These were tenements or holdings within towns allotted to the ownership of outside nobles, magnates or manors, which gave them a stake financially in the town and a reason for supporting its defence. Faversham itself had 32 such *hagae*. Thirdly, charters re-granted to local churches their manorial holdings, which were first granted by the king before the Viking incursions began. In 941 King Edmund restored land at Preston and at Graveney to Christ Church, Canterbury. (Anglo-Saxon Charters 1968, 185). Here we have clear indications of the destruction caused to the area by 60 years of Viking attacks and occupation.

Finally, we have the hands-on evidence of the Graveney boat. In 1970, when improvement works were being undertaken by Kent River Authority to Hammond Drain and White Drain on the Graveney marshes, an Anglo-Saxon clinker-built boat was found in the mudflats (Pl. 10a). The boat was carefully removed by the National Maritime Museum to be conserved and stabilised by the Mary Rose Trust. It was a cross-channel cargo vessel, 13.6 m long, 3.4 m wide and 1 m in draught (*c.* 44 × 11½ × 3¼ ft). Later studies, including dendro-chronology, determined that it was built from oak, in the late ninth century and was abandoned in the mud in the mid-tenth century. One of the last cargoes it carried was hops. Other remains include fragments of quern-stones made from Mayen lava, quarried in the Rhineland (Care Evans and Fenwick 1971, 86–96). This well-built little boat is solid evidence that trade, the life blood of Faversham, was alive and well in the mid-tenth century. The hops and the quern-stones both show links with the other side of the North Sea, up the River Rhine – hops at the time were also a German product.

Unfortunately, the peaceful recovery was not to last.

Ethelred the Redeless or Unraed

> Here came Cnut with 160 ships ... over the Thames into Mercia at Cricklade then turned into Warwickshire in which they burned and killed all that they came to ... after Easter, Cnut turned towards London with all his ships
>
> *ASC* AD1016 Canterbury Manuscript

Ethelred is regarded as almost the worst king in our history. His nickname means he had lacked good counsel (rede, raed) not that he was *readyless*, i.e. *unready*. Historians are divided as to whether his personal performance was all that bad, but misfortunes seemed to come at him from all sides with astonishing regularity. He was to be king for nearly 38 years, the longest reign of any Saxon king.

Ethelred had barely become king when it seemed that divine wrath descended on England. In 980 the Vikings reappeared and ravaged the Island of Thanet (*ASC*, 124) and the next decade saw an increasing frequency of their attacks. Ominously, these were no longer led by warlords venturing out on their own for plunder, but by the newly created kings of Denmark and Norway. The Danes were often able to use Normandy as a base, where the duchy had been handed over to their leader Rollo in 911 by the Franks, to save the rest of their kingdom.

In 991 Olaf Tryggvason, later king of Norway, and ironically later made a saint, arrived at Folkestone with a mighty force of men and 93 ships. He ravaged the area and then moved on to Sandwich. His next recorded landing was at Ipswich. Olaf won a decisive victory at Maldon in Essex the next year (*ASC*, 127). In 994 Olaf was joined by King Swein Forkbeard of Denmark and their hostile fleet appeared in the Thames. They moored their ships either at Sheppey or Grain, ready for an assault on London. King Ethelred's two armadas approached from London and East Anglia to catch the invading fleet within a pincer movement, but whether through treachery or incompetence, the Danes and Norwegians escaped almost intact. They were thus able to ravage the coasts of Kent, Sussex, Hampshire and Essex with impunity and we must assume that Faversham was again targeted.

The Viking main base for the following years appears to have been the Isle of Wight. In 999 the Danes came back into the Thames, ravaged much of Kent, and attacked Rochester (*ASC*, 131). They defeated a local army, which fled, according to Florence of Worcester (1848–9), when help promised by the King failed to appear. Then King Swein of Denmark launched a series of campaigns in 1001 and 1003 along the south coasts. Between these two dates Ethelred handed the Danes a great propaganda boost, by ordering a massacre throughout England of all Danish settlers, many of whom had been settled since Alfred's agreement with Guthrum in 878. Little damage was done, apart from a massacre in Oxford, but the so-called massacre of St Bride's Day was not to be forgotten.

Ethelred's last stand

In 1008 Ethelred ordered ships to be built all over England and for them to assemble at Sandwich the next year. As with those few initiatives that Ethelred displayed it was inevitable that this one should also come to nothing. It is probable that Faversham Bay will have played its part as a mustering point for ships in transit from London or the north and East Anglia, on their way to Sandwich. By 1009 the new fleet was moored at Sandwich to withstand any attackers from Denmark, as it was known that Swein was planning an imminent assault. The navy was in prime condition but the crews were not. Wulfnoth, a South Saxon, led a mutiny and 20 long ships took off raiding. The *Chronicle* says that Ethelred abandoned his ships, but this seems exaggerated (*ASC*, 138–9).

Shortly afterwards, another immense army of raiders, led by Thorkill and Olaf Haraldsson, another future king of Norway, arrived at Sandwich in August. They secured Thanet and marched on Canterbury, where the terrified citizens paid them £3000 to go away. They moved their winter quarters back to Sheppey and spent the winter devastating Kent and Sussex, trying to attack London and eventually returning to Sheppey, where they awaited the spring of 1010, to repair their ships and mount an offensive on East Anglia. The following winter they returned victorious to Sheppey and spent their time ravaging both banks of the Thames.

During 1011 Ethelred begged for peace, promising another large tribute; indeed, so much of the country was now occupied or in ruins that he had no other option. But even while negotiations were taking place, the Vikings descended on Canterbury, and laid siege. After 3 weeks, they broke into the city and sacked it. Simeon of Durham describes an appalling massacre (Thomas Arnold 1885, 143). Of the few that survived, the Archbishop Alphege had a ransom of £3000 placed on his head, and sums were demanded for the Abbess of Minster in Thanet and the Bishop of Rochester (which indicates that the army had already pushed westwards along Watling Street). Florence of Worcester tells us that a plague struck down the Vikings within the city, and the wrath of God killed several thousand (1848–9). The Archbishop refused to be ransomed and was transported to Greenwich where he was martyred on 19 April 1012 when the Danes flung ox heads, bones and stones at him. His corpse was carried off hastily for burial at St Paul's, London. Meanwhile the largest sum of tribute in this country was paid over to the Danes, Florence of Worcester says £48,000 (1948–9, section on 1012) and the invading army left these shores.

The invasions of Swein and Cnut

In 1013 the Danish King Swein Forkbeard returned with a massive invasion fleet and army. His base was set up at Sandwich and this time he had come to stay. He began an extensive campaign across the north of England whilst Thorkill's ships remained moored at Greenwich to intimidate London. Then on 2 February 1014 Swein died unexpectedly at Gainsborough. In a surprising reversal of events the Danes were caught unprepared and sailed for Denmark. The English were left to pay a tribute of £21,000 to Thorkill and his ships at Greenwich.

However, this was not to be any sort of glorious end to Ethelred's dismal reign. Cnut immediately began his plans to regain 'his' kingdom. During the autumn of 1015 he arrived off Sandwich and set off down the Channel raiding the coasts (*ASC,* 146). Ethelred's health was declining fast, and the future was being discussed. Ethelred's likely heir, Edmund, was not even sure of his father's approval and was an unknown quantity. So, when Ethelred finally died in April 1016 there were two possible claimants to the throne: Edmund his son and Cnut his rival.

Cnut was chosen king at Winchester, the nominal capital, but the Londoners chose Edmund II, whom we know as Ironside. Cnut hurried with his fleet up to London. He encamped on the Isle of Sheppey and using his ships at Greenwich had a great ditch dug around London Bridge to blockade the city (*ASC,* 148–50). Edmund, meanwhile had, recovered Winchester. Soon, the Danes were driven back to Sheppey. Cnut seems to have had some grudging respect for his adversary Edmund Ironside and they agreed to meet to partition the kingdom, with Edmund receiving Wessex and Cnut, probably, Mercia, East Anglia and Northumbria, but 6 weeks later Edmund Ironside was dead. Cnut's possession of the kingdom was thus undisputed, the only other possible heirs being two young sons of Ethelred, in exile abroad. The younger of these, only 13 at the time of his father's death, was Edward, later to become Edward the Confessor.

The period between Cnut's accession in 1016 and the Norman Conquest in 1066 was relatively peaceful, although the struggles for power at the top intensified with the rise of the Godwin family (who by 1066 owned much of England) and the ever-increasing power of the Normans. Most of the troubles seem to have been in other parts of the country to Faversham. King Edward the Confessor ruled for 24 years (1042–1066), and was declared a Saint in 1161 because of his pious ways. This is the King who features in the twelfth century wall painting in Faversham's St Mary of Charity. He died without an heir and that is when the troubles returned with a vengeance.

It hardly needs repeating that, whatever fate was suffered by Sheppey, Sandwich, Canterbury and Rochester, was also felt in Faversham and throughout north Kent. With Cnut came more stable conditions and Faversham resumed its position as head of the hundred. We also know that Ospringe Church acquired a Danish round tower (like the numerous examples we find in East Anglia) which fell during the reign of William and Mary during the pealing of bells to celebrate a victory.

During this period, many of the Danes and Normans had supposedly become Christian, including Swein and Cnut. In 1023 the martyred Bishop Alphege's relics were removed from St Paul's back to his cathedral at Canterbury (*ASC,* 156). Cnut's queen, Emma, a Norman princess and formerly Ethelred's wife, and her Danish son, 5-year-old Harthacanute (later king, 1040–1042) accompanied the body to Gravesend by barge and thence by road to Canterbury. There is a tradition that it last rested in Seasalter Church before reaching Canterbury.

The last invasion: Faversham and the Norman Conquest

> Then Earl William came from Normandy into Pevensey. This became known to King Harold … but William came across him by surprise … and there was great slaughter on either side
>
> AD1066: *ASC* Worcester Manuscript

This section is about how the crushing Norman victory over King Harold Godwinson II at Hastings on 14 October 1066 ultimately affected Faversham, as it did the whole community of England.

The invasion route

Only 19 days before the Battle of Hastings, Harold Godwinson's army had fought and won a bitter battle in the north near York at Stamford Bridge, against an invading army lead by his brother Tostig and King Harald Hardrada of Norway. With many of his warriors lost or wounded, he hastened south, calling all and sundry to his cause. We are told by William of Jumieges, in his *Gesta Normannorum Ducum* written in 1070, that men came from Kent and Canterbury to join him – maybe they came from Faversham?

William had left his navy at Pevensey where he landed, and had built a fort at Hastings, to which he retired after the battle to rest his troops. He realised that he had won a major battle but by no means won the war. He moved on to Dover, after he had demonstrated his brutality at Romney, and then to Canterbury, which surrendered even before he arrived. During his stay many areas of Kent, Sussex and even Hampshire offered their submission, including the nominal capital of Winchester. However, it was the capture of London that he decided was the key to his success. He burned down the suburb of Southwark and set off westwards to find a crossing point of the Thames. The way was now open to London where he was duly crowned king by Archbishop Aldred in Westminster Abbey on Christmas Day, 1066.

Details of his route through Kent are not known (though see Banyard 2004, 34) but it seems likely that he took the route along Watling Street past Faversham and Milton, and through Rochester. It is also possible that he or his troops scouring the countryside from Canterbury came to Faversham. If either of these suppositions is correct it may help to explain his decision to keep Faversham and Milton as two of his only four royal manors in Kent. More of this later.

A legend with some truth?

Thomas Sprott, a monk from St Augustine's, stated in his thirteenth century chronicle (1719 edition) how his Abbot and Archbishop Stigand of Canterbury lay in wait for William and his army at Swanscombe beyond Rochester. They were camouflaged to a certain extent by waving green boughs aloft (the similarity to the moving wood of Birnam in Shakespeare's *Macbeth* has not escaped attention) and held swords in their right hands. The Normans, on their way to Dover, sometime after the coronation, were surrounded by this forest. The desperate band promised William their allegiance in return for the confirmation of their ancient laws and privileges. Otherwise a deadly fight would ensue. William, who at this stage of his reign was anxious to win over possible supporters, agreed and Kent thus won its motto *Invicta, Unconquered.* Although the story is clearly fictitious, this accounts for the right of Kent to retain its legal system known as *Gavelkind*, different in many ways from the law in the rest of the country and giving rise to patterns of rural settlement that are unique to Kent: this is discussed in the last section of this chapter (Sprott 1719).

Faversham remains a Royal Manor

Why did King William keep Faversham Manor for himself? He also kept Milton, nearby, a manor comprising Sheppey as well as Milton. The crucial point was probably the strategic position. He who holds the manors of Milton and Faversham controls the Swale, then the main shipping route to the Medway estuary and thence to London. The Danes were still a possible threat even in the late eleventh century and it was probably not forgotten that Sheppey proved to be their last base in 1016. Faversham was to be the king's last remaining port in Kent. A quick survey of the Domesday Book entries for Kent show the astonishing number of manors held by King Edward the Confessor which King William handed over to his followers as a reward for their loyalty, including many of the 225 he handed to his half-brother, Odo, Bishop of Bayeux, with William retaining only Faversham (£80), Milton (£200), Dartford (£80) and Aylesford (£20).

Faversham at the end of the eleventh century AD 1085–1100

> Then he [King William] sent his men all over England ... and had them ascertain how many hundreds of hides there were in each shire .... he had it investigated so narrowly that there was not one single hide, not one yard of land, not even (it is shameful to tell – but it seemed no shame to him to do it) one ox, not one cow, not one pig was left out. And all the records were brought to him afterwards'
>
> *ASC* 1085: Worcester Manuscript

By 1085, the invasions were largely over and the vicious pacifying of the conquered country completed. Admittedly there was still the civil war to come, between the forces of King Stephen and his sister the Empress Matilda over the right to the throne, but the shape of the social and physical landscape was beginning to take lasting form under the highly competent and ruthless management of the Normans. The most remarkable record of these skills in action is the Domesday Book (Williams and Martin 1992).

Domesday charts minute details of the land of England – numbers of pigs that can be supported by a manor, numbers of herring caught a year. Its purpose was to identify, list and quantify anything and everything that could be taxed. Thus, we have details of former owners and tenants (pre-Conquest) and the present-day owners and tenants in 1085. Post-Conquest, most of Kent including

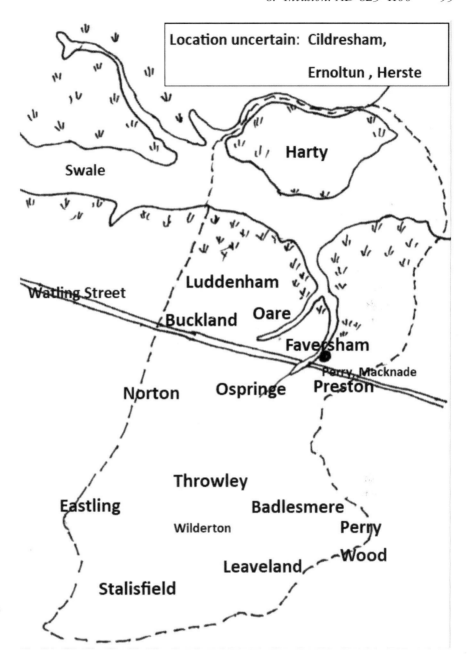

Location uncertain: Cildresham, Ernoltun , Herste

Swale

Harty

Watling Street

Luddenham

Buckland   Oare

Faversham

Perry Macknade

Norton   Ospringe   Preston

Throwley

Badlesmere

Eastling   Wilderton   Perry

Wood

Leaveland

Stalisfield

FIGURE 6.2. The Hundred of Faversham as listed in the Domesday Book, 1086.

much of Faversham Hundred was owned by William's half-brother Odo, Bishop of Bayeux, but some parts of the Faversham Hundred were owned by the Archbishop of Canterbury (Preston), St Augustine's Abbey (Leaveland and Wilderton) or by King William himself (Faversham manor and town; Lawson 2004, 36–9). Only very rarely does the original Anglo-Saxon tenant survive, and the names of new tenants are very much Norman in character: for one of the

Buckland manors Turstin de Gironde replaces Thorgot and for Norton, Hugh de Port replaces Osweard.

Domesday gives the size of each of the manors within the Faversham Hundred in 'sulungs' and 'yokes'. These are Kentish units, not used elsewhere in England where the hide and virgate are standard measures. Up until the eleventh century, units such as sulungs and hides were not absolute sizes as we are used to, but are defined as the area of land needed to support one family. Thus, in fertile areas a hide/sulung is a much smaller area than in moorlands which are much more unyielding and more land is needed to support a family. The Normans would have none of this, though, and sulungs and hides became absolute units, always the same size. A sulung (2 hides) is reckoned about 120 acres (*c.* 48.5 ha), and with four yokes to the sulung, a yoke is about 30 acres (12 ha).

The total acreage for the Faversham hundred, adding up the listed manorial holdings in Domesday, is 44 sulungs, equivalent to around 5000 acres or nearly 2025 hectares. What is striking is the variation in size of the manors. Thus, there are very small holdings such as Mackenade, Perry and Oare with only 1 yoke (30 acres/12 ha) of land each. The largest holding is one of the Ospringe manors, probably the one centred on what is known as Queen Court nowadays, at 8 sulungs (960 acres/388.5 ha), with Faversham itself, the Royal Manor, at 7 sulung (840 acres/340 ha). Then come some of the big Downland holdings such as Throwley (3 sulung), another Ospringe one (4 sulung) and Norton (4 sulung). The Anglo-Saxon idea of a relative-to-fertility unit seems to be holding somewhat as the tiny holdings are in the fertile foothills, with the marked exception of Faversham itself, and the larger ones tend to be on the less fertile and heavily wooded downland.

This downland is of special interest. The underlying porous chalk means that there are no springs or streams higher up in the downs – the Westbrook rose near Painters Forstal and higher up than that, deep wells must be dug and/or dewponds and cisterns created to have a water supply. To make the downland situation even more hostile to farmers, much of the North Downs is capped by a thin layer of sticky residual clay loaded with flints, as discussed in Chapter 2. Alan Everitt asserts that the high downland was not settled until after the Norman Conquest (Everitt 1986, 344). What is especially interesting, then, is Domesday Stalisfield, high up on the top of the Downs.

Stalisfield is listed as having 2 sulungs (240 acres/97 ha), of which 2 acres/0.8 ha were meadow. The manor had woodland enough for 60 pigs to feed on pannage, a number exceeded only by the manors of Faversham (100 pigs) and Ospringe (80 pigs). There is only one plough listed, compared with 43 in Faversham Manor and 31 in the biggest Ospringe manor, so there clearly was not much arable farming in Stalisfield parish. Nearly all the land must have been woodland with pigs snuffling around and scattered huts in clearings.

There are ten villans listed for Stalisfield. Villans were bound in duty of service to their lord but had a good deal of freedom once that had been discharged and under Kentish customary law (*Gavelkind*), they could pay a rent in goods or coin and get out of the actual labour. Domesday also lists six slaves for Stalisfield. A particularly interesting point is the presence of a church at Stalisfield that still stands today as the church of St Mary. This church is nowadays next to a large farm with the modern but telling name of Court Lodge – a name often given to manor farms due to the holding of regular law courts at the gate of the house by the local boss (in 1085, Adam, who had taken Stalisfield from Thorgisl). All the scattered houses would have been linked by footpath to the church and manor.

Stalisfield was obviously a proper little settlement by 1066, high on the Downs. The puzzle is, from where did they get their water? Boreholes drilled in the vicinity in recent times have gone down around 100 m before reaching water (e.g. at Cornhill, Stalisfield). Perhaps they used a dew pond system, or cistern storage? Perhaps their well boring skills were greater or the water table then much higher than I am assuming? What this does show is that folk were determined to colonise this remote and difficult place, an ambition perhaps related to the centuries of invasion down by the coast – perhaps the Stalisfield folk were refugees? Perhaps the slaves were descended from the original British?

The contrast with Domesday Faversham is powerful. The Manor of Faversham was huge, with 30 villans and 40 bordars (less free than villans) and five slaves living there. Only adult males were counted so a multiple of six to include women and children gives a population of about 450. There are 43 ploughs listed. A plough is a measure based on a team of eight oxen, so 43 ploughs is a lot of capital wealth, and there must have been much arable farming – cereals, root crops, peas, and beans. There is also, however, much woodland, with pannage for a 100 pigs and 2 acres/0.8 ha of meadow. Faversham also had a mill, yielding £1 a year, a salt pan yielding 3 shillings and 2 pence, a market yielding £4 and the town owned three properties (*hagae*) in Canterbury yielding 1 shilling and 8 pence. The hagae were tenements created in the tenth century to force other manors or magnates to keep an interest in the defence of the town by imposing upon them a financial stake.

There are two surprising omissions from the list of Faversham's assets. First, there is no mention of fishing. In the Hundred, fisheries are found at Oare, Luddenham (300 herring), Ospringe (10 pence worth) and, more surprisingly, Preston (250 eels), and Badlesmere (12 pence worth). The Preston catch can be explained by there being until recently a spring and stream next to St Catherine's church, up which the eels could swim. Badlesmere fishery, though, is a mystery unless they had a detached possession down by the coast.

The other even more puzzling omission in the Faversham listing is of a church. It seems most unlikely that manorial hamlets such as Stalisfield, Oare, Luddenham and Badlesmere should have churches and not Faversham, the 'King's little town'. Having had its own lathe at one time and later heading up a Hundred, it would also seem likely that Faversham church was the Minster church for the region. Documents known as the *Domesday Monachorum* and the *White Book of St Augustine* do include Faversham church in a dues list which the documents claim date back to the time of the Domesday Book but these are later copies and dubious – in Chapter 7 we will discuss the troubles that arose from such claims. Even if the *Monachorum* is taken as authentically 1070 in date, as claimed, the value of the dues from Faversham's church is only 28 pence, a sum which is typical for churches with no dependant churches and is the same as the dues from Preston, Graveney and Ospringe. On the other hand, Milton's dues are 10 shillings, although Luddenham and Oare are only 7 pence each. This is not pointing to Faversham's church being anything special (Ward 1933).

Nevertheless, the King's Manor must have had its own chapel. We have already seen that this is what happened in Stalisfield, where the Manor chapel became the parish church, and the same is true in Ospringe (where St Peter and Paul is close to Queen Court), Luddenham and other places not just in this Hundred but all over the Anglo-Saxon lands. Even in the towns, parish churches were usually originally founded by the lord who owned that block of tenements/messuages/hagae. There are exceptions to this, of course, e.g. the minster churches of the mid Anglo-Saxon period (see Chapter 5), but the proliferation of churches in the late Anglo-Saxon period was linked to the growth of feudalism and the associated manorial power structure, where the lord stood at the top of the pyramid in all affairs including the religious. So, Faversham's lack of a church in Domesday must surely have been a slip of a quill by the Norman bureaucrat.

The comparisons between the overall values of Stalisfield and Faversham according to those Norman accountants are striking (Table 6.1). Macknade, the least valuable holding in the Hundred, and the Archbishop's Manor of Preston are also included. Luddenham has been included to show that sometimes values went down, post Conquest. The figures for Middleton (Milton Regis), neighbour to the west and another Royal Manor, are there to put Faversham in its place.

The increase in value for Faversham is impressive, though proportionally Preston and Stalisfield have increased even more. Why Luddenham has fallen is not known, perhaps the herring failed?

Parish	value TRE (time of King Edward)	Value at time of handover to new owner	Value in 1080	up or down
Stalisfield	£3	£2	£5	67% up
Macknade	50d	?	60d	20% up
Preston	£10	?	£15	50% up
Luddenham	£10	£6	£6	40% down
Faversham	£55	£60	£80	45% up
Milton	£200	£200	£200	no change

TABLE 6.1: Changes in selected parishes as recorded in the Domesday Book

Macknade is one of those very small manors mentioned earlier in this section. Other very small manors of only one yoke (30 acres/12 ha) give the clue to why these small holdings, barely big enough to deserve the term 'manor', exist. They all consist of small portions of other larger estates – Ospringe, Perry, Oare and Buckland. The Kentish 'Invicta' origin myth, where the men of Kent were given permission by William the Conqueror to continue with their own customary laws concerning inheritance and disposal of land, was described earlier in this chapter. This system is known as *Gavelkind* and has many aspects but the most striking in terms of the landscape was a system of partible inheritance. This meant that when an owner died, his land was not left intact to a single heir but divided up amongst his sons. If he had no sons, it was divided amongst daughters. Dowagers and widows also had rights for lifetime use of parts of the estate. This system was very like that used by the Franks.

The outcome is obvious: smaller and smaller properties, often scattered; one small manor might come from a wife's side, others from a mother as well as chunks from the males in the family. The result is possibly the most confusing layout of ownership and parishes in the British Isles. Before the reforms and amalgamations of 1883 (the *Divided Parishes Act*), detached scraps and bits of a Kentish parish could be distributed all over the place. Luddenham turns up in all sorts of unexpected places – south of the A2 surrounded by Preston South Without, for example, and also the land on which the Marshside gun cotton works was built, surrounded by Oare and Preston North Without. The holdings too small to be proper manors, like Macknades and Perry, were grouped together into bigger units for a parish, Preston in this case with the ancient St Catherine's as church. Preston itself is in three parts, the detached Preston North Without which is really Hamme Manor: Preston South Without which is south of Watling Street and includes Copton, Macknades, Perry Court and Westwood manors: Preston Within, next to Faversham town itself. Chasing up family history from parish records prior to 1883 in this area is a nightmare.

Alan Everitt suggests that *Gavelkind* is why Kent never had agricultural villages or the associated common field system with ridge and furrow cultivation, as in the Midlands (Everitt 1986, 47–8). Instead, he argues that Kentish settlement was scattered with lots of hamlets and farmsteads, little winding lanes linking them and with a small market town to serve their commercial needs. The churches, he argues, are often isolated in the countryside, not because their village has disappeared but because they are serving a wide area of scattered settlement. When it came to the enclosures of the seventeenth–eighteenth century elsewhere in Britain where common land was fenced off from the villagers and often put under sheep, Kent was on the sidelines because the land was already privately enclosed in complex patterns.

What is interesting is that, in describing the mid-medieval landscape, Everitt could be describing the modern landscape of the southerly Faversham Hundred: winding lanes (quite often, even in 2017, with grass growing down the middle), lots of picturesque little manor houses, plenty of woodland, relatively small fields. The trees are different – both sweet and horse chestnut are later introductions – and there is not the same rustling and snuffling as in the Norman forest inhabited by wild boar and deer, although we are told that nowadays this can be heard in the forests of the Weald.

So, let us finish this chapter with a view of this area in around 1090, on the brink of the High Medieval period, the so-called twelfth century renaissance. We will stand on the point where Watling Street crosses the Westbrook in a shallow ford. To the north, downstream, we can see a small watermill, a scatter of little wattle and daub houses along the eastern side of the river and a patchwork of small fields stretching to the east, over the higher ground. Beyond this we can see the cluster of buildings around the Royal Hall and a large chapel: beyond that saltmarsh and the glimmer of the sea. On the west side of the river is forest, covering the plateau and stretching southwards.

To our south, looking up the Westbrook valley, is another impressive cluster of buildings including a church and another water mill. Here the valley is better drained and fully cultivated but the woods crowd in from either side. The hills beyond are thickly covered with trees. A track leads southward, however, past the manor and church, so there must be more people living up there in the woods. Another road runs down towards the downstream houses to the north, and Watling Street runs straight as ever from east to west.

It's a peaceful scene. Only 70 years ago, all you would have seen would have been burnt out ruins, weeds taking over Watling Street and the fields, the people gone leaving only the harsh squawk of the crows. Now, once the upcoming civil war has been sorted, we are at the beginning of some very good times.

Final comment

Chapter 6 has mostly drawn from historical documents and even then, Faversham's fate has been mostly inferred from recorded events nearby such as the over wintering of Vikings on Sheppey in 854 and the sacking of Canterbury in 1011. Even for these, there is, as yet, no archaeological evidence. The only recorded item of Norse material culture near Faversham is a piece of tenth century animal-face motif horse harness found recently in the Sheldwich area (Pl. 10c).

The situation by the end of the eleventh century, however, is very different. The Kings little town has acquired a splendid new parish church and is running a successful market. The transgressions of the sea have led to the beginnings of 'inning', the process of building bunds to keep the sea out and ditches to drain surplus water (Pl. 14b). The other effect of the transgressions has been to move the head of the tide ever closer to the town, giving advantages to shipping coming in and leaving with the tides. Peace at last: good times ahead.

a)

b)

c)

PLATE I. a) Edward Jacob, Mayor and author of the first full account; b) The Institute in East Street in 1900, from a tinted glass slide; c) 1734 etching of the two Abbey gates, looking southwards

a)

b)

c)

PLATE 2. Local field research by FSARG: a) fieldwalking at Ospringe; b) keyhole excavating and sieving in gardens; c) highly organised grid-based metal detecting at Davington

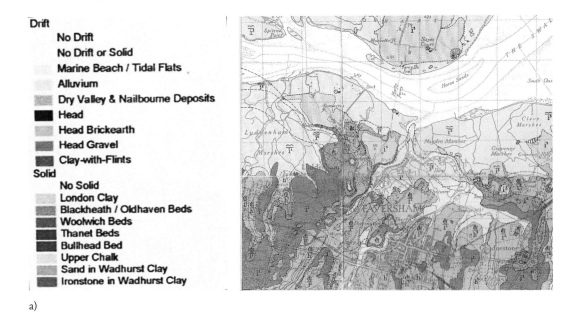

Drift
- No Drift
- No Drift or Solid
- Marine Beach / Tidal Flats
- Alluvium
- Dry Valley & Nailbourne Deposits
- Head
- Head Brickearth
- Head Gravel
- Clay-with-Flints

Solid
- No Solid
- London Clay
- Blackheath / Oldhaven Beds
- Woolwich Beds
- Thanet Beds
- Bullhead Bed
- Upper Chalk
- Sand in Wadhurst Clay
- Ironstone in Wadhurst Clay

a)

b) c) d)

PLATE 3. a) Geological map of Faversham area; b) Lower Palaeolithic hand-axes; c) *Bout coupé* handaxe (Middle Palaeolithic); d) crested blade (Upper Palaeolithic), from around Faversham

a)

b)

c)   d)

PLATE 4. a) Mesolithic flints from a Davington.garden; b) Neolithic grooved ware, scrapers, and aurochs teeth from Ospringe; c) Late Bronze Age flints from Davington; d) Clapgate Spring.

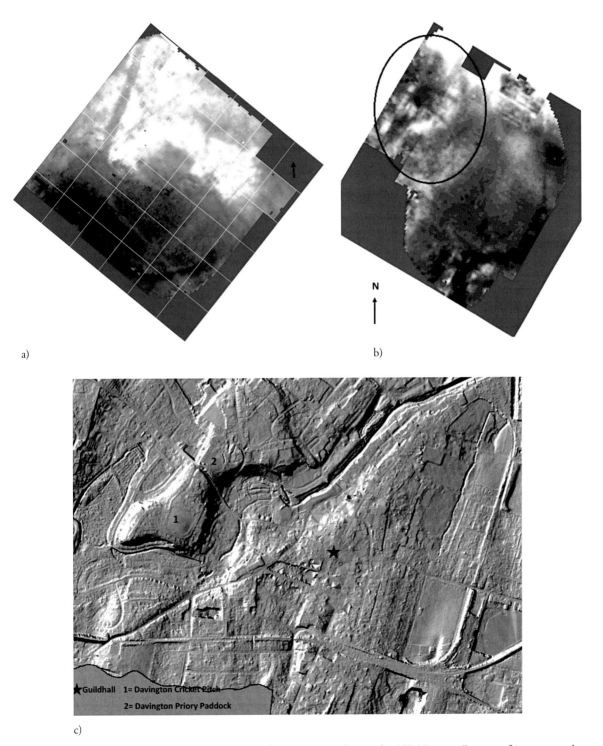

a)

b)

N

c)

★ Guildhall   1= Davington Cricket Pitch
              2= Davington Priory Paddock

PLATE 5. a) and b) The georesistivity maps were created at points 1 and 2 on the LIDAR map. Features of interest on the georesistivity map b) are circled. c) LIDAR map of the modern Faversham Town.

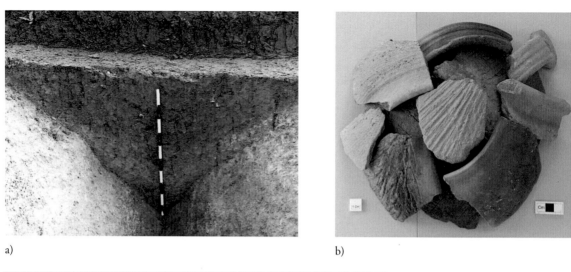

a)

b)

c)

PLATE 6. a) Late Iron Age (LIA) 'V'-shaped ditch near Macknades; b) LIA pottery from ditches below the villa shown in Figure 4.4; c) Roman villa at Sheldwich discovered in 2004: excavating a demolished hypocaust

a)

b)

c)

PLATE 7. Grave goods from the Roman period, found in the cemetery at Syndale: a) game counters and dice, found in the pot;
b) small selection of pottery; c) various glass vessels and fragments

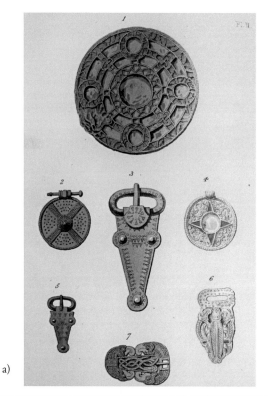

a)

b)

PLATE 8. Finds from the Kingsfield sixth–seventh century cemetery: a) buckles and other items drawn by Roach Smith in 1858: b) Saxon glassware displayed at the Maison Dieu, Ospringe

a)

b)   c)

PLATE 9. a) the Stone Chapel, near Syndale, with Roman masonry; b) Roman spolia at the west end of Luddenham church; c) Piece of an early Saxon cross from St Catherine's

a)

b)   c)   d)

PLATE 10. a) the Graveney boat being excavated in 1970; b) loom weight from the Post Office site, Faversham; c) Norse horse harness part from Sheldwich; d) shelly ware from Tanners Street

a)

b)

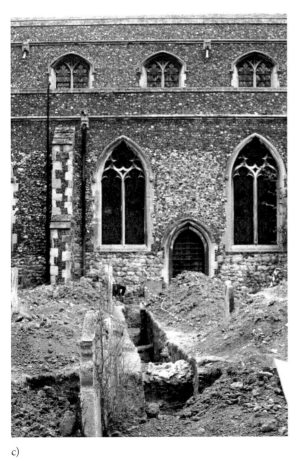

c)

d)

PLATE II. a) nineteenth century version of Town crest; b) thirteenth century seal matrix, Preston Street; c) twelfth century ruins in St Mary's churchyard; d) Mary on painted pillar of St Mary's

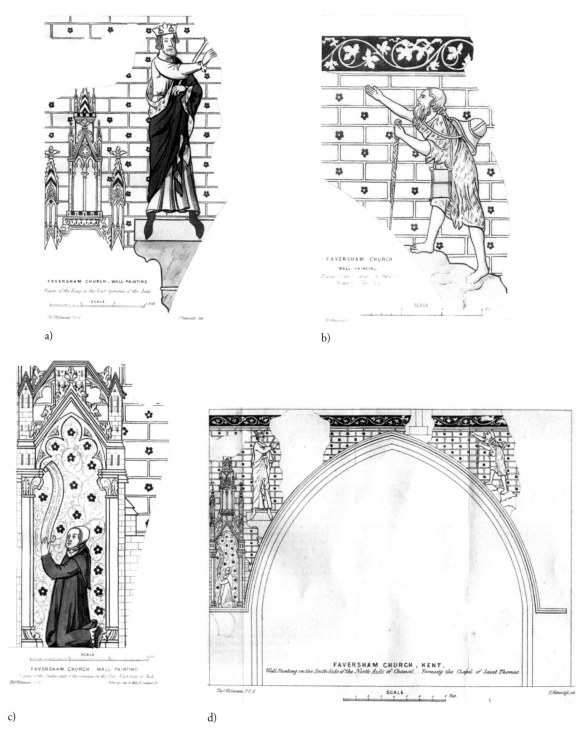

a)

b)

c)

d)

PLATE 12. Mural from St Mary's, dated to *c* 1300: a) King Edward the Confessor blesses b) pilgrim going to the shrine of St Thomas at Canterbury; c) Dod, the donor, prays to St Edmund; d) drawing of the full mural (Willement 1858)

a)

b)

c)

d)

PLATE 13. a) Davington Priory, viewing the east end of the church; b) Masonry at the Priory; c) the Maison Dieu, Ospringe; d) jug from the 1977 Maison Dieu excavations

a)

b)

c)

PLATE 14. a) Faversham's Cinque Port crest; b) building survivor from around 1340; c) across Luddenham 'innings' to Sheppey, Minster Abbey on a high point

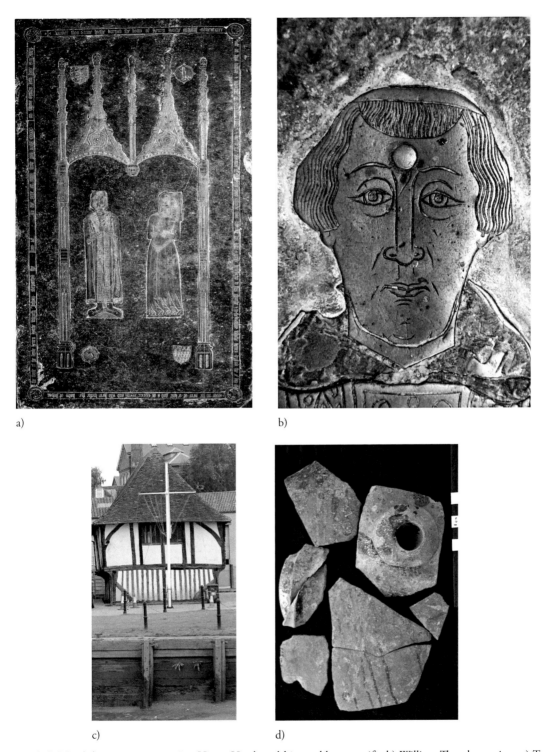

a)

b)

c)

d)

PLATE 15. a) St Mary's brass commemorating Henry Hatch and his troublesome wife; b) William Thornbury, vicar; c) Town Warehouse (Hazard); d) late medieval thumbed pot, Tanners Street

a)

b)

c)

PLATE 16 a) retaining wall behind the Limes in Preston Steet; b) base of 1624 wall surrounding Davington Manor; c) Tudor style gate created from Abbey demolition, Arden's House

Peace, patronage, and the hand of God: AD 1100–1400

Duncan Harrington

Introduction

Whether a visitor or a resident in Faversham, the mid-twelfth century would have seemed very vibrant compared with the surrounding countryside where daylight hours ruled the agricultural day and the bells of the local church announced the services. Boats came up the Swale arriving at the wharf carrying all manner of products and taking away others, especially grain to London. Among the items being unloaded were great blocks of stone for the Abbey that was being built. A great hive of activity greeted the onlooker with masons and their servants hard at work and vertical scaffolding not normally seen in domestic building. Stone had replaced wood initially for the most important buildings and then gradually for the humbler. Such building work was expensive but Royal patronage made the task easier. It was this infectious air of prosperity that engulfed the town.

During the period AD 1100–1400, some 2500 markets and 500 boroughs were created in England alone. From about 1180 to around 1250 there was rapid urban growth with new classes of documentary material giving an insight into regulation and self-governance. Despite England being in a period of intense civil war we find King Stephen and his wife Matilda founding various religious institutions, not just their Royal Mausoleum Abbey in Faversham. The marshland around Romney continued to be 'inned', i.e. drained, and later the area around Faversham, especially in the Luddenham marshes, was brought into pasture and arable.

The transition to peace

The period opens with the death, on 2 August 1100, through a hunting accident in the New Forest, of William II, King of England, otherwise known as William Rufus. On 5 August 1100, after much infighting amongst claimants, William's brother Henry was crowned King of England. Henry I then issued a charter of liberties (see below) and recalled Archbishop Anselm, who had been exiled by William Rufus in October 1097. Anselm landed back at Dover on

2 September 1100. In Rome, Anselm had witnessed a Council that affirmed the right of the Church, rather than local monarchs, to control appointments of clergy to churches. This was opposed vehemently by the Norman monarchs and was the cause of some of the bitter arguments and even bloody battles that took place on Faversham's streets in the High Medieval period and which are described later in this chapter.

Faversham itself had several religious institutions at this time. Besides the great Royal Abbey and the huge parish church, described below, there were several other kinds of religious institutions founded near Faversham during this period. The two most important lesser ones are also described below and their archaeology detailed in Chapter 9, as will be done for many of the local parish churches, long forgotten roadside shrines, and small remote foundations. The medieval built landscape is overwhelmingly religious.

The foundation of Faversham Abbey

Faversham Abbey was founded at the height of the twelfth century flowering of monasticism and it was one of many monasteries that sprang up in western Europe at that time. Christopher Holdsworth has reckoned that something approaching 180 monastic houses were founded in Stephen's reign, a huge number, probably more than any founded in a similar number of years in the middle ages (Holdsworth 2001, 216–7).

The Norman kings were liberal benefactors to the great and powerful chain of Benedictine monasteries centred on Cluny in Burgundy, France. By the late eleventh century Cluniac foundations had become preoccupied with liturgy and splendour. William Rufus founded only a single Cluniac monastery, that of Bermondsey. When Henry I re-founded the Abbey at Reading, he took monks from the Cluniac Priory of Lewes. Stephen, King of England (1135–1154) following the family tradition of founding a Royal burial Abbey, founded St Saviour's Abbey in Faversham with the help and support of his beloved wife Queen Matilda.

The initial problem was that, although Faversham was chosen as the site for the future Royal Abbey, Stephen had already given both Faversham and Milton to reward his great ally William of Ypres. Stephen and Matilda insisted on an exchange of estates so that William de Ypres had to give up Faversham and receive Matilda's manor of Lillechurch at Higham in Kent together with lands from the king's manor of Milton, which seems to have taken place without any discord.

Stephen then approached the Cluniacs and arranged that Clarembald, prior of Bermondsey, a Cluniac Abbey, should found Faversham accompanied by 12 monks. It was a long process, which may have been delayed by the dispute about whether the King or the Church had the rights to income from the Abbey. This argument, between the king and Theobald, archbishop of Canterbury, ended with Theobald being sent into exile. On 11 November 1148, very soon after his return, one of Theobald's primary engagements was to consecrate the new Abbot of Faversham in Kent before the altar of Christ Church Cathedral, Canterbury (Eveleigh Woodruff 1925, 64–70). Present were Simon, Bishop of Worcester; Robert, Bishop of Bath; Robert (Warelwast), Bishop of Exeter; Hilary, Bishop of Chichester; and Queen Matilda, the founder of Faversham Abbey. It is interesting to note that Stephen and Matilda refer in their charters to the Abbot and Monastery of St Saviour's, Faversham when normally Cluniac houses in England were simple priories. Woodruff remarks that Clarembald had a curious preamble to his profession: 'that it is only fair and reasonable that persons who expect to be obeyed by their subordinates should show the same spirit of obedience to their own prelates'.

Letters of permission were read out from Peter, Abbot of Cluny and the prior of La Charité-sur-Loire, addressed to Theobald. They said that they gave permission to Clarembald and the others to build the Abbey 'which they have already begun to found'.

The monks of Cluny already followed the Benedictine rule with modifications. Normally the bishop of the diocese in which the religious house was situated received the professions of obedience but this time it was to be the archbishop of Canterbury.

The new Abbey was on 'the north-east tip of tongue of hard ground that rises sharply from the east bank of the creek to a height of twenty-six feet [*c.* 8 m] above sea-level' and had the advantage of having Thorn Quay nearby (Telfer 1965). Although 1147 is often quoted as the date of foundation it is now generally accepted that it was 11 November 1148 on the consecration of Abbot Clarembald, the first abbot appointed by Stephen, who was in office from 1148 to 1177. The physical attributes of the Abbey will be discussed in Chapter 9 on the findings of archaeology about medieval Faversham.

A gallows and assize of bread and ale were included in the Abbey foundation grant but the homage and services of men of the town, apparently the men of the *hagae* or haws, were reserved to the king. This, again, caused many problems because it resulted in tenants who had previously held land directly from the crown now owing dues, rights, and service to the resident abbot as their lord. Since Stephen's line died with him, it was not the great foundation that he had hoped, but the fact that it owned most of the central core of Faversham had great consequences for the history of the town. (*VCH* Vol. II, 137). The Abbey in having the manor and hundred of Faversham ruled the lives of the medieval community at Faversham.

In 1148–9 Archbishop Theobald of Canterbury at the request of Queen Matilda and Abbot Clarembold consecrated a cemetery at Faversham for the use of the monks there without prejudice to the parochial rights of St Augustine's. There is no mention of Stephen which may confirm Henry Huntingdon's view that Matilda was the main instigator of the foundation. On the other hand, it may have happened because Stephen was at loggerheads with the church and under an interdict from Archbishop Theobald on 12 September 1148. William de Ypres was then acting with the queen as an intermediary between Stephen and the Archbishop. At their invitation, Theobald took up residence in the Abbey of St Bertin at St Omer, so that he could conveniently negotiate through messengers with the king.

Clarembald died on 4 April 1177. In 1177–8 the Abbey was in the king's hands for 20 weeks, during which time he would have received the income. The next abbot was Guerric, formerly a prior of Bermondsey. Elected in 1178 he was blessed by Archbishop Richard of Dover. Guerric died 23 August presumably in 1188. He was followed by Ailgar, elected 15 September 1189, at Pipewell and blessed by Archbishop Baldwin in 1190. There followed Nicholas (1215– 1234) and Peter de Linstede (1234–1267), each of whom had been cellarer to Faversham Abbey and both retired due to old age and sickness. Abbot John de Horapeldre (1268–1271), another cellarer, was followed by Peter de Erdeslose (Herdeslo) (1271–1272).

From a volume of the *London Topographical Record* we learn that the Abbot of Faversham acquired most of the site of an inn in London by the Fleet from William de Baseville at the time that the Abbey was first founded, and right

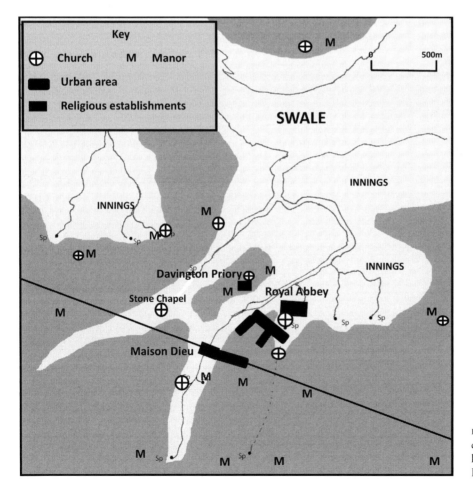

FIGURE 7.1. Thirteenth century distribution of key landscape features in Faversham area

to hear courts was endowed by Matilda, the wife of king Stephen, upon its property in London and Southwark (*LTR* 19, 73–4). The abbot established his London inn with a private wharf at this Fleet site. It is not known when the inn was built, quite possibly shortly after the site was acquired, but it was not mentioned until 1244 when the abbot bought some more land from the Templars. An outgoing charge of 19d to the Templars in respect of a messuage given to them by Brother Soloman refers either to the land on which the inn was sited or land contiguous to it.

From the work of Michael Frohnsdorff in *The Royal Charters of Faversham* (2013), the Abbey foundation charters, transcripts, and translations, together with a commentary upon them, show that King Stephen's initial major endowment to the Abbey was the manor of Faversham. Subsequently his wife, Queen Matilda of Boulogne, more than matched his gift with properties from her own wealthy Honor of Boulogne, the most important of which was the manor and town of Tring in Hertfordshire. This was probably in 1151. It remained with the Abbey until 1340. The land purchased from Fulk of Newnham could well have formed part of the original endowment. On 17 August 1275, under Peter de Rodmersham (Redmersham), Abbot in 1272–1275, Fulk Peyforer and magister Hamo Doges were appointed to the custody of the Abbey which had fallen into debt (CPL I, 470–1). Was this the point where income no longer matched expenditure, even though by 1278–9 the Abbey claimed, and was granted, the liberties and free customs of the hundred?

Foundation of St Mary's (popularly known as Our Lady of Faversham)

Although there is argument about the reasons for selection of the site and, indeed, over the date of its original foundation, it seems most likely that the present parish church grew from the chapel of the former Royal Manor, which is dated by document to have existed in AD 811. In Chapter 5 evidence is given for Saxon settlement in the immediate vicinity of the present-day church. This site, high above navigable streams to east and west, with a view to the coast to the north and forested hills to the south, with warm brickearth soils and a spring nearby, does seem to have encouraged 'central place' development for millennia.

Although the puzzling absence of this church from the Domesday book should not be forgotten, there is no doubt that, not long after the Norman Conquest, it was completely re-built. Our Lady of Faversham was built on a large scale with a total floor area of nearly 15,000 square feet (*c.* 4570 square metres), bigger than some of England's smaller cathedrals (Jacob 1774, 39). This splendid building, endowed with lands by Queen Matilda, was to play a central role in some of the most bitter and violent rows between church and state to take place in Kent during this period.

The problems arose, as always, over money. At the heart of the disputes was a claim by St Augustine's of Canterbury that it held the right to the considerable income from the churches of Faversham and Middelton, tithes from all the rents of those two manors and from all their appurtenances, i.e. from land, wood, meadows, and water; excepting the tithe of honey and money-rent. Thorne, the main chronicler of St Augustine's, writing in around 1397 stated that these rights had been given to the Abbey by King William I in 1070, and gave a long list of charters up to the fourteenth century which confirmed this right. Besides the tithes, the grant also gave St Augustine's the right to appoint the church's priest.

This charter is regarded 'of dubious authenticity and spurious' by Davis, writing a life of Thorne in 1934 (Davis 1934). Lewis, writing earlier in 1727, held strong anti-monastic views and he also thought that the Abbey deeds were forgeries and reckoned that all the incumbents before 1340 were rectors. It is certainly true that a certain Reginald was called rector or parson between 1122 and 1136. This accusation of a fake charter is, however, not simply a notion of modern historians, as the events of 1178 and after show. According to Thorne, in 1178 Roger, the Abbot elect of St Augustine's, Canterbury, 'in answer to the prayers of King Henry II' (and because he needed friends in his dispute with Richard, Archbishop of Canterbury), without consulting his convent gave the church of Faversham to a certain clerk of the king's chamber, Osborn de Camera. The condition was that he paid an annual pension of 6 marks to the monks of St Augustine's. Osborn considered himself a rector. This, Thorne said, was the cause of the dispute that followed. Osborn died on 3 May 1201. That year the king presented Simon Fitz Robert to the church, but he was not admitted. He was a royal administrator, Provost of Beverley, and Archdeacon of Wells in 1199.

Meanwhile, the Abbot of St Augustine's had sent monks to claim possession and put forward a chaplain. Herbert, an official of the archdeacon of Canterbury, disputed the claim. Seeing the danger, Abbot Roger of St Augustine's went himself to claim possession on Thursday, 10 May 1201. According to Thorne, the people of Faversham were on Abbot Roger's side in the dispute and were consequently excommunicated, that is, cut off from all participation in the sacraments. The Archbishop of Canterbury then visited the town. This was followed up by angry letters from King John. He ordered the church and parsonage houses to be set on fire. He relented but, instead, commanded the sheriff of Kent to eject the monks.

The siege lasted from 31 July until 15 August, when the Abbot of St Augustine's came in person and the besiegers fled. The Abbot now took possession until 24 September when he, in turn, was ejected. He appealed to the Archbishop, who relented but, on 24 October, the archdeacon pulled down the altars. The Abbot then appealed to Pope Innocent III, who sent commissions to the Bishop of Ely and the Abbot and Prior of Ely, appointing them judges on his behalf in this case. The sheriff of Kent, in turn, appealed, in the king's absence, to Geoffrey Fitz Peter, Earl of Essex, the king's justiciar.

When the king heard what had been happening, he again wrote angry letters to the Abbot and to the judges, who all stood their ground, at which point the king seized all the possessions of the Abbey of St Augustine's. John, the papal legate for Scotland, became involved. Eventually, the king turned for advice to Hubert Walter, Archbishop of Canterbury, and the patronage was restored to the Abbey and its charters were confirmed.

There had been contention over a whole range of issues for a long period but, as far as Faversham was concerned, the question was about who had the rights to the revenues of the church during a vacancy. The dispute dragged on until 1237 when a composition or agreement was made between Archbishop Edmund Rich and Abbot Robert which, among other things, arranged that the income during a vacancy should be divided between them.

The tranquillity of the church was shattered again in 1301. Peter de Milstede, having been presented and instituted to the vicarage of Faversham and taken his authorised oath of obedience to the Abbot of St Augustine's, afterwards took a fresh oath to the Archbishop of Canterbury as his subject, for which and other malpractices the Abbot of St Augustine's excommunicated him and sent some monks from the Abbey to replace the vicar.

Soon after, on the death of one of the parishioners, the corpse, at the desire of Peter de Milstede, was intended to be buried at St Catherine's, Preston, but the monks of St Augustine's assembled at the house where it lay and caused it to be carried to Faversham parish church. The townspeople, headed by the Mayor, assembled with a great noise and armed with swords, hatchets, and clubs, etc. maimed, beat and wounded the monks and their attendants. They destroyed the furniture in the church and, in revenge, set fire to the transepts and chancel of the church of Faversham and attempted to set fire to the Parsonage House. The church and cemetery were placed under an interdict which brought on litigation as to the authority of the church which lasted for several years. In 1308 St Augustine's and St Saviour's came to an agreement over the advowson and tithes of the parish. Finally, the church was restored by 1327 and a handsome, well-lit chapel was added at the west end of the south aisle at about the same time.

These are fascinating stories. The trouble is that they come from accounts written by monks of St Augustine's and, of course, find everything in St Augustine's favour. They also were written many years later than the events described: William Thorne, mentioned above several times, wrote in the late fourteenth century, finishing in 1397. Historians point out that the claims on Our Lady of Faversham and the Manor postdate the serious fire of 1168 that devastated St Augustine's and, presumably destroyed the library. Michael Frohnsdorff (2016), quotes from the monk Thorne's *Chronicle*:

> In A.D. 1168 on the day of the decapitation of St. John Baptist [i.e. August 29] the church [the Abbey of St Augustine's] was in great part burnt, and in this fire, many ancient documents perished ... In pity for its misfortune, Pope Alexander (III) confirmed the church of Faversham for the repair of the church thus destroyed by fire and set aside the church of Menstre [Minster in Thanet] and Middleton [Milton] to the sacristy for the repair of this church (Cronne *et al.* 1968, xxxix)

Frohnsdorff then says:

> This certainly implies admission that the king, Henry II, had not confirmed the
> gift, and that this must be new money and property, otherwise the Abbey would
> already have access to this source of income!

Whatever the truth, this story of Faversham's parish church is a fine illustration
of the tensions running almost non-stop between the power brokers of the
medieval period. Add into this the extreme and long-standing hostility between
Christchurch Canterbury and St Augustine's, and the fact that of all the
Abbeys in Britain, St Augustine's was the only one answerable directly to the
Pope thereby by-passing the Crown, and Faversham only saw a fraction of the
conflicts. To quote Michael Frohnsdorff once again:

> we cannot imagine how during the turbulent thirteenth century the townsfolk
> of Faversham put up with the presence of two Abbeys in their midst, seeking to
> control their lives and enrich themselves.

The Hospital of St Mary, Ospringe (otherwise known as the Maison Dieu)

The Hospital was in the parish of Ospringe and bordered on that of Faversham,
positioned on the main London–Dover road with its remaining buildings
located beside Water Lane. The Hospital was fed from a spring at Whitehill,
below Painters Forstal, flowing past Ospringe Church and behind Queen Court
and then into the northern part of Water Lane. It crossed Ospringe Street (now
part of the A2) by a ford until a bridge was built. On the northern side of
the street it then passed through the main complex of the medieval Ospringe
Hospital of St Mary.

Large numbers of pilgrims have visited Canterbury since the foundation of
the first cathedral on English soil in 597 and would have passed the Hospital,
which provided a refuge for the traveller, the poor and the infirm. After the
death of Thomas á Becket, murdered in 1170 and quickly venerated as a saint
and martyr, the number of pilgrims visiting the city rose rapidly. In 1220, on
the fiftieth anniversary of his death, Becket's remains were moved from his first
tomb to a shrine in the Cathedral.

Michael Frohnsdorff has written extensively on the foundation of the
Hospital of St Mary of Ospringe. (Frohnsdorff 1997, 10–13). Founded by Henry
III, the probable date is 1234 but before that there are early thirteenth century
charters to the Cartulary of Ospringe Hospital. Frohnsdorff says:

> Let us accept that Henry III did provide for himself and his successors such
> accommodation because quite clearly there were many royal visits to the hospital
> … His father, King John, seems to have come to the vicinity and stayed on several
> occasions, and it has been generally thought that he stayed at Queen Court, the
> manor house of Ospringe.

Lewis, writing in 1727, tells us that:

> the hospital consisted of a master and three brethren who are called secular priests who had taken on them or were professed to be of the order of the holy cross and two secular clerks whose office was to pray or celebrate for the soul of their founder and the souls of his royal predecessors and successors. The design of this foundation seems to be for the entertainment of the King when he went to Dover and France and of the Knights Templars when they came into or went out of the kingdom to conduct the pilgrims who went to Jerusalem. For this purpose, there was in this house a chamber called the *Camera Regis* or the King's chamber of which mention is made in an ancient perambulation of the town of Faversham which chamber, very probably, was a room whereby the king was want to repose and refresh himself when he travelled this road. (Lewis 1727, 81)

Frohnsdorff (2016) points out that:

> it was not a large establishment to deal with the demands of the travellers, sick and the poor, that thronged the hospital, as well as the occasional illustrious visitor with his or her retinue. The master was at first often an outside appointment, but soon it became a requirement that the master should have served in the hospital as a chaplain or priest. Lay sisters and brothers administered to the sick, while the posts of the secular priests were initially set up to say prayers and masses of the souls of Aymer de Valence and his wife. By far the most interesting members of the establishment were the three brethren in holy orders. They are said to have been Austin monks, and that was certainly the case at the Oxford hospital, because their order was less strict and allowed greater contact with the poor and the sick. As the role of a medieval hospital was less concerned with healing or treating the sick, in which the staff had little skill, than with preparing their souls for the after-life and purgatory, the three brethren had a vital part to play in the life of the hospital.

Davington Priory

During the reign of Henry I (1100–1135) Newnham manor was held by Hugh de Newenham, as lord of the manor, from St John's College, Cambridge who were the king's tenants in chief (Hasted 1798, 414). Fulk de Newenham, son of Hugh, succeeded his father in the possession of this manor and, during the reign of king Stephen in 1153, founded the nunnery at Davington. Dedicated to Saint Mary Magdalene, it was a Benedictine Priory. (Knowles *et al.* 1972, 210). Whilst Fulk gave the church of Newnham to the nuns, the Abbey of Faversham claimed it under another grant with Luddenham and the dispute was referred to Hubert Walter, Archbishop of Canterbury (1193–1206) who gave the church to the nuns, subject to the annual payment of 2½ marks to the Abbot and Convent of Saint Saviour.

Henry III, by a Charter dated 22 April 1255, confirmed the possessions of the nuns and granted liberties to them which they claimed successfully, through their attorney Richard de Boylaund, in 1279. Archbishop Peckham, on 10 October 1279, committed the custody of the Priory to the vicar of Faversham, ordering him to be careful of its possessions and to see that the provisions made by himself and his predecessor at their visitations should be observed. The Priory is not mentioned in the *Taxatio* of 1291. Further lands were acquired in perpetuity in 1341 and 1392. In 1343 the king re-mitted to the Prioress and nuns the demand made upon them for wool, sheaves and lambs, granted by the commons, and the tenth granted by the clergy. They had complained of their poverty and a return of their possessions had been made; it was found that these hardly sufficed for their maintenance and the support of alms and other works of piety ordained. Archbishop Langham briefly reported all things well after a visitation on 20 April 1368. A return in 1385 shows that the Priory then owned the churches of Harty, Newnham and Davington worth £12, the church of Bardfield worth 13s 4d and temporalties yearly worth £14 6s 5d (Burke and Young 2003, 14–26).

Faversham Manor and hundred

So that the royal descent can be understood, our narrative returns to the reign of Henry I. Faversham manor and hundred remained part of the royal demesne until the civil war (commenced 1138), which was caused by disputes over the succession to Henry I. His son and heir, William the Atheling, drowned in the wreck of the *White Ship* in 1120. There were two main contenders: Henry I's daughter Matilda, the Empress of Germany, and Stephen, Henry I's nephew, who married Matilda of Boulogne 'of spectacular lineage' in 1125. Henry I insisted, in 1126, on an oath from the nobility and the church headed by Stephen and the Archbishop of Canterbury that Matilda the Empress should be queen.

Henry I died during the night of 1–2 December 1135. As soon as Stephen received news of this he moved speedily from Boulogne to England to claim the crown. He probably left Wissant on the 4th or 5th of December 1135 but found that Dover and Canterbury were held against him. His entourage presumably must have stopped on their way to London and the royal manor at Milton Regis (Sittingbourne) or the royal manor of Faversham may have been their first stop, although we have no evidence from the itinerary of King Stephen (Cronne *et al.* 1968, xxxix).

Is this why Stephen (1135–1154) chose Faversham to build his great Abbey? He might have chosen Milton, a neighbouring wealthy royal manor instead. Certainly, Kent, with Essex and London, was the heartland of his power. Faversham provided ease of access and publicity as it lay on one of the great highways of western Christendom. It also had important trading connections with Boulogne and Flanders.

The story continues with the help of Faversham's unusually comprehensive set of Town Charters. These are important documents which set out the legal position of towns – rights and obligations – and give it the status of borough. Mindful of ship-service that had been provided by Faversham, King Henry III granted a charter to Faversham on 4 June 1252. Ballard wrote:

The time-honoured distinction that was drawn by our forefathers between a chartered borough and a market town shows the importance that they attached to the possession by a community of a document granted by the king. (Ballard 1913, xiii)

A translation follows of the original charter, in the Mayor's parlour at Faversham:

Henry by the Grace of God King of England Lord of Ireland Duke of Normandy and Aquitaine and Count of Anjou to his Archbishops, Bishops, Abbots, Priors, Counts, Barons, Justiciars, Sheriffs, Reeves, Ministers, and all his Bailiffs and faithful of all England and Normandy Greeting! Know that we have granted and by this our Charter have confirmed to our Barons of Faversham quittance of toll and all custom for all their sales and purchases throughout England and Normandy into whosesoever land they come with soc and sac, thol and theam, infangenthef, wreckfry, witfry, lastagefry, locofry and quittance of shires and hundreds with den and strand at Yarmouth just as they and their ancestors their Combarons of the Cinque Ports have had more fully and more honourably in the time of King Edward and all other our predecessors Kings of England and they shall plead nowhere else than where they ought and were accustomed to wit at Shipway and that here upon no one shall wrongfully disturb them nor their merchandise, upon pain of forfeiting ten pounds. These being witness John Maunsell Provost of Beverley, Master William de Kilkenny Archdeacon of Coventry, Ralph son of Nicholas, Bertram de Crioll, John de Lessington, Robert Walerand, Elyas de Rabayn, Robert de Norreys, Nicholas de S. Maur, Anketin Malore, Roger de Lokington and others. Given by our hand at Westminster fourth day of June in the thirty sixth year of our reign.

This charter links the town to the Cinque Ports Federation, but it has been suggested that there was a much earlier connection. Tann, in his book *Royal Charters of Faversham* (2013), covers in much greater depth than is possible here all the charters that relate to the town. Professor J. Horace Round put the connection of the ports sometime during the reign of Henry I (1100–1135). Certainly by 1160–1 we find reference to the ships of the Five Ports. Faversham was already a limb of Dover in 1229, and Tann has argued convincingly that a date prior to the founding of the Abbey and possibly 1143 might not be unreasonable. It was the provision of ship service that was so important to the crown, this entailed providing vessels and men for the Channel crossings and for defence and warfare (Pl. 14a).

In return the Crown granted the head ports and their limbs substantial privileges both in taxation and trade. It made them free from toll and every custom on buying and selling throughout England and Normandy and confirmed to them the valuable privileges, which they, their ancestors, and their com-barons of the Cinque Ports had had from the time of king Edward the Confessor (Murray 1935, 50–4). None of this was in the interest of Faversham Abbey, as it conferred certain privileges and freedom from the obligations to the Abbot as lord of the hundred and manor.

So, what had the 32 householders of the old town of Faversham achieved by this charter? To be able to claim freedom of the ports and the title of Baron gave the inhabitants of an affiliated town a new standing. Backed by the confederation, which helped to bear the cost of obtaining confirmation of charters, maintaining suits, and providing expert legal advice, Faversham could defy its legitimate overlord and refuse him his dues in money and in service. Nonetheless the conflict between the abbot and townsmen reached a peak in the following century. This may have been not so much a result of a naturally emerging desire in the townsmen for urban liberty but of a desire to defend existing liberties and customs held from the pre-conquest period.

In 1310 the abbot came to an important agreement with the town whereby they no longer paid toll, although the toll of outsiders was still due to the abbot. Also, they were not to pay the custom duty of *Gavelcestre*, namely by receiving 1½d from every brewing of ale whatsoever exhibited for sale, nor to pay *Fenestrage*, window duty, namely receiving 1 farthing from every merchant displaying goods for sale in his window in the same town on any Saturday. The original deed has survived with a fragmentary seal of the abbot attached by a silk cord (KHLC/ZB 38). The townsmen in return granted the abbot £10 a year rent from land within the liberty. From the pleas before the king we find that in Edward II's reign, in April 1312, the agreement was recited and ratified. Following that, in 1315, Edward II confirmed the lands, manor, fair and liberties to the Abbot and his successors (Harrington and Hyde 2008).

In 1327 a tallage was made in the town. This was a manorial tax by the Abbot and was superseded by other forms of taxation in the fourteenth century. Two hundred and fifty-three people are listed under the various heading of Bakers, Brewsters, Butchers, Fishermen, Crying and selling at window, Tanners, Inn keepers, Tipplers, and Kingsmill (2) & Colemans Hole (1) with the Brewsters (all female) and Tipplers making up the greatest numbers. A tippler was basically a drinkseller, an ale huckster, a tapster or even a tavern-keeper.

In 1337 watch and ward were ordered to be kept on the sea coast and the Abbot was required to find two men at arms to keep ward at Walmer and 33 in Sheppey of whom 25 were to be of Milton and Marden, three of Boughton and the remaining five of Faversham. At the same time, the town hired the ship *Katerine* for the king's service. In 1346 Faversham sent two ships to the siege of Calais with 53 mariners (Giraud and Donne 1876, 21).

The Black Death 1348–9

The fourteenth century had already been less kind than the two preceding centuries in terms of weather. Heavy rains and low temperatures caused major crop failures between 1315 and 1318, a situation exacerbated by the big increase in population in Europe during the twelfth and thirteenth centuries. Millions are estimated to have died. Up to 1348 the situation gradually improved, although the climate was in general deteriorating and becoming colder and wetter in northern Europe. Then in 1348 came a far worse disaster, the epidemic known as the Black Death.

Chapter 7: Intermission: Weather forecast

Time to take measure of the weather again as there are big changes on the way.

That pleasantly warm medieval period is nearly over, and we are on the brink of what is called nowadays the 'Little Ice Age'. In Greenland, the glaciers are advancing again, and those tough Norse farmers have left the land to the Inuit by 1400. England will see some appalling cold wet weather in the fourteenth century, leading to widespread famine.

On the good side, the sea is easing up on its invasion of the land as sea level falls again.

There is, however, something much worse on its deadly way into Europe …

The latest theories are that this was an Ebola type virus rather than the bubonic plague spread by fleas on rats but, for the 40% or so of the population that died, the distinction is not important. This virus, named haemorrhagic plague, or bubonic plague *Yersinia pestis*, swept through Britain in 1348 and ravaged Europe where up to 25 million lost their lives. For centuries, almost every text book stated that the disease, which caused an agonising death within five days of the symptoms first appearing, was spread by fleas carried by rats. In the humorous but apt words of Ziegler commenting on poor peasant wattle and daub houses: 'The medieval house might have been built to specifications approved by the rodent council as eminently suitable for the rat's enjoyment of a healthy and care-free life' (Benedictow 2004, 348).

The epidemic, in fact, began with an attack that the Mongols launched on the Italian merchants' last trading station in the region Kaffa (today Feodosiya) in the Crimea. In the autumn of 1346 plague broke out among the besiegers and then penetrated the town. When spring arrived, the Italians fled on their ships and the Black Death slipped unnoticed on board and sailed with them (Benedictow 2005).

The epidemic reached England in the latter part of 1348 in Melcombe, Dorset. Geoffrey the Baker recorded:

> And at first it carried off all the inhabitants of the seaports in Dorset, and those living inland and from there it raged so dreadfully through Devon and Somerset as far as Bristol that the men of Gloucester refused those of Bristol entrance to their country, everyone thinking that the breath of those who lived amongst people who died of plague was infectious. But at last it attacked Gloucester, yea and Oxford and London, and finally the whole of England so violently that scarcely one in ten of either sex was left alive. (Simpson 1905, 24–6)

It has been suggested that the overall death rate was between 30% and 45% and contemporary writers give an apocalyptic account of its effects. The plague raged to such a degree that the living was scarcely able to bury the dead.

> Sometimes it came by road, passing from village to village, sometimes by river, as in the East Midlands, or by ship, from the Low Countries or from other infected areas. On the vills of the bishop of Worcester's estates in

the West Midlands, they (the death rates) ranged between 19 per cent of manorial tenants at Hartlebury and Hanbury to no less than 80 per cent at Aston. ... It is very difficult for us to imagine the impact of plague on these small rural communities, where a village might have no more than four or five hundred inhabitants. Few settlements were totally depopulated, but in most others, whole families must have been wiped out, and few can have been spared some loss, since the plague killed indiscriminately, striking at rich and poor alike. (Bolton 2003)

The inhabitants of Faversham and the surrounding districts have left little record to posterity of their own personal account to this new disaster in the town. We have one proof of the effect of the Black Death in our locality: this was the death of the master of the Maison Dieu, John de Lenham and the entire hospital staff in March 1349 (Frohnsdorff 1997). The Black Death decimated an already vulnerable and unstable population which, even by the sixteenth century, had not recovered to the number of inhabitants of 1300. The plague added to the pattern of mortality where epidemics of smallpox, measles, typhus fever and dysentery occurred during the whole of the later Middle Ages. Pneumonia, whooping cough, influenza, and the enteric fevers were also epidemic at times. Death was a much more common phenomenon in family life than in the experience of those of us who live in a modern industrialised society. The great drop in population was further increased by more outbreaks of plague in the late fourteenth century and fifteenth.

A new social landscape 1350-1400

When Adam delved and Eve span
Who then was the gentleman?

John Balle, priest, 1381

The disasters of the early and mid-fourteenth century triggered many fundamental social and economic changes which, together with the greater availability of land, led to prosperity for some (Chaucer's doctor: 'he was a perfect practicing physician', made much of his wealth during pestilences) but for others, prices rose steadily whilst the labour force dwindled drastically. The land owners by trying to peg prices and to revert to labour services caused great resentment among the peasants. If the landowners wished to have labour, they found that they had to offer tolerable terms and so the process which turned the serf into a free peasant continued (Mate 2010).

Merchants resented the fact that continental traders sailed from Dover or the Thames with rich profits made in England. It seemed to them that these Lombard bankers, Hanse merchants and Flemish traders could only have grown rich at the expense of Englishmen. Anger and jealousy occasionally boiled over into rioting and murder and the Lollards were not the only people that resented the steady flow of money from England to Rome.

There were other problems for the survivors of the Black Death, trying to create a new world. In 1370, Christchurch Canterbury organised a special pilgrimage to celebrate the 200th Jubilee of Thomas Becket's death. With such large crowds, however, the event had been a disaster with extortionate food prices, due to a local famine. 1368–70 was the only instance since 1315–17 of a triple harvest failure, due to the weather and the single longest run of below average harvests was from 1364 to 1372 (Campbell 2010, 46).

Unlike the plague, famine hits the poor hardest and unsurprisingly there were protests. In 1381, Faversham and its neighbourhood were engulfed in the Peasants Revolt led by the commoners Wat Tyler, Jack Straw and John Balle. They had a political agenda that included some very revolutionary ideas: its famous slogan, ascribed to the preacher John Balle has been used to head this section. Dartford and Maidstone were occupied by the rebels who, on 10 June 1381, moved towards Canterbury committing great damage.

It was now that John Gardener, a tailor of Faversham, met the rioters 'he well knowing that they had perpetrated felonies and treasons and rendered them aid and favour' and he, with many others, entered the grounds of William Makenade at Preston next Faversham and assaulted him and would have killed him had not James de Frogenale and Thomas Seyntleger become sureties for John Gardener's requirement. John Gardener also went with others to Lymost (Lime oast?) in the village of Preston next Faversham, ejected Stephen de Makenade from his land and destroyed lime sacks and utensils found there belonging to Philip Bode, to the value of 40s. Moving on to Ospringe, John and his party ordered Richard Bertelot to pay him instantly 20s or else he would pull down his house and kill him; they bound him under the obligation of an oath, and carried away wine flagons and other utensils to the value of 100s.

The hundreds of Boughton under Blean and Faversham fared little better. The king's Bench records tell us that Laurence de Breule the constable of the Boughton hundred was almost killed. William Smyth of Boughton, baker, on Monday the 10 June broke into the house of Thomas Garwynton of Welles and plundered his goods. John Brown of Faversham, Limeburner, on that Monday with others pulled down the house of John Kateby in Boughton. Within the hundred of Faversham there are accounts of the houses of Thomas Holbeame of Stalisfield, Richard of Eslyngge and many others being broken open and their goods carried off.

Perhaps what is surprising is how this affair was so short lived. (Hilton 1973). W. E. Flaherty says:

> Their accounts would lead us to suppose that the mighty commotion sprang entirely out of a dispute about three groats, and in the course of a single week subsided as quickly as it had arisen; – the murder of the tax-gatherer at Dartford being the first act of the drama, and the death of Wat Tyler the last; – after which the King and his nobles had nothing to do but to take unrestrained vengeance on the insurgents as long as they pleased. (Flaherty 1860, 90)

Final comments

We are now on the brink of a new century, the fifteenth, which will see a continuation of the unrest and change that we have seen in the latter part of the fourteenth century. The Lollards have already been mentioned and their form of religion, related to the doctrines of Wycliffe that anticipate socialism, will gather in strength, but also be suppressed with a greater and greater degree of brutality: the first burning for heresy is in 1401 and the frequency will increase greatly in the fifteenth century.

During the post-Black Death period Faversham's membership of the Cinque Ports was re-inforced in return for their ship service. In 1346 Faversham had sent to the siege of Calais two ships and 53 mariners, although their quota was only one ship. Edward III, on 12 July 1364, in return confirmed the town charters of 4 June 1252 (mentioned earlier) and 14 November 1302, on the strength of this continuing service. This gave Faversham big advantages, in that close links between the merchants in Faversham and London created a vigorous trade, sending considerable produce to the metropolis and thence to other parts of the country and overseas, especially Calais. Faversham exercised a strong market attraction for wheat, the most commercial of grains but clearly other trades and crafts also flourished in this period.

Meanwhile, at this transition stage to the late medieval period, the Abbey of St Saviour is still very much there, as are the Hospital of St Mary, the Convent of the Poor Nuns at Davington, Our Lady of Faversham, tied to St Augustine's in Canterbury, and St Catherine's of Preston, tied to Christchurch, Canterbury. Perhaps from the viewpoint of a casual visitor, the town does not look very different to what it looked like in 1320, when Our Lady of Faversham's re-build was completed and the Black Death was unimaginable, though perhaps it looks scruffier and with derelict houses around. Under the surface, however, the differences are profound, as Chapter 8 will show.

CHAPTER EIGHT

Faversham Town reborn: AD 1400–1550

Duncan Harrington

Introduction

Relatively few local documents for Faversham have survived from the early fifteenth century so that we know only a little about the town at the start of this period but as the century continues considerably more administrative public records become available enabling us to tease out an historical thread.

The natural resources of Kent made it one of the most prosperous counties in England by the end of the fifteenth century despite it being only ninth in size and having areas such as the Weald and North Downs where settlement was still sparse. The fertile and varied soils, especially the increasingly 'inned' (protected by sea walls and drained by ditches) marshland made it a rich and diverse agricultural region. As London grew so Kent supplied the markets. In the fifteenth century, however, there was a reduced demand for grain, unsurprising given that a population for England of around 6 million in AD 1300 was down to an estimated 2.5 million in 1400 as consequence of the ravages of the Black Death and famines in the preceding century (see Chapter 7). Because of this reduced demand for food, farmers were now encouraged to produce more wool, using those new 'inned' lands for grazing sheep. Rebellions and civil war arising from the social turmoil caused by the loss of so many people, rich and poor alike, however, lessened as the worst outrages were controlled.

By the end of the fifteenth century, Faversham was on the way to becoming a prosperous and independent minded town, but it still lay literally in the shadow of the great Royal Abbey of St Saviour and its church Our Lady of Faversham, still belonged to St Augustine's. As discussed in this chapter, the tensions between Town and Abbeys not only continued but intensified, a reflection of wider tensions in the country about the role of the Church versus State. By the end of this chapter, that great Abbey, nearly 400 years old, had gone, as had St Augustine's, and the town was embarking upon a new, free phase of its existence.

An age of transformation

As Croft says: 'The Faversham evidence comes early in the explosion of urban ritual and ceremony of the fifteenth century' (Croft 1997, 260–3). For example, on the 8 March 1406, the king granted to the mayor and commonalty of the town of Faversham within the liberty of the Cinque Ports that they may have a mace borne before the mayor within the said liberty with the arms of the Cinque Ports fixed on its head. Even more significantly, on 2 September 1408 a charter was granted to the town:

> Whereas among other franchises granted to the Barons of the Cinque Ports of the town of Feversham by charters of the king's ancestors and confirmed by the king with clause *licet*, it was granted to them that if anyone wished to plead against them, they should not answer or plead otherwise than they did in the time of King Henry I, and that they should only plead, where they ought to plead, to wit at Shipewey, as in the said charters is more fully contained [Tann 2013, 118] and although the said Barons have used these franchises up to these times, yet now the steward, marshall and clerk of the market of the household and other officers and ministers of the king have entered the town of Feversham to do their offices there to the damage of the said Barons; now therefore the king grants to the said Barons that the steward and marshall of the household and the clerk of the market or any other officer of the king's shall not enter the said town to do any office there nor intermeddle in any matter there by colour of their office, but that the said mayor and Barons shall have all their franchises without impediment. (*CCR* 5, 1341–1417, 440)

From the early fifteenth century, comfortably off merchants came onto the Faversham scene. Two served as mayor of the Town several times and were obviously movers and shakers of their period. All of them were buried at Our Lady of Faversham where their fine memorials can be seen to this day (Pl. 15a, b)

We first hear of William de Ledes, a prosperous merchant, when he was arrested to appear before the king and council in November 1398 with six others. He had wide support from four merchants and a pardon was issued in March 1399. One letter speaks of him as a ship-owner, which may have been between 1400 and 1404 when he was twice mayor. He was not heard of again until 1416 when he was provided with a royal commission, with Richard Cliderawe of the county of Kent esquire to buy 1000 quarters of wheat 'with all convenient speed' for the victualling of Harfleur and take them to the town of Sandwich. He died on 28 October 1419 and was buried in St Mary's church in Faversham (Jacob 1774, 146).

Next, Seman de Tong is listed in the 1373 lay subsidy within the hundred of Faversham (TNA, E179/225/4). This is presumably the same Seman de Tong named in a commission in 1380. Another, or the same, was witness in various charters in 1389, 1397, 1399 and January 1408 (Croft 1998, 257–9). In 1392–3 there is an *Inquisition Ad quod Damnum* concerning Seman de Tonge's grant of a messuage and land in Faversham and Boughton-under-Blean to the master and brethren of the Hospital of St Mary, Ospringe (TNA, C143/419/13). Seman de Tonge succeeded William de Ledes as mayor in 1401 and was again mayor in 1403. He may well have held office in Faversham before 1401 as he was chosen with William Makenade as part of the royal commission in the case of malefactors in January 1380.

It was now that the Faversham Custumal was created. A book, otherwise known as the Common Place book, recorded documents, oaths, proclamations, legal proceedings, and charters that the town considered important (Harrington and Hyde 2008, 1–76). Justin Croft considers a substantial portion, which includes the custumal itself, is likely to have been produced between *c*. 1382–*c*. 1405. For 1448, the second town book refers to this as 'in the olde quayer that was Seman at Tonge'. In 1409 Seman was granted a royal licence, on payment of 80 marks to found a substantial chantry at the altar of the Holy Trinity in St Mary's Church. Lands were provided in Wye, Godmersham and Boughton Aluph. Later in life he made the benefactions to the Hospital of St Mary, Ospringe. He died in Faversham on 6 January 1414 aged 42 having been born in Throwley. His will is dated 14 November 1413 and was proved in 1415.

Then there is the bold sailor known as 'Arripay', a nickname based on his real name of Henry (Harry) Pay. In 1406 the ships of the Cinque Ports were under the command of 'Arripay' of Faversham, when they surprised 120 French ships, laden with salt, iron and oil. 'Arripay' ended his career with an appointment as water bailiff of Calais with a royal yearly pension of £20. He was buried in Faversham and, from a reconstruction of the inscriptions we know that he died on 26 March 1419 (Weever 1631; Cozens 1793). Why was he buried at Faversham? The explanation may be that he had married Isabel daughter of

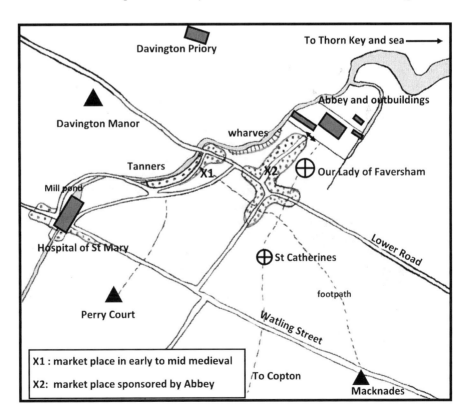

FIGURE 8.1. Close-up of Faversham Town around 1400

Seman de Tonge who, in his will written 14 November 1413, left them both £40 and to Isabel various household goods and 200 mother sheep, with 40 marks to her son Seman. He also left Henry Pay £40 of the money 'in which he is held bound to me.'

Another inhabitant of Faversham who achieved fame a few years later, Sir William Cantelowe, was a merchant who achieved prominence as an administrator appointed by the crown; from 1436 to 1440 he was Victualler of Calais. He also had many complicated dealings with foreign merchants and made many substantial advances to the crown, including £800 to the new college at Eton. He was master of the Mercer's Company in 1450, 1456 and 1462. He was briefly imprisoned after the London riots against the Italians in April 1456, but, after the accession of Edward VI, he was knighted in 1461. In his will dated 1464 he was described as of St Mary Magdalen, Milk Street, London and of Faversham.

These strong and successful self-made men were not aristocrats, and their rise to wealth and status shows very clearly that the old feudal system was fast disappearing and, increasingly, power resided elsewhere. For example, through mediation an agreement was reached on 1 August 1438 between the mayor and commonalty of the town of Dover and the mayor and commonalty of the town of Faversham over the impositions that could be made upon the town by the Head Port (Statham 1902, 185–95). It was agreed in future that Faversham would pay 40s per annum for all contributions, assessments and demands. At every summons to parliament after the date of the agreement Dover was to notify Faversham to provide four 'discreet sufficient and able barons' and Dover would choose one 'whom they at their discretion shall see and know to be the better and more suitable' and return him to the said Parliament as one of the Barons of the said town of Dover. The town of Dover was to pay 20d a day to any Baron of Faversham for each day that he is in parliament. There are endless clauses and caveats to this document.

After a slow start in the fifteenth century, regulations governing trade poured out. In 1437 Henry VI wrote to the sheriff of Kent saying that no person should sell any wool, skins, fleeces, or other merchandise pertaining to the staple of Calais except from appointed ports, such as Faversham. Faversham had less overseas trade than Sandwich, but it vied with Henley-on-Thames in carrying grain to London and Calais. Its oyster fishermen engaged in this coastal trade. The merchants, such as the men described above, also carried wool, cloth, firewood, and timber by ship to London. In about 1450 there was a recession with an agricultural slowdown that led to land being taken out of cultivation, tenant farmers being affected, and ecclesiastical landlords being persuaded to lease out their lands, but matters began to improve by 1500. There was further development of pastoral farming after yet more marshlands were inned for pasture in the 1490s.

There was also a dramatic increase in ale brewing. In 1327 brewing, had been mainly carried out at home by women but by around 1500 it had become

FIGURE 8.2. 'Arripay's' memorial from 1419; a) the very worn real version; b) nineteenth century replica

commercialised and carried out in specialised premises. In 1540 the most common drink was still ale but the use of hops instead of spices produced a stable and long-lived beer brew that travelled well. Hop growing started in Germany – indeed the tenth century trading ship recovered from the marsh at Graveney had hops along with lava quern stones of German origin in a cargo that had originated in the Rhineland. By the early 1500s, however, hop growing had been taken up by the English and by 1540, small quantities of hops were being exported back to the continent (Mate 2006). Despite the spread of beer production into both small and large towns, beer did not immediately replace ale but nevertheless from this point on, Faversham became well known for its brewing, a reputation it carries to this day.

Large quantities of fresh, smoked, or dried fish from Faversham were provided, sometimes under protest, to both the Abbot of St Saviour's and the Lord Warden of the Cinque Ports. This matter seems to have caused endless

FIGURE 8.3. Solid evidence exists for the *Vaults* being a brewery 500 years ago and, except for the nineteenth century when it was a rope and sacking manufactory, it has been a public house ever since. The passage way to the right is the ancient Gatefield Lane connecting the Domesday Manor of Macknades to the pre-Abbey market place in Tanners Street

disputes and so eventually we find the matter settled when King Henry VI on 28 December 1446 granted a further charter to the town (Tann 2013, 128–9). The charter not only reinforced the requirement that 'they should not pleas anywhere other than where they were accustomed and ought to plead, namely at Shepway'. The charter also recalls that the present mayor, barons, and commonalty have been compelled to pay annually to the Constable of Dover Castle and the Warden of the Cinque Ports 2000 herring and sometimes 100 salt fish (called grayling) sometimes to the value of 12 marks annually, all this having started out many years before as a gift. Under the charter the town was immune to payment of any kind and any officer trying to over-rule the charter was liable to a heavy penalty.

The Church and Faversham Town

Meanwhile, the battle between town and the 'blake monks' (Leland 1710) continued. A concerted attack on the Abbot's rights was made in 1412 and 1413. At this stage, Faversham was supported by the Cinque Port Barons in a major protest about a ruling made by the Abbot of St Saviour's. The Cinque Ports barons called in support from the City of London and in an undated petition in chancery, probably of 1389–1413 (Hyde and Harrington 2002, 33–4) the mayor and commonalty of London complained that the Abbot of Faversham had newly imposed, contrary to custom, a charge upon the gathering of shell-fish. The case lasted 8 years, but there was never a judgement.

Up on Watling Street, trouble was brewing at the Hospital of St Mary. The *Patent Rolls Calendar* records that, on 17 December 1418, a commission was granted to the Abbot of St Savior's, William Cheyney of Shepey and the escheator in the county of Kent to enquire into the report that:

> divers defects, dilapidations, wastes and destructions have been committed in the hospital of Osprenge, of the foundation of the king's progenitors and of the king's patronage, and in the houses, enclosures and other buildings pertaining to it at the time when John Fakenham, deceased, was warden, by his carelessness and negligence and divers lands and rents granted to it of old for the maintenance of the poor there and many relics, ecclesiastical ornaments, books and jewels of the hospital have been dispersed, sold and carried off by the said warden and his executors.

This was only 3 years after Henry V had stayed at the Hospital in 1415 on his way back from Agincourt. We also know that Faversham Abbey was held of the King *per Baroniam*, meaning that the Abbots were supposed to attend Great Councils but only a few Abbots of Faversham ever received a writ to attend Parliament and as far as is known none ever sat. The History of Parliament says 'Not many abbots, the heads of religious houses, were ever summoned to Parliament and most who were, never attended' (Davies *et al.* 1982, 91).

All of this shows the waning of the power of the religious institutions in the town, even though this is a hundred years before the Dissolution. The Hospital of St Mary at Ospringe was particularly badly hit by the Black Death and never recovered its former vitality. There were, however, still some benefits coming from the presence of a great Abbey in town. One of these was access to education. Whilst we have no direct records for education at earlier times, it might be inferred that those learned men who described themselves, as 'of Faversham' would have acquired Latin at an early stage in their lives. It is highly likely that boys in Faversham were schooled in the art of writing and reasoning in Latin. In the medieval university, the *trivium* was the lower division of the seven liberal arts, and comprised grammar, logic and rhetoric.

We gain the first documentary evidence of a grammar school master, Lawrence Barry, in the town of Faversham in 1420. Our knowledge of him comes about in a somewhat convoluted manner. Every 50 years there was a jubilee celebration of St Thomas of Canterbury's death which was attended by an immense concourse of pilgrims, some moved by religious fervour others by promises of indulgences for sin and the hope of cure of their ailments. As described in Chapter 7, the Jubilee celebrations of 1370 had been a disaster.

At the end of the Jubilee celebrations in 1420, having secured a successful conclusion that year, we find a variety of accounts of what transpired. The papal bull granting the dispensation to hold the Jubilee commemorating the death of Thomas Becket in 1170 was not to be found, apparently, it had been stolen in 1370, so that there was disagreement about exactly what it conferred. The rumours spread among the pilgrims that 1420 was not a proper jubilee year and that it was due in the next year, 1421. Some started to say that the indulgence only applied to the fortnight following the translation, and not the whole 12 months; and some said that since the papal bull had been lost, no benefits could be obtained at all. Laurence Barry set about elucidating the matter and fixed a notice, presumably in English, to the door of the chapel of the Maison Dieu at Ospringe so that the passing pilgrims would know his findings, although one wonders how many would have could read it.

On the notice, he describes himself as 'Master Lawrence Barry, headmaster of the Grammar School in the town of Fawerscham' (Foreville 1958, 135–7). He points out that he had a singular affection for the blessed martyr and having inspected the books in the monastery, wished to contradict the objections of 'least truth' that the jubilee was not in that present year. He confirms the indulgence, for those that have truly confessed and are sorry for their sins, is for the whole of the jubilee year and that the loss of the Papal Bull did not inhibit the indulgence. For a fuller account of the celebrations, which lasted 15 days from 6 July 1420, see the accounts by William Somner (1640, 51).

The Benedictine rule allowed boys to be taught in monasteries in the hope of making novices. From 1235, the Decretals of Gregory IX specified that the children of parishioners were to be educated in the parish church by the clerk. If, after one year, a pupil was found 'unapte to lerne' he was to be dismissed so that 'he vnworthely occupied not eny more eny rowme or place in the seyde scole'. The education which the boys received in these early schools in Kent would have included subjects which had a direct bearing on the Christian faith and the church services. The curriculum would have comprised reading and writing Latin, music and a knowledge of the Gregorian chant, a study of the scriptures with commentaries and methods of calculating the Easter festival. Others may well have been taught the art of copying the scriptures and other works onto vellum and for those with an artistic gift of illuminating them. This in effect would mean a school room and a school master and so monastic schools came about.

As far as Faversham was concerned, schooling at this stage seems to be related to the parish church of St Mary rather than the Abbey of St Saviour. We know from the orders of the church clerks in 1506 it was necessary for one of the clerks to be resident at night and a further clause deals with the education of boys in the town quire:

> *(Folio 7r) Margin:* x clause. Item the said clarkis or one of theym asmoche as in theym is shall endevour theymself to teche childern to rede and synge in the quyer and to do seruice in the churche as of olde tyme hath be accustomed thei takyng for their techyng as belongith therto. (Giraud 1893, 203)

The orders do not say where the teaching is to take place, but it may have been a chamber in the porch, now demolished, or an upper room by the west tower. However, Edward Jacob says 'On the south side of the west front is a room, formerly open to the church by semi-circular arches, wherein, as far back as I can trace any account of it, were taught reading and writing' (Jacob 1774, 43). He also says 'Probably in this place the wardmotes were holden, which are mentioned to have been in the church'. The parish guide book tells us that this school room was previously a chapel and is now the choir vestry. Below this room is a vaulted crypt. Jacob is no doubt right in identifying the crypt with the recorded chapel of St Mary-in-the-Churchyard. When the party wall dividing the room from the nave of the church was demolished in 1902 an iron grill was found embedded in the wall at the floor level of the room. Anything said in the room could be heard in the church. The beneficiaries would have been the church clerks and other willing to improve their Latin. There is a detailed account of the work by Charles Curling with a picture of the arch and grille.

Munden has suggested that the last two boys of any note who probably received their early education at this parish school were John Cole of Ewell Farm, who went up to Oxford in 1488 (Munden 1972, 461) and John Castlock the last Abbot of Faversham Abbey 1499–1538 (Owen 2014). In 1521 Master John Cole suggested that the grammar school at the parish church should be replaced by an endowed free grammar school attached to the Abbey almonry. A pupil would only be admitted to this school at the Abbey if 'he can sey and rede hys matens evynsong 7 psalmes lateyne dirige and commendacions', confirming that some formal education was taking place in the town well before 1526 (Giraud 1893).

The Hospital of St Mary at Ospringe, especially after secularisation in 1515, may have provided some early education. All that can be stated is that in 1544 the Reverend William Tomlinson besides his clerical duties was required to keep a school. The licences to teach from 1568 onwards has no-one from Faversham until 28 November 1581 when Richard Gill and Richard Wood are granted a licence, Mark Elfry then being the minister in the town. Willis comments: The number of licences increases substantially in 1581, perhaps connected with the *Act* of 1580 which laid down penalties for a schoolmaster who did not attend church' (Willis 1972, 3). Then, on 12 June 1582 Robert Stone BA, the second master of the grammar school, was licensed to teach.

The foundation documents of the abbey indicate Stephen and Matilda intended to free the monks of all secular responsibilities. The considerable body of information about Faversham Abbey yields no evidence of a novice school and it is only in 1527 that we find any mention of education for the monks (Harrington and Hyde 2014). Perhaps it was this inability to attract good novices that helped the Abbey's decline. Certainly, no monk in the time of Clarembald to Castlock emerges from anonymity as a writer of any kind, nor do we find any mention in the Leiger Book of the Abbey of a school until 1527. Recently Professor Nicholas Orme has written an account of John Cole (*c.* 1467–1536) who, with the Abbot, set up a school in the abbey (Orme 2016, 107–26).

Cade's rebellion

The great changes that were going on in England, most notably the rise to prominence of a new bourgeois social class in Faversham town and many similar places, unsurprisingly boiled over into violent action. At the end of Chapter 7, we heard about the abortive revolution known as the Peasants Revolt in 1381. The differences between that event and the rebellion lead by Jack Cade in 1450 are significant.

The 1450 Cade rebellion was a manifestation of the disorderly state of England at the time with many cases of murder, aggravated burglary and highway robbery: even those with a valid title to their property did not always have peaceful possession (Harvey 1991). The rebellion differed greatly from the rising of 1381 for it was supported by the respectable upper middle class and was aimed at oppressive officials who abused their power and, particularly, the sheriff of Kent.

In this popular rising the participants were not just poor rustics, but well-to-do farmers and tradesmen. We find that the following men just from Faversham were pardoned for being connected with Cade's rebellion: John Sencler, esquire; William Barbour, senior, gentleman; Simon Orwell, brewer; John Ulff, fishmonger; Richard Brayton, brewer; Richard Croft, gentleman; Richard Mascell, butcher; John Orwell, brewer; John London, yeoman; John Poland, glover; William Welles, butcher; Stephen White, tanner; Thomas Stede, yeoman. The calendar of Patent Rolls also gives Thomas, esquire; James God, plumber, William Horne, weaver; John Stanmer or Davy, yeoman; John Thornbury, esquire. Also mentioned as being of Faversham in the commissions were John Parminter, smith; William Parminter, smith and Robert Spenser, soap maker (KHLC: Fa/Z/3 and *CPR*, Henry VI Vol. V). If we compare occupations with the 1327 tallage, mentioned earlier, we can see even by this date that the brewing of beer is becoming an industrial process as opposed to the domestic brewing of ale discussed earlier.

It is also little wonder that, on 26 April 1451, the constable of Dover Castle and warden of the Cinque Ports (or his lieutenant) were to cause a proclamation to be made that all men not born within the liberty of the said ports nor having domiciles therein 'but coming thither of late and staying and wandering wither they will, intending no honest labourers there' were to return to their places of origin or abode and those that refused were to be committed to prison (*CPR* 30 Henry VI (III), 577)

Faversham town by AD 1500

Jacob (later copied by Hasted) tells us that, during the earlier medieval period, the market and guildhall (Yeldhall) were in Tanners Street, as mentioned earlier, along with the Abbot's gaol. There is increasing archaeological evidence that there were two clusters of settlement, one around the Stonebridge ford area and another in the upper town, very probably focused on the original royal manor. This is discussed further in Chapter 9. By the later medieval period, however, the market had moved from its original Saxon location to a wide space where Abbey Street and Court Street joined the ancient east–west road, a location in which it has stayed until this day. In Chapter 9 on the archaeology of medieval Faversham, the linking by late medieval times of the two earlier settlements of Faversham will be shown, giving much the same central layout of the town that we see today.

The new market place was encroached upon by the insertion of Middle Row during this late medieval period. This was common medieval practice, occurring in most towns with spacious market areas. When it occurred in Faversham is unknown, but late fifteenth century wills refer to permanent dwellings in Middle Row. The surviving buildings of this period suggest that Faversham was flourishing in 1500 – there was, for example, a wool market and prosperous merchants were erecting commodious dwellings that, a hundred years later, were still considered fit residences for leading citizens.

Some of the sixteenth century owners of these large houses are known to have had malt houses on their properties. These were possibly inherited from the late fifteenth century owners, as at that time there had been a substantial increase in London's consumption of barley, as a grain and as malt, both for brewing, and this could well the source of the new wealth. In the late fifteenth century, more houses with open halls were built, the largest being Nos 10 and 11 Court Street, now belonging to Shepherd Neame. Numbers 7–9, *The Sun* at 10–11, 47, 55 and 56 West Street are other examples. Around 1400 Preston Street and the market place were updated through the addition or re-building of several large and substantial timber-framed houses, with open halls, long wings and central courtyards (see Chapter 9 for more detail).

By the fifteenth century there was a Trinity chapel on the north side of the churchyard in which William Thornbury, vicar between 1459 and 1480, spent the last years of his life as an anchorite in solitary devotion (Pl. 15b). His was one of the commemoration brasses in the church, along with those of Seman de Tonge in 1414 and Henry Pay in 1419 mentioned elsewhere. According to Mill Stephenson, in 1926 Faversham had the largest number of late medieval brasses (26) of any parish church in England (Smith 2004b).

The last throes of medievalism: AD 1500–1550

The second town book records momentous events in the town in the sixteenth century seen through the eyes of the townsmen themselves. We can watch them in wardmote meetings and through the chamberlain's accounts becoming aware of a problem, facing up to it, dealing with it and then reckoning how to pay for it. On top of that, a long series of audited accounts (KHLC: Fa/Fac, 1–196) with vouchers and a variety of working papers have survived. For example, we find an unusual reference to tuitioners and this appears to be someone seeking sanctuary. In 1506 a certain William Basden came before Robert Wythiott mayor of the town 'and sought protection of the aforesaid town and it was granted to him and he agreed to pay for the aforesaid protection iijs iiijd', the money was collected by the mayor, as coroner, for this grant of protection. Such entries peter out by about 1564. We learn about town property from the chamberlains' accounts, which were considered before the auditors each year in the presence of the Abbot of St Saviour's and the mayor.

From these documents, we learn that the Abbey vs Town battles worsened. In 1511, Lawrence Streynsham, gentleman, being chosen mayor refused to be sworn before the Abbot of St Saviour's. Streynsham was by the decree enjoined to take the oath per ancient custom 'truly to obey the abbot and convent, lords of the town, in all lawful commandments, and truly to maintain and keep to his power the freedom and rights of the monastery.' if he did not obey the decree he was to be fined by order of the Star Chamber £100. Because of his continued refusal on 13 November 1511 he was sent to the Fleet prison and the Warden of the Cinque Ports was ordered to arrange a fresh election of the mayor (BL, Landsdowne MS, 639:41). We have no doubt about the veracity of this oath because from 1258 until the dissolution of the abbey the jurats chose three suitable men to be mayor and then the abbot confirmed one of them (Murray 1936, 93–5). Streynsham appears amongst the list of Mayors for 1511 together with William Sparrow.

On 10 August 1514 a proclamation was read in the town declaring that peace had been made with France. A few days later, 18 August, Henry VIII's sister Mary, was married by proxy to Louis XII, King of France and it was a very reluctant Queen who visited the town in October with her train and trousseau (Harrington and Hyde 2008, 98). Henry himself was there briefly in 1520 with Queen Catherine and his chancellor, Cardinal Thomas Wolsey, en route to meet Francis, King of France, which culminated in the *Field of the Cloth of Gold*. In May 1521 King Henry met the Holy Roman Emperor Charles at Dover and they visited Faversham on the way to London. Henry allowed the king's minstrels to play in Faversham every year from 1515 to 1532, but then there is a gap until 1540 when we also find record of the King's players (Gibson 2002 vol. 2).

The year 1533 saw another momentous event in the life of the town. A rich, childless merchant adventurer and wholesale fishmonger called Henry Hatch, who had property both in London and Faversham, died leaving his estate to the town after providing a life tenancy for his widow, Joan (see Pl. 15a for the splendid brass). In 1533, the bequest took the form of £26 13s 4d for a new set of organs for the parish church and the residue for making a new jewel house. Although his widow, who remarried to become Lady Amcotts, fought the terms of the will, eventually his dreams such as the improvement of the creek and the building of a market house came to inspire his townsmen for the rest of the century and indeed up the present day (Hyde 1985).

The wealth of the Parish Church is a measure of how far the town had come in the assertion of its new prosperity. Amongst the records that have survived in the parish collection is an inventory of all the goods and ornaments that belonged to the parish church of Faversham on 8 December 1512. A further inventory of the goods and ornaments in the parish church of St Mary of Faversham was made in 1549 (CCA, U3/146/6). Amongst the few remaining parish records for this period we have three undated accounts by Nicholas Fyshe and Giles Liedgegood for attending the visitations at Sittingbourne and being cited to attend the church courts at Canterbury. A priest's vestry and treasure house were added to the parish church in 1513. There would have been stained glass windows, mural paintings of which one survives, and no pews. There were 12 altars which some of the townsmen remembered in their wills and a school in the chapel at the end of the south aisle.

As for the Abbey, its doom was approaching fast. For centuries before the building of the Abbey the Manor of Faversham had belonged to the crown until king Stephen granted the manor and hundred to Faversham Abbey in 1148 and at the same time set up some form of its own admiralty court with a water bailiff (CCA: U3/146/5/13/1-3). Not only were the lands and possessions transferred to the Abbey but also its various courts and jurisdictions. The *Act of First Fruits and Tenths* passed in 1534, however, gave the Crown financial control over the church and was one of the seminal acts which transferred power from Rome to the English Crown. Henry VIII more than doubled his annual income of £40,000 by this Act of Parliament even before he attacked the monasteries. He continued to get the new annual tax of a tenth even after the monastic property was sold. This led to the 1535 survey in which, on 30 January 1535, Cromwell appointed mainly local gentlemen as commissioners in every shire with specific instructions about what to do.

This culminated in the dramatic event of 1538, the dissolution of Faversham Abbey against whose rights the townsmen had fought so hard and so long. John Sheppey, Abbot of Faversham, wrote to Cromwell on 16 March 1536 in response to a letter on 8 March asking for his resignation. The Abbot points out how his predecessor left the abbey with great debts and that since that time they had been greatly impoverished not only with costs and charges of the crown but also many great repairs, law suits and actions recovering rights of the monastery and money detained by the tenants. He calculates this sum to be £2000 of which the house still owed £400 to its creditors. Despite an impassioned plea to let him continue in his office on 8 July 1538, Faversham Monastery was surrendered to the king. The first account of the ministers for the crown covers the period from Michaelmas 1537 to Michaelmas 1538. Transcripts of these and other documents relating to the surrender can be found in Harrington and Hyde's *Faversham Abbey, collections towards a history* (2014).

The dissolution of the 400-year-old Abbey, about which the town had always had very mixed feelings, completed the transformation of life in Faversham. The main building, a familiar landmark, was soon destroyed and the stones were sent to shore up the defences of Calais, Ambleteuse and Guisnes in France. The town's civic, religious, social and economic way of life was irrevocably changed: the town was now master of its own destiny and some could see that there was money to be made. Yet the townsfolk had to contend with the new owners of the Abbey lands. What of the men who bought the abbey property?

On 10 May 1539, the site of the abbey with the demesne lands was leased for 21 years to a gentleman called John Wheler of London at a rent of £3 18s

8d a year to be paid in four equal portions a year. On 16 March 1540 the reversion was granted to Sir Thomas Cheyne together with other property. As we would expect, however, the would-be purchasers had already been on the scene before the Dissolution, anxious to increase their landholdings. In 1540, when sales began in earnest, the government laid down certain rules. First, it said that all the estates were to be held by knights' service, which obliged the holder to pay wardship for an heir under 21 and the marriage of a ward as well as the marriage of the widow. knights' service was bitterly resented but was only abolished in 1660. Secondly, the holder was to pay a tenth of the net annual value of the property to the crown each year. Thirdly, the holdings were to be sold at a price of 20 years' purchase of the annual value for agricultural land and 15 years' annual value purchase for urban property. Three of the men belonging to the dozen families who were granted half of all the crown lands in Kent were involved in Faversham: Sir Thomas Cheyne, Anthony St. Leger, and Sir Anthony Aucher. The Abbey lands had been farmed by lay farmers long before the dissolution, and, in most cases, the sitting tenants remained in possession even as the landlords changed.

Davington Priory and the Hospital of St Mary met less dramatic ends, gradually fading away through lack of money and support. Archbishop Warham had made a visitation of Davington in the autumn of 1511, when Elizabeth Awdeley (Audley) was prioress. The convent had rents to the value of £31 14s. besides demesne lands which they held and cultivated to the value of £10 yearly. The house had to pay 20s to the archbishop for board at the time of his visitation. Elizabeth Awdeley, professed at Cambridge, had been there 20 years, and Elizabeth Bath, professed at Milling, 10 years; and they said that all was well except that the revenues of the house decreased. There were also two other inmates, not professed, who had been there for 15 and 10 years respectively.

Davington eventually succumbed to poverty. It was found by inquisition on 26 October 1535 that, whilst there had been there a priory of Benedictine nuns dedicated to St Mary Magdalen, where one Maud Dynmarke was prioress, Elizabeth Audley a nun, and Sybil Moonyngs a novice, Elizabeth had died on 12 June 1526, and no more nuns had been professed there. When the prioress Maud died on 11 March 1535, after her death Sybil walked away from the priory, so that it was forsaken and extinct (Wood-Legh 1984, 241–2).

The Hospital of St Mary, Ospringe became a secular institution in 1515, owned by the College of St John's, Cambridge. Its sorry state was described earlier in this chapter and the destiny of its buildings will be described in Chapter 9, along with the very little known about other local religious institutions apart from the churches.

Even the parish church did not escape change. After the Reformation the great wooden rood screen, that separated the congregation from the celebration of mass in the chancel was pulled down, the stained glass was destroyed, and the murals obliterated. The emphasis was now on preaching the Word.

The final stage: A Royal Charter in 1546

After the dissolution of the abbey it became essential for the town to obtain a new charter for two reasons. In the first place, it had to establish its claim to rights formerly enjoyed by the Abbot. On his way to the war in France in July 1545 King Henry VIII stayed the night in Faversham and was presented with two dozen capons, two dozen chickens and a sieve of cherries. On 27 January 1546 Faversham received its Charter of Incorporation. The mayor and jurats had not only regained their earlier rights but now had rights and responsibilities for law and order in the community, duties formerly the responsibility of the Abbot. They were given the right to nominate two jurats from whom the freemen were to elect a mayor on 30 September each year. The King appointed John Seath as mayor, who had the oath of office given to him by the Lord Warden of the Cinque Ports in the palace at Westminster.

The town was to be governed by a mayor and 12 jurats, 24 commoners (12 chosen by the mayor and jurats and 12 by the commoners), four churchwardens, two chamberlains, two porters, two searchers and sealers of leather, two searchers of flesh, one common meter of corn, four auditors and finally two presenters of Court Street, West Street, and Preston Street (Jacob 1774, 69–74). By 1581 they were joined by two overseers for the poor and of their stock of money, two overseers of the stock of corn for the poor and two overseers of the poor each in Court Street, Preston Street, and West Street, two receivers of Master Henry Hatch's lands and lastly two receivers of the school lands. The town was so governed until 1835, nearly three hundred years later.

We are fortunate, since the Cinque Ports were exempt from most taxes, that a Faversham taxation list from 1545 has survived for the town. Boulogne had recently been conquered by England and money was sought for its defence and the continuing war with France. Thus, we see some of the selling off the Abbey's treasures. In 1548, a cross and silver chalice were sold for £22 15s 5d and John Wreke paid for 300 quarters and 22 lb (*c.* 10 kg) of old latten candlesticks. Part of that sum was used for painting of the rood loft and providing the north aisle with scriptures. Finally, after various disputes, John Seath paid £40 for the silver pyx (the container in which the consecrated bread of the Eucharist is kept). Probably before then, and after its dissolution in 1538, the townsmen moved the Abbey's fifteenth century misericords or church stalls into the chancel of St Mary of Faversham. Linenfold panelling from the Abbey was used to furnish sixteenth century Dorney Court in Buckinghamshire.

Southouse (1671, 141) comments:

for although some profit was raised by the pilching of the monasteries of their plate et cetera to the Kings Exchequer, yet the far greatest part of the prey came to other hands. Insomuch that many private men's parlours were hung with altar cloths, their tables and beds covered with copes instead of carpets and coverlies, and many made carousing cups of the sacred chalices, as once Belshazzer celebrated his drunken feasts in the sanctified vessels of the temple.

Final comments

The period covered in this chapter showed the outward continuing prosperity of the town, with money spent on public and private buildings and general refurbishment of quays, sluices, and pavements to be found detailed in the town books. But the skyline was very different, no longer could the magnificent Abbey of St Saviour be seen, just a few remaining useful domestic buildings. Its loss created a mixed set of emotions, for some no longer required for work, others having different landlords, and finally the mayor, jurats and commonality no longer answerable to Abbey in so many ways, they were after 1546 starting life under a new charter.

The archaeology of medieval Faversham, above and below the ground: AD 1100–1550

Introduction

This chapter is written as complementary to the last two chapters on the history of medieval Faversham. Duncan Harrington has used surviving documents to tell us a great deal about life in those times. Until the last 50 years, the medieval period was thought of as entirely the province of the historian, with the contribution of archaeologists limited to the pre-documentary periods of prehistory, Romano-British times and the 'Dark Ages'. Increasingly, however, the skills of both historians and archaeologists in interpreting the past are joined to make an ever more vivid picture. Reading documents about the past is fascinating but touching and seeing its material world also makes a major contribution.

Faversham is itself exceptionally rich in 'standing remains' dating back in some cases nearly 1000 years, and still in use. Furthermore, the gardens of later properties often yield the remains of former houses demolished to make way for new ones. The very first keyhole pit dug by FSARG in 2005 at 78, West Street revealed a horizontal, demolished wall of laths, plaster, and daub with a 1643 rose farthing conveniently sitting on top (FGW, TP 23A). In those days and indeed until the early twentieth century, any kind of discard, whether the rubble of a former house, the cinders from the grate, broken pots, animal bones or oyster shells, were dumped in the garden, whose depth was therefore constantly increasing.

The lands around the town are more difficult to interpret. As emphasised earlier, huge tracts around the town have been ravaged by brick earth removal, gravel extraction and chalk quarrying, all of which destroy archaeology. South of Watling Street, on the lower slopes of the chalk downs, very little archaeology has been carried out, although metal detectorists have been active in recent years. North of Faversham town are the North Kent marshes where recent alluvium masks earlier archaeology.

Chapters 7 and 8 have covered the turbulent history of medieval Faversham town, starting with a busy little market town and port that became a member of the Cinque Port federation as a limb of Dover in the twelfth century (possibly earlier) and ended up as a later version of the same by 1550. In between those dates, the town was overshadowed by a huge Royal Abbey. This was built overlooking the Creek just as the Late Iron Age homestead, then the Roman villa, then the Kings Manor did during the thousand preceding years.

Chapter 9: First Intermission: Weather forecast

The warm weather is to continue for a while yet, warm summers and mild winters. The down side of this is that glaciers and ice sheets are melting rapidly, south-east England continues to subside, and the sea is coming in relentlessly.

The archaeology of High Medieval Faversham (AD 1100–1400)

The major religious buildings

In the mid-nineteenth century, Edward Crow had attempted to find the remains of the Royal Abbey, uncovering chalk and flint foundations in Sextry Orchard, plus much stone and tile and a length of wall. In 1965, the site now used as the playing fields of the Queen Elizabeth Grammar School was still occupied by this orchard. The school building plan was to clear the orchard and level the ground. Brian Philp mounted a rescue operation to take place in what turned out to be a bitter winter. Funded by the then Ministry of Works and aided by volunteers, he excavated the main body of the great Royal Abbey, exposing it to view for the first time in over 400 years (Philp 1968, 1–60).

With the foundations exposed, the puzzle became that some of these foundations seemed never to have been used. The chalk foundations of the west wall, for example, were about 6 m (*c.* 20 ft) further west than a still-standing west wall fragment standing on mortar foundations. Furthermore, it became clear that at its east end, the original Abbey, had three apses (curved extension chapels) built on chalk foundations but, at some point, these had been demolished and the whole east end of the church shortened considerably and squared off. Cut into the original 1148 chalk foundations of the chancel apses were many later graves. Philp calculated that these and other modifications reduced the size of the Abbey by 28%. Originally, it had been planned to be around 110 m (*c.* 361 ft) long, longer than Rochester Cathedral, though nowhere near as long as Canterbury Cathedral at 158 m (492 ft). After the changes, however, the length came down to about 80 m (*c.* 263 ft and remained at that size until demolition. This shrinking made it comparable to the middle ranking Abbeys such as Romsey Abbey in Hampshire.

This major re-build is dated by Philp to the early to mid-thirteenth century, less than 100 years after the original build and the burial of King Stephen, his wife Matilda and son Eustace. He attributes this revision project to the need to create a less ambitious building because of shortage of money: the Abbey would have money problems throughout its life. Probably, however, this scaling down and poverty was because Stephen's dynasty, for which he had founded this Royal Mausoleum Abbey, had come to nothing and a grand building was no longer appropriate (Philp 1968, 36).

FIGURE 9.1. Plan of
Faversham Abbey (from
Philp 1968)

About mid-thirteenth century the Minor Barn and the palfrey stables were built in the north-east corner of the precinct. Presumably there was a medieval Grange farmhouse as well although, as Southouse tells us, Lord Sondes replaced this in the seventeenth century. Philp also attributes the building of the inner and outer gatehouses to this time, although the surviving Lodge adjoining the outer gate is later. A portion of the precinct wall, running down to the Creek from the outer Gatehouse, was briefly exposed in 2007 when the site was cleared for the building of Goldings Wharf (Wilkinson 2007b, 24).

The 1965 excavation produced a great many finds, most of which are currently (2017) curated in the Faversham Society archives. Carved stone, peg tiles, slates and column bases were found, with stonework from an area identified as the royal burial chamber bearing traces of white, red, gold and purple paint. In the living areas for the monks, pottery fragments were found, some of it shelly ware from the earliest period, then the sandy ware from Tyler Hill. From the later period were various imported stonewares from Germany. These types of pottery are common in Faversham and will be discussed in more detail later in this chapter.

The prize collection materials from the Abbey were the floor tiles. Mostly these were broken fragments but sometimes still in place in the nave and transepts. They included a range of early incised tiles, similar to ones from Canterbury Cathedral and probably made nearby in special kilns at the time of building. Then there were fourteenth century glazed tiles, some from kilns in the Thames valley and other thirteenth–fourteenth century ones made in the large kilns at Tyler Hill, up in the Blean woods. These carried decorations of *fleur de lis*, flowers, animals and monsters and were often grouped to make bigger patterns. For some of the decorated tiles the place of manufacture has been hard to define. Finally, there are plain tiles, mainly yellow or green (see Philp 1968, 40–1 for details).

The excavators disinterred ten human skeletons. The Abbey had a large cemetery so this is only a very small sample, representing eight adults and two children of about 7 and 10 years of age. Sex identification was possible with five individuals, all male. The adults were 169–182 cm tall (5 ft 7 in–5 ft 11 in), and strongly built so had been well fed but their skeletons did show pathologies, such as osteo-arthritis and very worn and damaged teeth (Philp 1968, 51–4)

The second religious foundation in Faversham, built in 1154, was the far more modest Davington Priory on the other side of the Westbrook valley (Pl. 13a, b) the Abbey and Priory being very much intervisible. Its foundation and early history has been described in Chapter 7 and its end in Chapter 8. The Nuns' end of the Priory Church was demolished, we are told, immediately after the Dissolution. In 1977, Peter Tester on behalf of the Kent Archaeological Society carried out an excavation and survey to try and learn more about this demolished section and to reconstruct the form of the original church before the mid-nineteenth century refurbishment by Willement (see Chapter 1) (Tester 1980).

Tester found that the nuns' part of the church had extended around 16 m (52½ ft) on from the present church, giving a total length of around 34 m (111½ ft) (at this time, the Parish Church of Our Lady of Faversham was 55 m/*c.* 179 ft long). To the north side lay a chapel and vestry. To the south lay the chapter house, which faced westwards onto a small cloister. South of the Chapter House some small sections of wall suggested a large building, thought to be the dormitory. To the west of the cloister, a wing of the original priory still exists, though very much altered in post-medieval times. Completing the square of

FAVERSHAM ABBEY c.1400
A RECONSTRUCTION BY JOHN BURKE.

FIGURE 9.2.
Reconstruction of Faversham Abbey by John Burke, as it probably looked around 1500

buildings around the cloister there is a nineteenth century wing of the house, built by Willement on the remains of the refectory which was severely damaged in the nearby massive gunpowder explosion of 1781. No finds are mentioned except for many roof slates found in a robber trench on the north side of the possible vestry. These would have been imported from the West Country.

The surviving part of the church, used nowadays as the Davington Parish Church of St Lawrence, has been much modified by Willement, but still has a small, fine Norman west door. Tester (1980) suggests that the aisles were added in the thirteenth century. As discussed below, such thirteenth century additions or even complete re-builds are common in local parish churches.

The third major medieval religious institution in the area was the Hospital of St Mary at Ospringe, commonly known as the Maison Dieu (Pl. 13c). As explained in Chapter 7, this was a very different kind of foundation to the Abbey and the Priory, in that it had a practical function, i.e. the giving of hospitality to travellers going along Watling Street to the pilgrimage centre of Thomas Becket in Canterbury or going between London and Dover en route to or from the continent.

The Hospital site has been excavated at various times: extensively in 1977 (Smith 1979, 81–187) and in more limited ways in 1990 (Parfitt 1990) and 2014 (SWAT Archaeology 2014). The 1977 excavation by the Central Excavation Unit of the then Department of the Environment was very thorough, far more so than the useful but limited investigation carried out by Tester in the same year at Davington Priory. All three investigations arose from development proposals for parts of the site. All in all, with excellent document survival, the Hospital is the most thoroughly understood of these three Faversham religious institutions.

Figure 9.4 shows the layout of the site according to the 1977 investigation, and has become the standard representation even though later work has shown that there are problems with the depicted orientation (FGW, *Understanding Ospringe, Final Summary*). The 1991 investigation took place in the joint cellar of a block of eighteenth century houses facing onto Watling Street and aligned to the road, not to the stream that flowed through the site from south-east to north-west as shown on the 1977 plan. In the 1977 plan, it was hypothesised that the Church (unexcavated at that time) was indeed on this site but aligned to the stream. The 1991 discovery re-aligned the whole block of buildings west of the stream to run along Watling Street. Excavations by FSARG in the garden of the *Ship Inn* in 2009 (FGW, KP43) revealed a section of medieval wall that also ran parallel to Watling Street. The 2014 report on the feature identified as the Common Hall uses the 1977 plan in an uncritical way, so the question remains unresolved.

Nevertheless, the identification of buildings and interpretation of their functions in 1977 remains very convincing. To the west of the stream, which was running in a culvert under the buildings, was the profane – a single storey Common Hall with an earth floor and stone pillars; the kitchen; the *necessarium* (Latrine); the bake house; the brewery; the cemetery. To the east of the stream

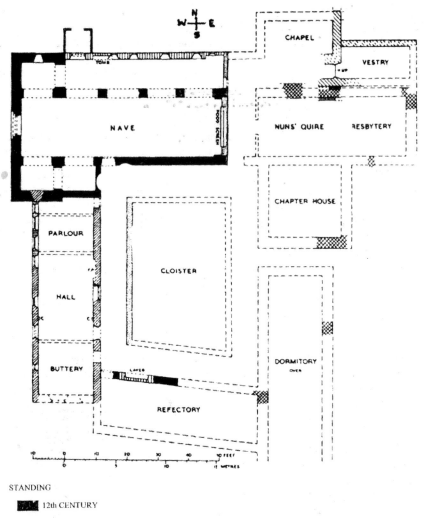

STANDING

▇▇	12th CENTURY
▥	13th " "
▨	14th " "
▤	15th " "
▢	POST DISSOLUTION

EXCAVATED

▩	PRIMARY
▩	LATER
▨	ROBBED

Davington Priory
Reconstruction of the Medieval Layout
From the original by P.J.Tester FSA
(1979)
Archaeologia Cantiana XCV
by courtesy of the Kent Archaeological Society

FIGURE 9.3. Tester's plan of Davington Priory after his 1977 investigations (from Tester 1980). The refectory survived until the massive gunpowder explosion at the Stonebridge Pond next door in 1781

is the sacred – the church, the chapel, the priests' accommodation. Interestingly, the two-storey structure identified as the Camera Regis or Kings Room is in this sacred zone, away from the common people. As discussed in Chapter 8, it is well documented that many high-class folk stayed here.

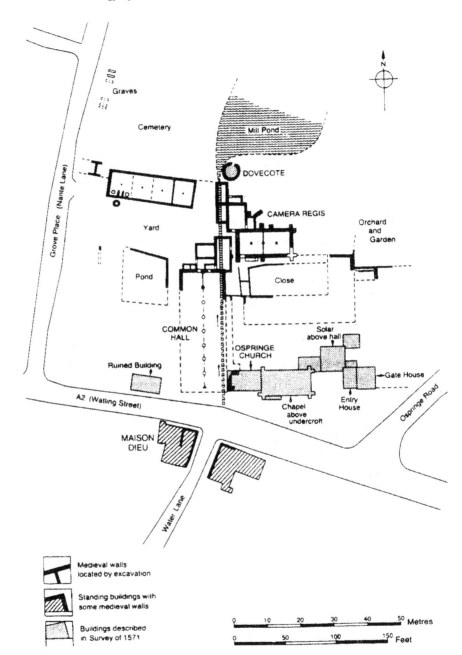

FIGURE 9.4. Plan of the Maison Dieu, based on the 1977 excavation led by G. H. Smith (from Smith 1979)

North of the site the stream was dammed to create a pond. Although direct evidence for a mill was not found by archaeologists, running a flour mill is mentioned in documents for the Maison Dieu. What the archaeologists did find was a circular dove cote. Doves provided food during the hard months of late spring/early summer when the crops were not yet ripe and winter salted meat stores had run out. The doves also provided guano for use as fertiliser throughout the year.

If we assume that Chaucer (1343–1400) was looking back to the early fourteenth century when he wrote his *Canterbury Tales* late in the century, we can fill the complex with people – the Wife of Bath, the Miller, the Knight, the Merchant, the Clerk, the Prioress, all of whom are familiar to us as the kind of people we know today. There they are, some sitting down to a meal in the Common Hall, laughing and talking at the tops of their voices and telling their tales, others sitting aside more privately but soon to be drawn in to tell their own stories.

Finally, there are the small institutions. The Priory at Throwley was built on land donated along with Throwley Church to the Abbey of St Benoit in St Omer, France in the mid eleventh century and dissolved as a foreign foundation by Henry V in 1414 (*VCH* Vol 2, 239–40). It has never been investigated archaeologically and almost nothing seems to be known about it. Two small chapels on Watling Street dedicated to St Nicholas are similarly uninvestigated, but, as according to Arthur Hussey (1911, 250) they were built to serve pilgrims performing the Becket pilgrimage, they are probably late twelfth century in origin.

The churches in the High Period

In 1085 the Domesday Book told us that nearly everywhere around Faversham (with the startling exception of Faversham itself) already had a church (Chapter 6). Nevertheless, almost no archaeology has been undertaken on church sites in this area and there have, so far, been no traces of early pre-Conquest structures except for the Saxon Cross fragment at St Catherine's (Chapter 5). For the most part, material evidence for the churches comes from the standing buildings, almost always heavily 'restored' in the nineteenth century so that spotting early build and re-constructing the early church can be near impossible. Details of the churches have been taken from information lodged on the Kent County Council HER, available online at http://webapps.kent.gov.uk/KCC.ExploringKentsPast.Web.Sites.Public/Default.aspx

These parish churches were not left out of the religious fervour of the High Medieval period. Post-Domesday is when these churches, probably originally wooden with shingled roofs, were re-built in stone with tiled or slated roofs. Sometimes this is not until the thirteenth century, sometimes earlier in the twelfth. Early churches to be re-built were Luddenham (mainly using stone and tile from a nearby Roman villa), Throwley, Eastling, Ospringe, Preston and the now ruined church of Buckland. In the thirteenth century Oare, Badlesmere, Stalisfield and Leaveland were brought into the new world. Two churches listed in Domesday – second ones in Eastling and Oare – seem to have died away, but sometimes the founding of a new church happened in this period, for example, St James's at Sheldwich around 1100.

Luddenham, Throwley and Badlesmere preserve small but impressive Norman archways in their west walls and Norton in its north wall but, on the whole, very little is left of the first Norman stone built phase. As time goes by, the medieval churches added aisles (e.g. Ospringe) and chapels (e.g. Throwley), extended chancels (e.g. Sheldwich) and put in new fashionable windows (e.g. Preston and Norton). Between 1100 and 1350, the message seems to be one of a rapidly increasing and affluent population up on the Downs and around Faversham.

Two churches have not been included in the discussion so far. One is the Stone Chapel, dedicated to Our Lady of Elwarton. This church went out of use around 1540. The controversies over the origin of this little church near Watling Street have already been discussed in Chapter 5. In the thirteenth century a chancel was added to the building and in the next century the nave was extended but because of the ruined nature of the church little more can be said. The other omission is the great parish church of Faversham, dedicated, according to Hasted (1798, 362) to the Assumption of St Mary and known as Our Lady of Faversham in the medieval period. James (1990) makes a case for the name St Mary of Charity being a post-Reformation conceit.

Our Lady of Faversham is a remarkable church, both as a building and as a community. Its extraordinarily stormy history in the thirteenth century involving battles between St Augustine's, the Archbishopric, the King, the Pope and (always!) the people of Faversham has been outlined in Chapter 7, a tale of riot, excommunication, fraud and quite extreme violence. It is told in fascinating detail by James (1990). As far as the modern church is concerned, hardly anything remains above ground of the Norman building that must have witnessed these extraordinary events. James makes a case for some traces of this Norman church in the west wall and points out the mention of a bell tower in a description of the 1301 riot but he goes mainly for a major fourteenth century re-build, starting around 1340. As James says, this was a tremendous undertaking which is all the more puzzling when the horrifying events of the mid-fourteenth century and the difficult, changed times that followed are considered. The thinking now seems to be that this enormous re-build took place rather earlier, towards the end of the thirteenth and the beginning of the fourteenth century i.e. towards the end of a confident and creative period rather than across one of the most disastrous centuries this country has known (Benedictow 2005).

A vivid piece of evidence for this earlier date is a mural surviving in an alcove of the chancel, hidden behind the organ since a nineteenth century re-shuffle. This large and accomplished wall painting is of the classic thirteenth century image of Saint Edward the Confessor giving a ring to a pilgrim/beggar. In the corner of the mural is a small kneeling figure named in his scroll as Robert Dod. The scroll also contains a prayer to Saint Edmund of Bury. This very distinctive wall painting has been dated to around 1300–1320 and must have been created to adorn the new chancel that survives to this day (Pl. 12).

One solid piece of archaeological evidence for the old Norman church has, however, come to light in recent years. In 2006, considerable excavation took place in the churchyard to install an improved drainage system, including new soakaways (SWAT Archaeology 2006). Stretches of wall were revealed north of the nave, much interrupted by later burials. In places, the walls showed signs of vaulting. The walls appear to have been built on foundations set into a trench and were composed of flint and chalk, bound together with shelly mortar (Pl. 11c). No datable finds were associated with these walls but twelfth–thirteenth century seemed likely from the nature of the mortar, very like that used in the original building of the Abbey.

What were these buildings? There is documentary reference to chapels in the graveyard north of the church in the fifteenth century (James 1990, 32), for which these could be an undercroft. If so, these were early chapels for it seems likely that these walls represent a survival of the original Norman build. These are also probably the so-called 'Roman remains' listed on the Kent HER as 'foundations of Roman buildings (that) have been observed north of the nave of the church during the eighteenth century rebuild', now seen to be medieval in date.

How could we find out more about these mystery structures? Even in the twenty-first century graveyards like this are still very much sacred places and research archaeologists would not presume to ask for permission to dig. Non-invasive survey techniques such as georesistivity or magnetometry would be greatly hampered by layers of burials with iron coffin fittings. Nevertheless, it would be good to know more about these striking remains, the only convincing survivals of the Norman church.

Everyday life in the High Period

In Faversham's surrounding villages, hardly any archaeology has been carried out that reveals details of everyday life in this High Medieval period. Although the early manor sites mentioned in Domesday and the numerous small manor farms that were established later, as the population grew and estates were subdivided, have nearly all remained in occupation right up to the present day, the modern buildings are all replacements of the High Medieval accommodation, such as at Abbey Farm. Mostly these replacements are seventeenth century but some Domesday manors such as Makenade and Perry are more modern structures. Occasionally, earlier buildings have survived e.g. at Copton Manor which has some fourteenth century structures; Luddenham Court, which is a fifteenth century building re-faced in the eighteenth century; and Queen Court in Ospringe, which still has its sixteenth century timber frame. Several of the re-built old manors still retain medieval outbuildings such as the stables and barns at Abbey Farm, mentioned earlier.

The only exception to the lack of investigation of local medieval manors involved the search for the 'real' Davington Manor, next door to Faversham on the Davington plateau. This manor was well documented for the medieval period (Hasted 1798, 372–81). In the late 1960s, a large, seemingly ancient timber framed property with Tudor style chimneys, was demolished at the top of Dark Hill to make way for housing. Faversham people assumed that this property, known as Davington Court and having a large medieval barn nearby, was the medieval Davington Manor. In 2010, FSARG became aware

FIGURE 9.5. The twelfth century wall with arched gate, photographed in Stephens Close after the building of the 1960s houses but before the demolition of the 'fake' Davington Court seen in the background in 1963

that this was a wrong assumption, and that this so-called Manor was in fact a farm bailiff's house (Willement 1862, 49), grossly gentrified around 1900

Investigations over the next year revealed the remains of a very substantial stone-built property just to the west of the fake manor. Figure 9.5, taken in the 1960s, illustrates this paradox very well, with a surviving section of the stone wall of the 'real' manor in the foreground, brand new development either side and the 'fake' manor in the background, just before demolition. Keyhole excavations and surveys in all the surrounding gardens identified the earlier property being replaced in 1624 by a brick and tile mansion with brick-built cellars. Medieval walls too substantial for demolition were left as garden features. Willement (1862) tells us the Jacobean house was demolished in the 1650s, probably because of the rapidly growing gunpowder industry nearby with its constant explosions. A lot of red brick, blue glazed brick and red tile demolition materials were found in local garden excavations, as well as stone and flint wall foundations from the medieval house. (FGW, *The Davington Mysteries*).

The rest of this section concentrates on Faversham, Ospringe, Davington and Preston which nowadays make up the Borough of Faversham. It covers small scale work carried out by commercial archaeological units and by FSARG. As has been said before in this volume, the lack of any large scale development in Faversham to date has meant an unusual degree of preservation of archaeology in gardens, except in parts affected by brickearth extraction, but it also means that no large open areas have been available for commercial or research investigations.

Apart from churches and manor sites, there are few properties surviving in the Faversham area that can be dated to the period 1100–1400. In Ospringe, there are two on the south side of Watling Street, opposite the main Hospital complex, with lower parts that can be dated to around 1250 although their superstructures are post-medieval (Pl. 13c). These buildings lie either side of Water Lane, down which the Westbrook used to flow until it was culverted in the 1960s and they may have been part of the Hospital complex. The most easterly one is known as the Maison Dieu nowadays and is a Scheduled Ancient Monument that houses an impressive display of Roman, medieval, and post-medieval finds from the immediate area (see Chapters 7 and 8). The most notable feature of the Maison Dieu is the stone undercroft, through which the stream flowed in the past. Other early buildings are in Faversham town centre: one is part of a complex centred on a courtyard next to the Market Place, again thought to date to around 1250, and the other is the descendant of a large medieval Hall House on Abbey Street, dating from around 1330. This latter, much updated, has been used as the *Phoenix* public house since the nineteenth century (Pl. 14b).

Evidence for occupations comes mainly from the waterside area. The importance of Faversham as a port has been emphasised throughout this volume, especially in Chapter 7 when membership of the Cinque Ports Federation became vital to the town's sense of identity. As Harrington states earlier in this volume, there must have been movements of enormous amounts of building materials by water during this time, as stone was brought by water from the ragstone quarries near Maidstone on the Medway, and Caen stone quarries of Normandy. Other kinds of goods coming in will be described later on in this section, and must have given a lot of employment, both on land and in the ships. Unfortunately, the site of the 'great key at Thorne' mentioned by Edward Jacob (Jacob 1774, 14) as the point at which ships offloaded cargoes that then came upstream in smaller vessels in the medieval period, is nowadays the site of a large sewage works, and not susceptible to archaeological investigation.

In Tanners Street, FSARG found a post-medieval tanning yard with a courtyard of rammed chalk. When the chalk was removed, a deposit of horn cores was revealed. In medieval tanning hides were delivered to the tannery with skulls and feet still attached. The tanner would sell the outer layer of the horns to make knife handles and lanterns, and dump the cores. In the Tanners Street core dump were fragments of medieval pottery that dated the dump firmly, solid evidence for tanning as a livelihood back as far as the thirteenth century (FGW: TP25).

Another set of occupations centred on milling. The charting of a pond next to the Maison Dieu is physical evidence for this, although in the Westbrook

FIGURE 9.6. Horn core dump beneath the rammed chalk floor of a later tannery. The tabs indicate finds of pottery, the earliest of which was thirteenth century

valley itself the later gunpowder industry, equally dependant on water power, has erased all signs of medieval flour milling downstream from Ospringe.

The most abundant find by far for this High Medieval period in Faversham gardens is pottery. Pottery is useful not only for telling us about what people owned and used and thus their standard of living, but also because pottery is distinctive and can therefore usually be assigned to a place and approximate date of manufacture. It therefore tells us about trade contacts at specific times. Archaeologists can judge from the size of sherds and freshness of the broken edges whether the pot was simply broken and discarded, never to be looked at again, or whether it had become part of the midden compost spread across the fields. In this latter case, the pottery sherd becomes broken up by the plough over the years into small, very worn pieces. Finding such 'midden scatter' is a reliable sign that a piece of land was used for agriculture during the medieval period.

Up till around AD 1200, the main kind of pottery used in Faversham was, as mentioned in Chapter 6, a surprisingly primitive kind with simple pot shapes and with crushed shell used to temper the clay. The outside is often a pinkish colour (Pl. 10d). This shelly ware was usually handmade and slow wheel finished and although no kilns have been found in north Kent, it is reasonable to suppose that it was made locally (Cotter 1999). By the end of the twelfth century the shelly ware contained less shell and more sand and by 1225 it had gone out of use, never to return, so in the places where we find shelly ware we know that people were living there around 1000–1200. So far, three top spots have emerged in Faversham for this kind of pottery: Tanners Street, northern Preston Street and Abbey Place. It has already been said that Tanners Street is seen as the site for the original Saxon settlement (Jacob 1774, 15–16; KCC Heritage Conservation Group 2003, 14) and the shelly ware confirms that this habitation continued until the early Middle Ages.

Shelly ware was abandoned in favour of a new kind of pottery known to archaeologists as Tyler Hill ware after its place of manufacture. Tyler Hill, up in the Blean woods above Canterbury, had become the provider of the newly invented and instantly popular Kent peg tiles from about AD1200 onwards, and the tilers soon began to make pottery as well (Cotter 2001). This was a hard, sandy ware, orange on the outside and grey inside, often decorated with finger printed strips, stabbing and splashed glaze. Around 80% of FSARG's archive of medieval pottery is of Tyler Hill origin (Pl. 15d).

To begin with, the Tyler Hill potters dusted the outside of their pots with crushed shell, as a kind of imitation of the doomed shelly ware, but soon they were using their own designs. Once again, Tanners Street comes out with a lot of the High Medieval Tyler Hill ware but large amounts have also been found in gardens in East Street, Preston Street and at Abbey Place, close to the west front of the Abbey. The largest amount, however, from a single small scale excavation came from Ospringe. Excavation in the garden of a property opposite and east of the main Hospital site had startling results (FGW: KP63A). What seems to be the edge of Roman Watling Street, about 7 m (22 ft) south of and parallel to the present south edge of the A2 was itself flanked by a parellel adjacent ditch, as is usual with Roman roads. The ditch was loaded with pottery of both early, middle and late medieval date, the earlier material being dumped well before the start of the Becket pilgrimages after his martyrdom in 1170 and the building of the Hospital of St Mary. Perhaps this is associated with an earlier Templar foundation in Ospringe?

To the south, up Water Lane, a High Medieval midden scatter was found, indicating agricultural use at that time, as was also true in most of the Preston sites and the open areas behind Preston Street, Lower West Street and Tanners Street.

Other kinds of pottery indicate trade with places outside Faversham. Some are Kentish in origin, such as pinky-beige Wealden ware. Green glazed jugs with a distinctive white fabric, known as Surrey White Ware, came down the Thames from what is now Kingston. Most eye catching of all, however, is a flamboyant, richly decorated kind of pottery called London Highly Decorated Ware. Here is another one of those lucky Faversham events. In 1965, a new shaft was being bored at the pumping station in Conduit Street, next to the Creek. As the shaft went down, the workmen spotted a large dump of pottery and other materials in the mud at around sea level. By happy chance, this discovery was made at the same time as the Abbey was being excavated so there were archaeologists in town. One came immediately to see, and not only helped to rescue a mass of pots and leather goods such as shoes but also recorded a vertical section of the shaft as far down as 16 ft (4.9 m) below sea level. This is the only Creekside borehole undertaken in the town so far.

The pottery (dated to around 1300) and other goods were quite likely part of a cargo from London ferried into the Town Quay on a small ship which, for some reason, sank at the quayside. Wooden posts were spotted in the shaft, remnants of the quay. The leather goods have long gone missing, but the Faversham Society has curation of the pottery, which includes not only a range of beautiful and very well made pots in kiln-fresh condition but also the smoke blackened simple cooking pots of the crew. Who was this cargo for? Not the Abbey, which had its own quay. Were they for wealthy merchants, local bigwigs? No other finds from Faversham sum up the creativity, confidence and prosperity of the High Medieval period as much as these lost artefacts (Philp 2003, 57–68).

These good times, however, were about to end. As outlined at the end of Chapter 7, the fourteenth century saw famine, the Black Death, wars and rebellions. It has been estimated that the population of England in 1400 was less than 50% of that in 1300 (2 million compared with 5 million in 1300; Broadberry *et al.* 2015, 205). At the beginning of Chapter 8, Harrington remarks on the absence of documents for late fourteenth–early fifteenth century, implying a very different tone to what had been a busy prosperous town. We do not even know if people stayed in the town or took to the hills.

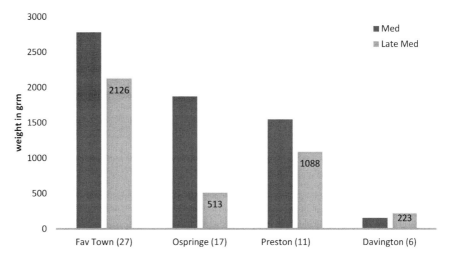

FIGURE 9.7. Comparing pre- and post-Black Death quantities of pottery in Faversham (FSARG finds of medieval pottery (1225–1400) compared with late medieval pottery (1400–1500) from the same keyhole pits)

The archaeological equivalent of the missing documents relates to medieval pottery. FSARG has found a lot of medieval pottery in Faversham gardens which can be classified into two periods of roughly the same length i.e. 1225–1400 for the High Medieval and 1400–1550 for late medieval. Only 61 pits with both medieval and late medieval pottery were considered at first. In this case, 62% of the total by weight was High Medieval and only 38% late medieval. There were also 19 more pits with High Medieval pottery but no late medieval at all. The graph in Figure 9.7 shows the changes in the four main parts of the Faversham area, suggesting that Ospringe showed the greatest change in pottery amounts whilst in Davington the quantities are very small and increase slightly.

The comparative studies in eastern England that inspired this exercise found a similar fall off in pottery finds in the mid–late fourteenth century and attributed it to the calamitous fall in population after the Black Death and other fourteenth century problems (Lewis 2016, 48–55). In Faversham, there is also a marked decline in the diversity of the pottery: this will be discussed further below.

Meanwhile, we can only imagine the empty houses, the quiet harbour, neglected fields, and the church bells tolling, if there were priests left to ring them.

Chapter 9: Second Intermission: Weather forecast

As predicted, the warm spell is ending, average temperatures are beginning to fall. Arctic ice is beginning to advance again, and those Norse colonists have started to leave Greenland. Meanwhile, bad-weather famines have been happening.

There is far worse than bad weather around. The Black Death has swept across Europe, reaching Kent in 1349. Around 40% of the population of Faversham have died. As a survivor, you would be surrounded by empty houses and weed grown fields: for a while, few boats will come into the semi-deserted quays.

On the good side, at least the advance of the sea has slowed down.

The archaeology of Late Medieval Faversham

The religious institutions in Late Medieval times (AD 1400–1550)

The archaeology along with the documentary history (Chapter 8) tells us that this period is an increasingly difficult time for the three religious institutions, Abbey, Priory and Hospital. By the end of this period they have gone, leaving scanty ruins.

For the Abbey itself, Philp does not identify any major building projects during the fifteenth to early sixteenth century (Philip 1968, 35–6). Significantly, the only ones that can be clearly identified are the Major Barn and the Abbots Lodge, both concerned with money and the outside world rather than spiritual needs. The Major Barn, built around 1500, is a huge, timber framed aisled barn that must have held large quantities of grain and other products. In 1999 the Abbey Barns featured in English Heritage's '100 most threatened buildings in the world' list. At that time, they were owned by Wadham College, Oxford University. Since then, they have become grant aided by English Heritage, much restored and house a joinery works. They are open to the public several times a year, usually on Faversham Society Open Days.

 Arden's House, as it is still known, was still fairly new when Thomas and Alice Arden moved there in 1544. It had been built in about 1475, probably as a guest-house, for the great Benedictine Abbey. Until 1772, it stood against the outer gateway which itself stood astride Abbey Street. With a handsome beamed parlour and hall above, it was the epitome of late fifteenth century domestic comfort, the kind of place in which Cardinal Wolsey would have felt at home during his visits to the Abbey in 1520, 1527 and 1528 (Hyde 1996).

It has been little altered since. The stub of the outer gateway, dating probably from the thirteenth century, forms part of the house and features a small oratory. A south wing of the building has been demolished, leaving just a handsome remnant known as Arden's Cottage. By the eighteenth century it had become a farmhouse, remaining so till the early twentieth century. By the 1950s, in common with other properties in once-prestigious Abbey Street, it had fallen on hard times and was threatened with demolition. Even at £950 it would not sell till a public-spirited purchaser came forward to restore it. Structurally it was sound but thorough restoration was needed

Pottery has been found in a variety of contexts on the Abbey excavation site and although nearly all of it is from the High Medieval period and is mostly Tyler Hill, there are a few interesting imported ceramics from the later period, particularly the German and Flemish stoneware and a piece of high quality Dutch majolica dated to the early sixteenth century.

Faversham Abbey, as explained in Chapter 8, lasted until the second phase of Dissolution in 1538 but was then quickly demolished, with much of the stone sent to Calais, still at that time an English possession. This demolition began with the removal and selling of everything of any value – timbers, fittings, carvings, window frames, lead etc. Then the stone body was broken down with pick and shovel. What happened to the bones of King Stephen and his family is unknown though legend says that they were either thrown into the Creek or secretly reburied in Our Lady of Faversham. The site of the Abbey lies nowadays under the playing fields of Queen Elizabeth Grammar School. The functional areas of the cloisters, kitchen and brewhouse, lasted into the seventeenth century. In Chapter 1 we heard from Southouse (1671) how, in 1671, the bakery and other service rooms were still standing though very ruined. These had gone by the end of the century.

The two gate houses survived longer with the inner gate being demolished in 1771 and the arch of the outer gate in 1772. Less well known is the fact that part of the west wall of the Abbey itself survives to this day, reaching to a height of 2–3 m (*c.* 6½–10 ft). It runs along the foot of the gardens of a terrace of west facing cottages. On its east (former inside facing) side it is cut off from sight by a mass of brambles and small trees. The lower front wall of a pair of seventeenth century cottages in Abbey Place is also thought to be part of the western wall of the Great Court, running on from the West Front. Finally, under Abbey Road and seen from time to time in road diggings over the years is the Great Abbey Sewer, still running down to the Creek as it has for 800 years.

The fates of the Hospital of St Mary and Davington Priory are sadder. Even by the time of the first Dissolution in 1535, both of these had faded away, as described in Chapter 8. In the case of Davington, the Convent of the Poor Nuns was left empty and abandoned until taken over by Sir Thomas Cheney in 1540 whereupon the whole Nuns quire and chancel end of the complex was demolished. A small FSARG excavation in 2006, when a lean-to building against the outer chancel wall was demolished, showed a complex early post medieval water system running right underneath the chancel wall, implying the destruction had been even more drastic than is thought (FGW, *Davington Priory*). The nuns' living quarters survived but were, over the years, given a second storey and now comprise an attractive private house with some scattered ruins to please the eye (Pl.13a, b).

The demise of the Hospital of St Mary was even earlier: by 1515, St John's College Cambridge had taken over the premises and secularised them. A survey of 1571 describes what was still standing: quite a lot but in a ruinous state. Most of it is now long gone, except for two properties on the south side of the street but some of the foundations are preserved above ground in the gardens of a Sheltered Housing development that was built on the site after the main excavation in 1977.

What became of the little chapels to St Nicholas is unknown, although Chapel House on the corner of Brogdale Road and the A2 is on the site of one of them. Throwley Priory faded away as well, with its buildings later being incorporated into the parsonage. A similar end came to the little medieval chapel of St Antony at St Catherine's, where the stonework can still be seen inside the Vicarage, encapsulated by Georgian and Victorian updates.

The churches 1400–1550

The story of the parish churches in this period is very different to the story of the religious houses, particularly for those churches such as Sheldwich, Throwley and Preston that were taken up by increasingly powerful local families. In prime place was the enormous Our Lady of Faversham. The most popular updating in the fourteenth–fifteenth century involved the adding of chapels, both in the churchyards and around the chancel, and the insertion of large perpendicular windows.

All updates were paid for by prosperous locals, who would then expect to be buried with some ceremony and masses said in perpetuity for their souls. Thus, from the early fifteenth century onwards, churches became crowded with monuments marking the life and death of a wide range of folk, not simply the local feudal landlords. At St Catherine's, Preston, there are brasses to the owners of that small but ancient manor Perry Court (1440) and to William Mares who married into the Macknade family and was squire to King Henry V. At St James', Sheldwich, we have the tombs of Sir Richard and Lady Dionysia atte- Lees (1394) of Lees Court but very soon there are tombs for the untitled John and Elizabeth Lesley (1426) and Joan Mares (1431). Throwley has some unmarked chest tombs dating from this period.

The chief beneficiary from this new confidence and display was Our Lady of Faversham. The earliest brasses in the church are to Seman Taylor 1419 (three times Mayor of Faversham) and Henry Paye, known as 'Arripay' (Admiral of the Cinque Ports; see Fig. 8.2, also Smith 2004a). From this point on, the interior of Faversham church became covered with brasses, monuments and plaques to the local elite. The fifteenth century misericords ('mercy seats' for the choir) are ornamented by a startling collection of carved medieval faces and activities, everything from a fox running off with a goose to a jester playing the bagpipes, to a naked man fighting a griffin (Smith 2004b). These misericords probably came from the dissolved Abbey in 1538.

The story of the High Medieval period had been one of nonstop battles between the townspeople, represented by the mayor and jurat, the Royal Abbey, represented by the Abbot, and the Abbey of St Augustine. In late medieval times, the interior of Our Lady of Faversham tells us that this balance of power shifted and that the people of Faversham were in the ascendant.

Everyday life 1400–1550

For the first time, we are in a period when many of the newly built houses have survived to the present day, albeit often re-faced, with medieval halls boxed off and brick chimneys inserted. The Kent Historic Towns Survey in 2004 (KHTS 2004) identified 35 fifteenth century and 40 sixteenth century houses still standing in Faversham, all but one in West Street, Abbey Street, Court Street, the northern end of Preston Street or around the Market Place. Tanners Street and Lower West Street houses are mainly post-medieval (with the notable exception of the *Bull* public house) but FSARG has found the demolished earlier properties under the gardens: they were probably the victims of post-medieval gunpowder explosions. By 1550, the centre of Faversham Town had much the same layout as it does today.

Many of the late medieval properties are nowadays pubs, such as the *Sun* in West Street, the *Bull* overlooking the Stonebridge Crossing, the former *Castle Inn* (now 75 West Street), the *Bear* in the Market Place and *The Vaults* in Preston Street, all originally fifteenth century buildings. The former *Flower de Luces* pub in Preston Street is now the Fleur de Lis Heritage Centre, home to the Faversham Society. The former *Ship Inn* in Market Place, with a fifteenth century wing, is now a boutique. One of the most striking survivals, however, is what used to be the Town Warehouse, on Town Quay, built around 1450 (Pl. 15c). This is a handsome, timber framed building end-on to Faversham Creek. It is used today by the Faversham Sea Cadets and known as *Training Ship Hasarde*, after the ship that Faversham supplied to the fleet that defended England from the Spanish Armada in 1588 (see Chapter 10 where the older spelling *Hazard* is used)

Parts of Ospringe were not included in the KHTS due to parish boundary oddities but, apart from the survivals from the Hospital, the rest of Ospringe is mostly post-medieval (seventeenth century) onwards. The exceptions are a property in Water Lane, opposite the site of a former mill, and a larger property along Mutton Lane. Both are fifteenth–sixteenth century survivals, the former maybe associated with the mill and the latter probably with nearby Queen Court, the main Manor of Ospringe.

From the gardens of these late medieval houses, overlying the remains of earlier properties now long gone, we find more personal items than from the earlier stage – buckles, ear scoops, a decorated bone handled knife, belt mounts, a dagger guard and lots of lead tokens. The owner of 75 West Street, the former *Castle Inn*, found a fifteenth century child's turnshoe under the stairs whilst doing renovations: 'concealed shoes' in new build houses were part of a widespread fertility tradition of late medieval/post-medieval times in north-west Europe.

The Tyler Hill pottery industry never recovered from the fourteenth century calamities and late Tyler Hill pottery is dark grey, gritty and brittle (Pl. 15c). Although it often has a splashed glaze giving a greenish effect, the fanciful decoration has gone. By around 1530 pottery was no longer made at Tyler Hill although peg tile manufacture continued until the nineteenth century (Cotter 2001). In Faversham, it was replaced by imports from the late fifteenth century onwards. Some of these are from the London area in a distinctive red pottery with a yellowish splashed glaze. An attractive London-made red ceramic chafing dish came from the garden of 75 West Street, the house of the child's turnshoe. Other pottery came from the Surrey/Hampshire border, the highest quality variety being known as Tudor Green. A new trend, however, was for a lot of stoneware coming in across the North Sea, notably a Belgian type called Raeren with thumbprints around the base. Large well-made floor tiles glazed in dark green or rich yellow, still to be seen in Faversham churches, were imported from Flanders.

The distribution of the late medieval pottery and houses is, unsurprisingly, very similar: East Street, West Street, Tanners Street, South Preston Street, Court

Street and Abbey Street. The Ospringe garden that had produced so much early
and High Medieval material continued to produce late medieval pottery, as did
excavations on Dark Hill on the site of the medieval Davington Manor. A real
surprise, however, came from the garden of a mid-nineteenth century terraced
cottage on the eastern side of the Mall, well away from the medieval heart of
Faversham or known manors.

A small excavation, expected to show typical mid-nineteenth century
deposits overlying a medieval agricultural level, turned out to be much more
complicated. A brick dust mortar floor was revealed, underneath which was a
mass of mostly late medieval fresh break pottery sherds, yet there did not seem
to be any medieval habitation nearby that could account for this deposit. Then,
nearby and close to St Catherine's church, the remains of a disappeared and
forgotten farm complex were found. Here were the stone coursed foundations
of a medieval farm house, demolished and rebuilt in brick (like so many others)
in the late sixteenth century (FGW, KPs 99, 99A and Preston Farm report) and
nowadays quite gone except for an imprint in plot boundaries.

Those magnificent stone built medieval religious and domestic buildings
did not, however, entirely leave us when they yielded to the emergence of a
business-based middle class. Most of the stones from the Abbey might well
have gone to Calais but many of them are still in Faversham. In Chapter 1,
we found them forming the wall base of the Old Granary at Standard Quay.
Plate 16 shows some other examples of Faversham walls with the lower courses
built of medieval stone and peg tile. The retaining wall behind the Limes is a
particularly good example of 'archaeology above the ground' with a sequence
of layers built up one on the other over the years, each with its distinctive
materials, from medieval stone at the base mixed with sixteenth century brick,

FIGURE 9.8. a). the
mortar over brick
dust floor, having
just been penetrated;
b) the ceramics that
were densely packed
beneath the floor. The
large item in the centre
is a medieval peg tile
fragment.

a

b

overlain by seventeenth–eighteenth century local red brick, then topped by nineteenth century yellow Kentish Stocks and finally modern machine made bricks used in repairs. From a Royal Abbey to propping up a revetment behind a pub – so the mighty are fallen and a new era begun.

Final comment

Combining the archaeology with Harrington's research, we have a singularly vivid picture of medieval Faversham. We have people, their houses, their churches, their market and a knowledge of what made them angry and what pleased them (note that in the 1327 tallage that listed occupations, the biggest category was Brewsters, mostly women). We can envisage the Abbey towering over the prosperous town and its almost insolently large church, and Davington Plateau crowned by the Priory with a stone built manor house just to the south. We can see larger ships coming and going from Thorne Quay and smaller vessels being towed up to the Town Quay where, in 1450, a warehouse was built.

There is, however, still much to find out. We know little about farming methods around Faversham at this time: the archaeology and historical research has concentrated on urban features. Only the characteristic midden scatter tells us where there were fields during the medieval period and we have not yet identified a ridge and furrow ploughing pattern, for example. Investigations into the changing uses of what is now inned marshland are also much needed, especially as rising relative sea levels are currently putting such lands under threat of reclamation by the sea.

Nevertheless, clear messages come through about medieval Faversham. There is a tendency to think of Faversham as primarily a port in the past. Yet the evidence from both history and archaeology points to a wide range of non-marine occupations, many of which are industrial such as brewing, malting, tanning and milling. Others are related to trade, retail, and marketing, serving a wide rural hinterland through a thriving and ancient market. Further trade could run east and west through Watling Street and the Lower Road, and southwards over the Downs on droveways to Ashford and Maidstone.

The next and last chapter will present a glimpse of where Faversham was heading after the Dissolution.

Epilogue: winds of change: AD 1550–1600

Introduction

The ending of the main part of this book with the fall of the Royal Abbey of St Saviour is the opposite of arbitrary: this event was Faversham's most important recorded change point. Over the next 50 years, a flowering of the Borough of Faversham took place at a greater rate than before or since and much of what we see as a distinctively local 'Faversham' identity came into being in this transitional period.

The key that unlocked the door to self-governance was the 1546 Charter issued by Henry VIII. This Charter cleverly and thoroughly made the town of Faversham into a Corporation, as explained at the end of Chapter 8. Reference was made at the beginning of the 1546 Charter to the fact that in 'many years past' Faversham had been governed by its Mayor and Jurats alone and that this Charter intended to return the town to that condition after what was a temporary interruption by the Abbey of St Saviour.

The Charter went on to name the first Mayor, the 11 other jurats and the 44 freemen who were the backup for the system. The document then laid down in careful detail all the rules, obligations, and potential rewards for those involved in implementing the system. A year later his successor Edward VI re-issued much the same document. Through these Charters, Faversham was set up as a miniature city state that lasted until the mid-nineteenth century and, some would say, even to this day.

Chapter 10: Final weather forecast

The year 1550 sees the beginning of the coldest century that Northern Europe has seen for millennia. Rivers will freeze in winter, snow will fall not only every winter but sometimes in June.

This is the Little Ice Age at its most potent.

Continuity and change

The town centre

At the end of the last chapter, it was pointed out that the layout of central Faversham in late medieval times was much the same as today. During the 50 years under discussion, the final touches were put. Previously the Abbot as Lord of the Manor of Faversham had controlled the hearing of suits, and Jacob tells us that the Abbots Gaol was down near Tanners Street (Jacob 1774, 15). In 1547, however, a Court House was set up at the north end of Middle Row, with a subterranean circular 'cage' for prisoners: the foundations of this were glimpsed in 2013 during excavation in Court Street for the laying of a new pipeline. At the same time, this southerly stretch of what was still called Abbey Street was renamed Court Street, in recognition of the newly erected Courthouse building that embodied the power transferred back to the town.

Nearby, central in the market place, a Market Hall was built in 1574 through a community effort by local people, including 13 nearby parishes. The cost of construction was partly met from the fortune that the merchant Henry Hatch had left to the town in 1533. Meanwhile, the general markets continued 3 days a week, with a fish market every day and regular corn and cattle markets. The town also inherited the right to hold two major fairs a year on St Valentine's Day and Lammas (early August), each lasting 3 days. Order was kept at the markets and fairs through specially appointed officers and criminal activities were tried at an ongoing Piepowder court, presumably held in the Courthouse with the 'cage' awaiting miscreants. Also, in the interest of keeping law and order were a pillory and a ducking stool, though the exact location of these is unknown.

Education

Around the same time as the building of the new Market Hall in 1574, Queen Elizabeth stayed for 2 nights in the town as part of a progression around Kent. She was presented with a petition to restore facilities for education to the town, the Dissolution having wiped out the schooling available in the Abbey and the Church of Our Lady of Faversham. This petition was granted through yet another Charter, this time pertaining only to education. A fine timbered school was built in 1578 along the lane between the re-named Church of St Mary of Charity (the former Our Lady of Faversham) and the remains of the great Abbey. The Charter detailed all kinds of practical rules and protections for this school, ranging from who was to appoint the teacher (All Souls College, Oxford) to the name of the school (the Queen Elizabeth Grammar School), how it was to be funded and how it must offer free education to local boys. The Queen Elizabeth Grammar School, a state school, still flourishes next door to the old building (Munden 1972, 9–13).

The port of Faversham

During this period, the port of Faversham came into its own. Faversham Creek itself saw many changes. The wharves were spruced up, especially the ones in the town itself. Most drastic, though, was the first attempt to manage the creek in favour of navigation through the building of a major sluice (Wilkinson 2006, 22–3). This was around the site of the present-day swing bridge. From then onwards, scouring became possible, this being the process of removing silt by ponding water upstream after high tide and, after around 3 hours, letting it rush forth. This scours the mud from around moored vessels and carries it out to sea. This method of keeping the Creek clear of silt has been used until very recently.

The sluice and consequent silt removal made the downstream Thorne Quay redundant. Now vessels up to 40 tons could come right up to Town along the deeper Creek. The chief exports in this period were corn, wool, charcoal and timber, much of it going to fast growing London. Imports were exotic items such as coal, butter and cheese, grocer's goods such as spices, wine, dyes and honey and manufactures from London such as textiles and metal work. Ceramics such as London red pottery, Belgian Raeren and other stonewares from the Rhineland were brought in. There were ever stronger connections across the sea to Flushing and Calais.

Coastal north Kent had long been famous for oysters and these were harvested in increasing numbers from the Swale and its inlets, some going to Holland as early as 1550. Oyster production was managed from the medieval period onwards by the Company of Dredgermen, a confraternity that survived well into the nineteenth century when changes in disposal of sewage polluted the waterways and brought an end to oyster cultivation in the Faversham area.

Fishing was also important locally: eels from the brackish ditches and herring from the sea are listed in the Domesday book as being supplied by local manors. Many other types of fish were abundant in the Estuary, dabs and cod in winter and herring, bass and sole at other times of the year. The main problem here, as always on the high seas, was continual acrimonious competition over fishing grounds between English, French and Dutch fishermen.

Underlying all this is a decline in importance for Faversham of its membership of the Cinque Ports federation. We have seen in Chapters 7 and 8 how in the power struggles between the Town and the two Abbeys, the position of the town faction was fortified by its Cinque port support and privileges. By the sixteenth century, however, the value of this membership was fading fast. The rise of a Royal Navy under central control (the Royal Naval Dockyards at Woolwich and Deptford were founded around 1510, with Chatham following in 1567) meant that the traditional reliance on the Cinque Port Federation to supply fully equipped ships in time of war was becoming obsolete.

Faversham did, however, send a ship to the fleet that would defend England from the Spanish Armada in 1588. This was *Hazard* (40 tons) complete with 'victuals, mariners and munition for two months'. *Hazard* survived the sea battle in July 1588 and was back in Faversham in August 1588. In 1596, Faversham equipped and sent the *Vineyard of Dover* to take part in a successful Anglo-Dutch attack on Cadiz. This, however, was the last time Faversham sent a ship at the call of the Federation. For a while the call was instead for cash but in 1641 even this was made illegal; Faversham could then concentrate entirely on its commercial activities.

The growth of industry

In a set of statistics for the Kent coast gathered in 1566, by the Privy Council, numbers of mariners for each settlement are given, along with numbers of houses and boats (Hyde 1997, 65). What is surprising about Faversham is that, although it is the second largest coastal settlement (380 houses only exceeded by Sandwich's 420 and followed by Dover with 358), it has a relatively small number of mariners – 50 compared with 62 from Sandwich, 130 from Dover and 160 from little Hythe (a puny 122 houses). The same is true for the numbers of ships: Faversham's 18 ships are exceeded by Hythe with 33 and Milton (130 houses) with 26. Taking these figures alongside the statement in the 1566 survey that Faversham had 'no persones lacking proper habitacone' i.e. no homeless folk, and recognising the favourable comments made by visiting sixteenth century topographers ('this town is well peopled and flourisheth in wealth at this day.' Lambarde in Chapter 1) clearly there are more opportunities for Faversham people than going to sea.

The shipping trade itself must have generated considerable land-based employment. Unloading cargoes, operating warehouses, working in the markets, fairs, and auction rooms, transporting goods to and from the town, providing supplies for ships and repairs to sails and other parts of the vessel must all have provided jobs and opportunities for money making. Whether there was actual ship building is very likely but not confirmed for this period.

Besides the commerce, there were industries which themselves provided goods for trade. Faversham is particularly well known as a brewing town. Records show that in 1525, William Castlock, the brother of the last Abbot of Faversham, was exporting and importing beer. By 1550 John Castlock, William's son, was leasing the ex-Abbey brew house. By 1570, he was the owner of 18 Court Street and beer featured as an export for Faversham that was sent not only to London but to Flushing. The export of malt made from barley was another local industry, with malt houses a long-standing feature of Faversham's urban landscape. Brewing has continued in Faversham ever since: the famous present-day Faversham brewer Shepherd Neame traces its earliest beer production on its Court Street site to 1698 (Owen 2012).

Another industry which continued from the medieval was charcoal production. This might have taken place beyond Faversham itself, up in the woods that were still present on the flinty slopes of the North Downs or even beyond in the forests of the Weald, but a particularly fine charcoal was produced from the alder and willow that flourished in the low lying marshy areas near Faversham itself. Charcoal is listed as one of Faversham late sixteenth century exports but a more interesting use for this material was in a new industry established in Faversham. This was the production of what Jacob called 'that dreadful composition GUNPOWDER' [*sic*] (Jacob 1774, 94).

Production of gunpowder, and eventually other explosives, became an extremely important industry in Faversham, expanding into the area to the west and north-west of the town. Again, it is Jacob who tells us that this industry 'hath continued to be made upon our stream ever since the reign of Queen Elizabeth if not before her time.' (Jacob 1774, 94). The advantages of the site for water power along the Westbrook had long been recognised and the presence of locally produced charcoal, the ease of importing salt petre and sulphur up the

Creek and then exporting the finished product up the Thames or Medway to the arsenals at the newly created Royal Naval Dockyards added to this. It is likely that the gunpowder for *Hazard*'s munitions in 1588 was made in Faversham.

Another local industry was the small-scale production of soft red bricks. Bricks and tile went out of use in Britain after the end of the Roman occupation. The return to popularity of the material can be traced to the revival of brick making in eastern England in the late thirteenth and early fourteenth centuries. This was a direct result of lack of local stone, an increasing shortage of good timber, and the influence of northern Europe where brick work was used extensively. By the Tudor period the brick makers and brick layers had emerged as separate craftsmen well able to rival the masons. From unsophisticated early work, brick building entered its heyday, rivalling stone in its popularity as a structural material.

In these early stages, bricks were generally made on site in wood or turf fired clamps by itinerant workers. The Tudors further patterned their brick work by inserting headers of burnt or vitrified blue bricks into the walling. Just south of St Catherine's Church in Preston Within, a mansion that Hasted described as a 'gentleman's seat' was built in the mid-sixteenth century and named Preston House. Archaeological investigation in and around the site of Preston House, which was rebuilt in Georgian style around 1790 and finally demolished in 1931, has found evidence for Tudor style red brick and a nearby early brickfield and kilns which went on producing red brick and tile up to the late nineteenth century (FGW, KPs 124 & 125).

Finally, industries like tanning, which had dominated Tanners Street in the High Medieval period, carried on well into the modern period, with a 1900 photograph showing a drying shed still in use next to the Stonebridge crossing (FGW, KPs 14, 17A, 25 and 5th Anniversary Report).

The people of Faversham

This epilogue, and indeed this book, must end with real people.

At the beginning of this period in 1550, the hated Thomas Arden, ex-comptroller of Sandwich, was living in the former Abbey Lodge, making money out of the Abbey's sequestered assets: he had been relieved of his mayoralty. He was, we are told, then murdered by his wife Alice and her lover. We have from this time a whole list of more successful mayors where surnames repeat themselves in years to come as sons succeed father: Streynsham, Finch, Upton, Philpot, Dryland (Jacobs 1774, 117–29).

We now have whole lists of ship's masters and their vessels, such as Henry Edwards, master of the *Mary*, and Abraham Snothe, master of the *Ellen*. Snothe, along with Edward Buddle, organised the provision of *Hazard* to the English fleet in 1588. We have many wills containing detailed inventories of the deceased's possessions, from 'fower flower pottes' to 'one little table and chayre' (will of William Peacock, dated 1570), so we can in our imaginations furnish houses accurately and understand what was valued by these people (Hyde 1997, 92).

Predictably, most of these named Faversham people are men, but women are named as beneficiaries in the wills. William Peacock leaves his daughters Rose, Margarett and Elizabethe dowries on their marriages and his wife Joane is entitled to all movable goods and chattels. His son Edward Peacock is, however, bequeathed the main part of his estate. Other named women are from the elite: Queen Elizabeth, of course, but also Henry Hatch's protesting widow who remarried to become Lady Amcotts. Then there are the notorious ones like Alice Arden. Finally, there are the ships – *Ellen, Anne Fraunces, Margett, Dorathie* and many others, surely named after the Masters' womenfolk (Hyde 1997, 105–18).

So, what was life like in the town for these Williams, Richards, Ellens and Margetts? Obviously, there were rich and poor, but the 1566 survey stated that no-one in Faversham at that time was destitute. All the wills leave something for the care of the poor and it was not long before the first alms-houses were built for six widows in 1614 using an endowment from Thomas Mendfield. Although there could still be good and bad years for crops, it is hard to think of Faversham people going hungry, with the huge amounts of foodstuffs going through the port and market, and ever-increasing job opportunities. The estimate of population size around 1570 is 2500.

With markets every week on Wednesday, Friday and Saturday, the daily fish market and the cattle and corn markets, there must have been people constantly coming and going, streets crowded with wagons and handcarts, noise and bustle. Many of the stall holders would be women, briskly managing the goods, cash and customers. Walking around and keeping an eye on everything would be the market officials, some checking that the correct weights were being used and others dealing with problems like pick pockets or drunks. Maybe there would be a pickpocket in the pillory.

On market days, then as now, there would be street entertainers – jugglers, acrobats, musicians. At special times in the year – May Day, Saints days and especially the 12 days of Christmas – groups of mummers and singers would perform. The twice annual fairs would attract even more exotic performers – maybe bears being baited, monkeys dancing, fire eaters and wrestlers. The most anticipated events of all would be colourful visitors – Queen Elizabeth herself at one point.

Maybe the most gripping entertainment was given by a group of travelling players who performed in Faversham in 1597 after a short spell in Dover. In the town accounts, they are down as being paid 13s 4d and performing in the Guildhall. This was probably the Court House in Middle Row, as the building occupied by the present Guildhall was still a Market Hall at that time, not being converted into a new Court House until 1603. This group were called the Lord Chamberlain's Men and one of the player/writers was a 33-year-old man, one of whose plays would likely have been offered in Faversham. Perhaps Faversham people enjoyed his latest work, *The Merchant of Venice,* a very apt production for Faversham (*Shakespeare on Tour* 2001, *Wherefore to Dover?*).

Let us take our last look at Faversham in this story of the early town through the eyes of this man, William Shakespeare. He may well have been more familiar with this town than one might expect. A play was published in 1592 called *Arden of Feversham* that told the scandalous tale of Thomas Arden's murder. Whether Shakespeare wrote the play is the subject of intense argument to this day, but, whatever the truth, he must surely at least have read it. So, he looks out across this busy town – only half the size of Canterbury but larger than Dover – and thinks about the great Abbey that used to loom over the town and the vultures such as Arden who swooped in to snatch up the entrails of its disintegration.

Probably, he takes a stroll down Abbey Street to view the 'tattered skeletons' of the still-standing service buildings of the Abbey and cast his eye over many ships moored along the wharves and the furious coming and going of people. If it is a market day then the noise will be enormous, the colours hectic, with goods for sale spread on stalls or on cloths on pavements, and the crowds parting to allow expensively dressed local merchants and their wives to pass through. Here and there he would hear snatches of Flemish or see simple country folk in from the Downs or the marsh, tongue tied in the face of this urban sophistication.

He may even see a well-dressed man apparently puffing smoke from his mouth as he rests on a bench; closer inspections show a small white bowl containing burning shreds and a long stem clutched in the smoker's teeth. The first tobacco has arrived in Faversham from the new colonies west of the Atlantic, at present a fascinating novelty but soon to be thoroughly condemned by a new King in his famous diatribe against tobacco.

The very fact that the Lord Chamberlain's Men are welcome here and, as the renamed Kings Men, were again welcomed to Faversham in 1606 and 1610, is a measure of Faversham's openness at that time. As the seventeenth century begins, however, the first tendrils of Puritanism begin to emerge in Kentish communities and start to bring these riotous and (to Puritans) pagan entertainments and pastimes under control, leading eventually to a ban under the Commonwealth … but that is another story.

Bibliography

Ancient and medieval texts

The Anglo-Saxon Charters: an annotated list and bibliography (ed.) P. H. Sawyer 1968. Royal Historical Society: London

ALCUIN. *The Letters of Alcuin* (ed.) R. Barlow Page 1909. Forest Press: Des Moines, IL

The Anglo Saxon Chronicle (ed.) M. Swanton 1996. Dent: London

AURELIUS VICTOR. *c.* 350. *Liber de Caesaribus* 39. Translated with commentary by H. W. Bird. 1994. Liverpool University Press: Liverpool

BEDE (venerable). *Ecclesiastical History of the English People*. J. A. Giles and L. C. Jane (eds) 1903. Temple Classics: London

DIO CASSIUS. *Roman History*, Vol 7, Books 56–60. Translated by E. Cary and H. Foster 1924. Loeb Classical Library Edition, Harvard University Press: Cambridge MA

EUTROPIUS. *c.* AD 350. *Abridgement of Roman History*. Translated by Rev. J. Selby Watson 1888. George Bell & Sons: London

FLORENCE OF WORCESTER. 1848–49 edition. *Florentii Wigorniensis monachi Chronicon ex chronicis (2 vols).* Benjamin Thorpe (ed). English History Society: London

GILDAS. *De Excidio Britannae* or *The Ruin of Britain*. A W Haddon & W Stubbs (eds) 1869. *Councils and Ecclesiastical documents relating to Great Britain and Ireland.* Oxford University Press: Oxford

JULIUS CAESAR. *The Invasions of Britain: The Conquest of Gaul*. Translated by S. A. Handford 1951. Penguin: Harmondsworth

MATTHEW PARIS. *Historia Anglorom*. British Library MS Royal 14.Vll folio 232

SIMEON OF DURHAM. *Symeonis Monachi*, Vol 2. Translated by T. Arnold 1885. Longmans: London

STRABO. *Geographies,* Book IV Chapter 5. Translated by H. Leonard Jones 1923. Loeb Classical Library Edition, Harvard University Press: Cambridge MA

TACITUS The Agricola and the Germania. Translated by H. Mattingley and S. A. Handford 1970. Penguin: London

WILLIAM DE JUMIEGES. 2002 edition. *Gesta Normannorum Ducum*. E van Houts (ed). Oxford University Press: Oxford.

ZOSIMUS. *c.* AD 420. Nova Historia, Book the Sixth. Oxford Edition 1814. W. Green & T. Chaplin: London

Secondary sources

ADAMS, S. 2017. The contents and context of the Boughton Malherbe Late Bronze Age hoard. *Archaeologia Cantiana* 138, 37–64

ALDISS, D. BURKE, H., CHACKSFIELD, B., BINGLEY, R., TEFERLE, N., WILLIAMS, S., BLACKMORE, D., BURREN, R. and PRESS, N. 2009. *Geological Interpretation of Current Subsidence and Uplift in the London Area, UK, as Shown by High Precision Satellite Based Surveying.* National Environmental Research Council: London

ALLEN, M., LEIVERS, M. and ELLIS, C. 2008. Neolithic causewayed enclosures and later prehistoric farming: Duality, imposition and the role of predecessors at Kingsborough, Isle of Sheppey, Kent, UK. *Proceedings of the Prehistoric Society* 74, 235–322

ALLEN, T. 2000. The origins of the Swale: an archaeological interpretation. *Archaeologia Cantiana* 120, 169–82

ALLEN, T. 2007. An archaeological assessment following excavation on the route of the Ashford Road to Canterbury Road water main, near Faversham in Kent. Unpublished report, Kent Archaeological Projects: Whitstable

ALLEN. T. 2009. Prehistoric settlement patterns on the north Kent coast between Seasalter and the Wansum. *Archaeologia Cantiana* 129, 189–207

ALLEN. T. and SCOTT, B. 2000. An archaeological evaluation on land at Abbey Fields, Faversham, Kent. Unpublished Report, Canterbury Archaeological Trust: Canterbury

ANDREWS, P. 2011. Springhead religious complex. In P. Andrews, E. Biddulph and A. Hardy, *Settling the Ebbsfleet Valley Vol. 1: the Sites*, 13–134. Oxford Wessex Archaeology: Salisbury

ANON. 1874. Report on the 1872 AGM of the Kent Archaeological Society held at Faversham. *Archaeologia Cantiana* 9, lviii–lxxxv

ANON. 1961. Entry for Roman iron working site at Brenley Corner. KCC HER entry: TR 05 NW 3: Maidstone

ASHBEE, P. 2005. *Kent in Prehistoric Times.* Tempus: Stroud

BALLARD, A. 1913. *British Borough Charters 1042–1216* Cambridge University Press: Cambridge

BANYARD, G. 2004. Duke William's Conquest of Kent 1066, in Lawson and Killingray (eds) 2004, 34

BEHRE, K.-E. 2007. A new Holocene sea-level curve for the southern North Sea. Boreas 36(1), 82–102. DOI: 10.1111/j.1502-3885.2007.tb01183.x

BENEDICTOW, O. J. 2004. *The Black Death 1346–1353. The Complete History.* Boydell & Brewer: Woodbridge

BENEDICTOW, O. J. 2005. The Black Death: the greatest catastrophe ever. *History Today* 55, 75–77

BIDDULPH, E. 2011. Roman settlement in the Ebbsfleet Valley in Regional Perspective. In P. Andrews, E. Biddulph and A. Hardy, *Settling the Ebbsfleet Valley Vol. 1: the Sites*, 243–8. Oxford Wessex Archaeology: Salisbury

BOLTON, J. 2003. The World Upside Down: plague as an agent of economic and social change. In W. M. Ormrod and P. Lindley, *The Black Death in England*, 17–79. Shaun Tyas: Donington

BOOTH, P., BINGHAM, A. and LAWRENCE, S. 2008. *The Roman Roadside Settlement at Westhawk Farm, Ashford, Kent. Excavations 1998–9.* Oxford Archaeology Monograph 2

BRITCHFIELD, D. 2008. Syndale Park Motel, London Road, Ospringe near Faversham, Kent: Archaeological Evaluation. Unpublished report, SWAT Archaeology: Faversham

BROADBERRY, S. CAMPBELL, B. M. S., KLEIN, A., OVERTON, M. and LEEUWEN, B. van. 2015. *British Economic Growth 1270–1870.* Cambridge University Press: Cambridge

BROOKES, S. and HARRINGTON, S. 2010. *The Kingdom and People of Kent AD 400–1066.* History Press: Stroud

BURKE, J. and YOUNG, L. 2003. *A History of Davington Priory.* Privately published: Faversham

BUTLER, C. 2005. *Prehistoric Flintwork.* Tempus: Stroud

CALIEBE, A., NEBEL, A., MAKAREWICZ, C., KRAWCZAK, M. and KRAUSE-KYORA, B. 2017. Insights into early pig domestication provided by ancient DNA analysis. *Scientific Reports* 7, 44–55. doi:10.1038/srep44550

CAMDEN, W. 1610. *Britannia.* London

CAMPBELL, B. 2010. Agriculture in Kent in the High Middle Ages. In Sweetinburgh (ed.) 2010, 25–54

CARE EVANS, A. and FENWICK, V. 1971. The Graveney boat. *Antiquity* 45 (178), 89–96

CATT J. A. 1986. The nature, origin and geomorphological significance of clay with flints. In G. G. Sieveking and M. M. Hart (eds), *The Scientific Study of Flint and Chert*, 151–9. Cambridge University Press: Cambridge

CHAMPION, T. 2007. Prehistoric Kent. In J. Williams (ed.), *The Archaeology of Kent to AD 800*, 67–134. Boydell Press and Kent County Council: Woodbridge

CLARKE, H. and AMBROSIANI, B. 1995. *Towns in the Viking Age.* Leicester University Press: Leicester

CODRINGTON, T. 1903. *Roman Roads in Britain.* Society for Promoting Christian Knowledge: London

COLES, B. 1998. Doggerland: a speculative survey. *Proceedings of the Prehistoric Society* 64, 45–81

COTTER, J. 1999. Medieval shelly wares in Kent: a summary of recent research. *Canterbury Archaeological Trust Annual Report*, 56–60. Canterbury Archaeological Trust: Canterbury

COTTER, J. 2001. Medieval pottery kiln-site at Daw's Wood, Tyler Hill near Canterbury. *Canterbury Archaeological Trust Annual Report*, Part 3, Section 2. Canterbury Archaeological Trust: Canterbury

COZENS, Z. 1793. *A Tour Through the Isle of Thanet etc.* J Nichols: London

CROFT, J. 1998. The Medieval Custumals of the Cinque ports *c* 1290–1500. Unpublished. PhD thesis, University of Kent.

CRONNE, H. A., DAVIS, R. H. C. and DAVIS, W. N. 1968. *Regesta Regum Anglo-Normanorum 1066–1154.* Oxford University Press: Oxford

CROW, E. 2009. *Historical and Various Gleanings Relative to the Town of Faversham and Parishes Adjoining.* CD ed. and transcribed by P. Tann. Faversham Society: Faversham

DARWIN, C. 1845 [1997]. *The Voyage of the Beagle.* Wordsworth Editions: Ware

DAVIES, R. G., DENTON, J. and ROSKELL, J. S. 1981. *The English Parliament in the Middle Ages.* Manchester University Press: Manchester

DE LA BEDOYERE, G. 1993. *Roman Villas and the Countryside.* English Heritage: London

DEFOE, D. 1724. Letter II: Part 1. Kent Coast and Maidstone. In S. Richardson (ed.), *A Tour thro' the Whole Land of Great Britain* (2nd edition). Samuel Richardson: London

EDITOR, ARCHAEOLOGICAL JOURNAL. 1929. Proceedings at meetings: Roman Ospringe and Faversham. *Archaeological Journal* 86, 298

EMERY, K. 2010. *A Re-examination of Variability in Hand Axe Form in the British Palaeolithic.* University College: London

EVELEIGH WOODRUFF, C. 1925. Some early professions of canonical obedience to the see of Canterbury by the heads of religious Houses. *Archaeologia Cantiana* 37, 64–70

EVERITT, A. 1986. *Continuity and Colonization: the Evolution of Kentish Settlement.* Leicester University Press: Leicester

EVISON, V. 2000. Glass vessels in England AD 400–1100. In J. Price (ed.), *Glass in Britain and Ireland AD 350–1100*, 47–104. British Museum Occasional Paper: London

EVISON, V. 2008. *A Catalogue of Anglo Saxon Glass in the British Museum.* British Museum Research Publication 167: London

FARGES, F. 1998. Minerology of the Louvre Merovingian garnet cloisonee jewellery: origins of the gems of the first Kings of France. *American Minerology* 83, 323–30

FAULKNER, N. 2000. *The Decline and Fall of Roman Britain.* Tempus: Stroud

FITZSTEPHEN, W. (ed.). 1956. *Stow's Survey of London*, 501–9. (Reprint of 1598 edition). J M Dent: London

FLAHERTY, W. E. 1860. The Great Rebellion in Kent in 1381 illustrated from the Public Records. *Archaeologia Cantiana* 3, 65–96

FOREVILLE, R. 1958 [1995]. *Le Jubile de Saint Thomas Becket* (reprint). Editions de l'Ecole des Hautes Etudes de Sciences: Paris

FOWLER, P. J. 1983. *The Farming of Prehistoric Britain.* Cambridge University Press: Cambridge

FREESTONE, I., HUGHES, M. and STAPLETON, C. 2008. The composition and production of Anglo Saxon glass. In V. Evison and I. Freestone (eds), *Catalogue of Anglo Saxon Glass in the British Museum*, 29–46. British Musem Research Publication 167: London

FROHNSDORFF, M. 1997. *The Maison Dieu and Medieval Faversham.* Faversham Society: Faversham

FROHNSDORFF, M. 2013. The Royal Charters of Faversham. Faversham Society: Faversham

FROHNSDORFF, M. 2016. Monastic Fraud. Faversham Society Newsletter, October, 6–7

GAFFNEY, V., FITCH, S. SMITH, D. 2009. *Europe's Lost World: the rediscovery of Doggerland.* Council of British Archaeology Research Report 160: York

GIBBARD, P. 2007. How Britain became an island. Nature Precedings. Nature Publishing Group: New York

GIBSON, J. M. (ed.). 2002. *Records of Early English Drama: Kent, Diocese of Canterbury* (16th edition?). University of Toronto: Toronto, Canada

GIDLOW, A. 1969. = 1968 in chap 4 Excavations at Barnfield, Oare. *Archaeologia Cantiana* 84, 238

GIRAUD, F. 1874. Report to KAS AGM. *Archaeologia Cantiana* 9, lxvi

GIRAUD, F. 1893. On the parish clerks and sextons of Faversham 1506–1593. *Archaeologia Cantiana* 20, 203–10

GIRAUD, F. and DONNE, Rev. C. 1876. *A Visitors Guide to Faversham and Brief Notes on Surroundng Villages.* James Higham: Faversham

HAMMOND, J. 2007. How Kent's recently discovered causewayed enclosures impact on our understanding and interpretation of the Early Neolithic in the region. *Archaeologia Cantiana* 127, 357–82

HARRINGTON, D. and HYDE, P. 2002. *Faversham Oyster Fisheries: Through Eleven Centuries.* Arden Enterprises: Folkestone

HARRINGTON, D. and HYDE, P. 2008. *The Early Town Books of Faversham.* History Research: Folkestone

HARRINGTON, D. and HYDE, P. 2014. *Faversham Abbey: Collections Towards a History.* History Research: Folkestone

HARRINGTON, S. and WELCH, M. 2014. *The Early Anglo Saxon Kingdoms of Southern Britain: Beneath the Tribal Hidage.* Oxbow Books: Oxford

HARVEY, I. M. 1991. *Jack Cade's Rebellion of 1450.* Clarendon Press: Oxford

HARVEY, I. M. 2004. *Oxford Dictionary of National Biography.* Oxford University Press: Oxford

HASTED, E. 1797. *General History: Divisions of the County. The History and Topographical Survey of the County of Kent* Vol 1. Bristow: Canterbury

HASTED, E. 1798. *The History and Topographical Survey of the County of Kent* Vol 6. W. Bristow: Canterbury

HILL, D., BARRETT, D., MAUDE, K., WARBURTON, J. and Worthington, M. 1990. Quentovic defined. *Antiquity* 64, 51–8

HILTON, R. 1973. *Bond Men Made Free: Medieval Peasant Movements and the English Rising of 1381.* Routledge: Abingdon

HOLDSWORTH, C. 2001. Battle conference on Anglo Norman studies. In E. King (ed.), *The Anarchy of King Stephens Reign*, 216–7. Oxford University Press: Oxford

HOLMES, S. C. A. 1981. *Geology of the Country Around Faversham: Memoir for the 1:50 000 Geological Sheet 273.* Geological Survey of Great Britain. HMSO: London

HUSSEY, A. 1911. Chapels in Kent. *Archaeologia Cantiana* 29, 217–67

HYDE, P. 1985. Henry Hatch and the battle over his will. *Archaeologia Cantiana* 102, 111–28

HYDE, P. 1996. *Thomas Arden in Faversham: the Man Behind the Myth.* Faversham Society: Faversham

HYDE, P. 1997 *Faversham Ships and Seamen in the Sixteenth Century.* Faversham Society Paper 45: Faversham

HYDE, P. and HARRINGTON, D. 2002. Faversham's role in the Armada and Counter Armada. *Archaeologia Cantiana* 122, 183–95

JACOB, E. F. 1774. *The History of the Town and Port of Faversham.* J. March: London

JACOB, E. F. 1963. *The Fifteenth Century 1399–1485.* Clarendon Press: Oxford

JAMES, H. R. 1990. *Faversham Parish Church: a History and Guide* Faversham Society Paper 33: Faversham

JOHNS, C. M. and POTTER, T. W. 1991. The Canterbury late Roman treasure. *Antiquities Journal* 65(2), 312–52

KCC HERITAGE CONSERVATION GROUP. 2003. Kent Historic Towns Survey (KHTS): Faversham, Kent Archaeological Assessment Document. KCC Heritage Conservation Group: Maidstone

KENNETT, P. 2009. *Faversham from Old Photographs.* Amberley: London

KNOWLES, D., BROOKE, C. N. I. and LONDON, V. 1972. *The Heads of Religious Houses England and Wales, 940–1216.* Cambridge University Press: Cambridge

LAMBARDE, W. 1576. *A Perambulation of Kent.* R. Newberrie: London

LARSSON, M. and PARKER PEARSON, M. (eds). 2007. *From Stonehenge to the Baltic: Cultural Diversity in the Third Millenium BC.* British Archaeological Report S1692: Oxford

LAWSON, T. 2004. The Viking incursions. In Lawson and Killingray (eds), 2004, 32

LAWSON, T. and KILLINGRAY, D. (eds). 2004. *An Historical Atlas of Kent.* Phillimore: Chichester

LELAND, J. 1710 *Itinerary* (9 vols), Thomas Hearne: London

LEWIS, J. 1727 [2010]. *The History and Antiquities of the Abbey and Church of Faversham and the Priory of Davington.* Gale ECCO publications: Detroit

LEWIS, C. 2016. Plague pits, Pot sherds and the shock of the Black Death. *British Archaeology* 150, 48–55

LUBBOCK, J. 1865. *Pre-Historic Times, as illustrated by Ancient Remains and the Manners and Customs of Modern Savages.* Williams & Norgate: London

LYNE, M. 2001. The ceramics: excavations at Syndale Park, Ospringe. *Archaeologia Cantiana* 121, 176–87

MACPHERSON GRANT, N. 2008. Dating and assessment of the ceramic assemblage at Syndale Park Motel, London Road, Ospringe, near Faversham, Kent: Appendix 2 Archaeological Evaluation. In D. Britchfield, *Syndale Park Motel, London Road, Ospringe near Faversham, Kent: Archaeological Evaluation*, 43–59. Unpublished report SWAT Archaeology: Faversham

MATE, M. 2006. *Trade and Economic Development 1450–1550: the experience of Kent, Surrey and Sussex.* Boydell & Brewer: Woodbridge

MATE, M. 2010. The economy of Kent 1200–1500: the aftermath of the Black Death. In Sweetinburgh (ed.) 2010, 11–24

MEANEY, A. 1981. *Anglo Saxon Amulets and Curing Stones.* British Archaeological Report 96: Oxford

MEATES, E. and FLETCHER, G. W. 1969 The ruined chapel of Stone by Faversham (1). *Antiquity* 49(2), 73–94

MEATES, E. and FLETCHER, G. W. 1977. The ruined chapel of Stone by Faversham (2). *Antiquity* 57(1), 67–72

MILLETT, M. 2007. Roman Kent. In J. Williams (ed.), *The Archaeology of Kent to AD 800*, 135–84. Boydell Press/Kent County Council: Woodbridge

MUNDEN, A. 1972. *Eight Centuries of Education in Faversham.* Faversham Society Paper 9: Faversham

MURRAY, K. M. E. 1936. The Common-place book of Faversham. *Archaeologia Cantiana* 48, 91–114

MURRAY, K. M. E. 1935. *The Constitutional History of the Cinque Ports.* Manchester University Press: Manchester

OPPENHEIMER, S. 2006. *The Origins of the British.* Constable and Robinson (Little, Brown Books): London

ORME, N. 2016. John Coles 1467–1536 and the origins of education in Faversham. *Archaeologia Cantiana* 137, 107–26

OSWALD, A. 2011. *Causewayed Enclosures.* Introduction to Heritage Assets. Historic England: Swindon https://content.historicengland.org.uk/images-books/publications/iha-causewayed-enclosures/causewayedenclosures.pdf/

OWEN, J. 2012. *The Shepherds of Shepherd Neame.* Self published: Throwley

OWEN, J. 2014. *The Emergence of Shepherd Neame from the Earliest Days of Brewing in Faversham 1100–1732.* Self published: Throwley

PARFITT, K. 1990. *Archaeological Excavation and Recording at 14–18 the Street, Ospringe.* Kent Archaeological Rescue Unit Kent Minor Sites Series 2: Sevenoaks

PARFITT, K. 2006. Ringlemere and ritual and burial landscapes of Kent. In S. Needham, K. Parfitt and G. Varndell (eds), *The Ringlemere Cup and the Beginning of the Channel Bronze Age*, 47–81. British Museum Research Publication 163: London

PARFITT, K. and NEEDHAM, S. 2007. Excavations at Ringlemere Farm, Woodnesborough: the Anglo Saxon cemetery. *Archaeologia Cantiana* 127, 51–2

PARKER PEARSON, M. 2006. The Beaker People Project: mobility and diet in the early British Bronze Age. *Archaeologist* 61, 14–15

PARRY, C. 2004. *The Parliamentary Representation of Faversham* Faversham Society Paper 86: Faversham

PERKINS, D. 1999. A Gateway Island: An exploration of evidence for the existence of a cultural focus in the form of a Gateway Community in the Isle of Thanet during the Bronze Age and Early–Middle Iron Age. Unpublished PhD thesis: University College London

PETERSON, J. W. M. 2006. Planned military landscapes in Roman Britain. In Leveque, L., Ruiz, M. and Pop, L. (eds), *Jouneys Through European Landscapes*, 153–6. COST Action: Ponteferrara

PHILIPOT, T. 1659. *Villare Cantianum: or Kent Surveyed and Illustrated.* William Godbid: London

PHILIPOT. T. 1673. *Phylosophical Essay of the Most Probably Cause of that Grand Mystery of Nature, the Flux and Reflux or Flowing and Ebbing of the Sea.* At the Sign of the Three Bibles, London Bridge: London

PHILP, B. 1968. *Excavations at Faversham, 1965. The Royal Abbey, Roman Villa and Belgic Farmstead.* Kent Archaeological Research Group First Research Report: Crawley

PHILP, B. 1997. The Roman villa at Blacklands, Faversham: Part II. *Kent Archaeological Review* 130, 235–9

PHILP, B. 2003. Discoveries at Faversham Creek 1965. *Kent Archaeological Review* 153, 57–68

POLLOCK, S. (ed.). 2004. *Archaeologies of the Middle East.* Blackwell Studies in Global Archaeology: Oxford

PRIESTLEY BELL, G. 1994. *An Archaeological Watching Brief on part of the Faversham to Sittingbourne Gas Pipeline.* Archaeology South East: London

PRYOR, F. and BAMFORTH, M. 2007. *Flag Fen, Peterborough: Excavation and Research 1995–2007.* Oxbow Books: London

REID, P. 2013. Littles Manor Farm, Sheldwich, North Field: a newly discovered Roman site FSARG, Unpublished report lodged on KCC HER as SKE 24075: Faversham

RICHARDSON, A. 2005. *The Anglo-Saxon Cemeteries of Kent.* British Archaeological Report 391: Oxford

RICHARDSON, A. 2017. A prehistoric and Anglo Saxon Cemetery site at the Meads, Sittingbourne www.canterburytrust.co.uk/news2/projectdiaries/meads

RIDDLER, I. 2004. Late Anglo Saxon Kent: economic development. In Lawson and Killingray (eds) 2004, 33

RIVET, A. C. F. 1970. The British Section of the *Antonine Itinerary. Britannia* 1, 34–82

ROACH SMITH, C. 1842. Notice of recent discoveries of Roman antiquities at Strood, Bapchild, Oare and Upchurch in Kent with remarks on the site of Durolevum of Antonius. *Antiquity* 29, 217–26

ROACH SMITH, C. 1871. *A Catalogue of Anglo Saxon and other Antiquities Discovered at Faversham in Kent and Bequeathed by William Gibbs of that Town to the South Kensington Museum.* Eyre and Spottiswood: London

SAWYER, P. 2013. *The Wealth of Anglo Saxon England.* Oxford University Press: Oxford

SIBUN, L. 2001 Exacavation at Syndale Park, Ospringe. *Archaeologia Cantiana* 121, 171–96

SIMPSON, W. J. 1905. *A Treatise on Plague.* Cambridge University Press: Cambridge

SITTINGBOURNE AND SWALE ARCHAEO-LOGICAL RESEARCH GROUP. 1973. Castle Rough Training Project 1972 Part 1 and Part 2, the flints. *Kent Archaeological Review* 31–2, 15–19, 60–1

SMITH, G. H. 1979. The excavation of the Hospital of St Mary of Ospringe commonly called the Maison Dieu. *Archaeologia Cantiana* 95, 81–184

SMITH, L. 2004a. *The Parish Church of St Mary of Charity, Faversham: the Misericords.* Parish Church of St Mary of Charity: Faversham

SMITH, L. 2004b. *The Parish Church of St Mary of Charity, Faversham: the Brasse.* Parish Church of St Mary of Charity: Faversham

SOMNER, W. 1640 [1977]. *The Antiquities of Canterbury.* R. Knaplock at the Angel and Crown in St Pauls Churchyard: London

SOUTHOUSE, T. 1671. *Monasticon Favershamiense in Agro Cantiano or A Surveigh of the Monastery of Faversham in the County of Kent.* At the sign of the Three Bibles, London Bridge: London

SPROTT, T. 1719. *Thomas Sprotti Chronica.* T. Hearne (ed.) Oxford University Press: Oxford

STATHAM. S. P. H. 1902 [2017]. *Dover Charters and other Documents in the Possession of the Corporation of Dover.* Forgotten Books: London

STRINGER, C. 2007. *Homo Britannicus: the Incredible Study of Human Life in Britain.* Penguin: London

SUTCLIFFE, A. 1995. *Insularity of the British Isles 250,000–30,000 Years Ago: the Mammalian, Including Humans, Evidence.* Geological Society Special Publication 96: London

SWAIN, E. 1981. *Britain in Old Photographs: Faversham.* Budding Books: Stroud

SWAT ARCHAEOLOGY. 2006. Archaeological evaluation, excavation and watching brief at the Church of St Mary of Charity, Faversham, Kent. Unpublished report SWAT: Faversham

SWAT ARCHAEOLOGY. 2008. Syndale Park Motel, London Road, Ospringe, near Faversham, Kent: Archaeological Evaluation. SWAT Archaeology: Faversham http://www.swatarchaeology.co.uk/pdf/2008/26.Syndale.pdf

SWAT ARCHAEOLOGY. 2009. Former Whitbread Training Centre site, Abbey St, Faversham, Kent. SWAT Archaeology: Faversham http://www.swatarchaeology.co.uk/pdf/2009/20.ABStreet%20interim%20phase%201.pdf

SWAT ARCHAELOGY. 2014. Archaeological Evaluation of land at the Barkaway site 20–22 Ospringe Street, Ospringe, Kent SWAT Archaeology: Faversham www.swatarchaeology.co.uk/pdf/2014/Barkaway%20revised%20report%20complete.pdf

SWEETINBURGH, S. (ed.). 2010. *Later Medieval Kent 1220–1540* Boydell Press/Kent County Council: Woodbridge

TANN, P. 2013 *The Royal Charters of Faversham including Magna Carta.* Faversham Society: Faversham

TATTON BROWN, T. 1994. *St Catherines Church, Preston near Faversham: Canterbury Diocese, Historical and Archaeological Survey.* Kent Archaeological Society: Maidstone

TELFER, D. W. 1965. *Faversham Abbey and its Last Abbot, John Caslock.* Faversham Society Paper 2: Faversham

TESTER, P. J. 1980. A plan and architecural description of the medieval remains of Davington Priory. *Archaeologia Cantiana* 95, 205–12

TODD, J. B. and ERLANDSON, J. 2013. Human acceleration of animal and plant extinctions: a late Pleistocene, Holocene and Athropocene continuum. *Anthropocene* 2013. https://www.infona.pl/resource/bwmeta1.element.elsevier-848a4c67-fdf9-304a-a7a2-3c07e533b6d7

VICTORIA COUNTY HISTORY. 1926. *The Victoria History of the County of Kent: Vol 2.* W. Page (ed.). St Catherines Press: London

WARD, A. 1997. The Roman site at Ospringe *Kent. Archaeological Review* 129 199–205

WARD, A. 2008. Review of KAFS Stone Chapel, Faversham, excavtions in 2007. *Kent Archaeological Review* 175, 102–4

WARD, G. 1933. The lists of Saxon Churches in the Domesday Monachorum and White Book of St Augustine. *Archaeologia Cantiana* 45, 60–89

WARD, G. 1934. The topography of some Saxon Charters relating to the Faversham district. *Archaeologia Cantiana* 46, 123–36

WARD, G. 1947. King Wihtred's Charter of AD 699. *Archaeologia Cantiana* 60, 1–14

WEEVER, J. 1631. *Ancient Funeral Monuments.* W. Tooks at the Bible in St Pauls churchyard: London

WELCH, M. 2007. Anglo-Saxon Kent to AD 800. In Williams (ed.) 2007, 187–248

WENBAN SMITH, F. 2007. The Palaeolithic archaeology of Kent. In Williams (ed.) 2007, 25–64

WESSEX ARCHAEOLOGY. 2003. Syndale Park, Ospringe: Archaeological Evaluation and an Assessment of Results (Time Team report). Unpublished report. Trust for Wessex Archaeology: Salisbury

WESSEX ARCHAEOLOGY. 2013. Land at Littles Manor Farm, Sheldwich, Faversham, Kent. Unpublished report, Wessex Archaeology: Salisbury. Lodged on KCC HER as SKE 24076

WHITING, W. 1921. A Roman cemetery discovered at Ospringe in 1920 (1). *Archaeologia Cantiana* 35, 1–16

WHITING, W. 1923. A Roman cemetery discovered at Ospringe in 1920 (2). *Archaeologia Cantiana* 36, 65–151

WHITING, W. 1925. The Roman cemeteries at Ospringe (1). *Archaeologia Cantiana* 37, 83–96

WHITING, W. 1926. The Roman cemeteries at Ospringe (2). *Archaeologia Cantiana* 38, 123–51

WHITING, W. 1929. Proceedings from meetings: the Council of the Royal Archaeological Institute London. *Archaeological Journal* 86, 298–302

WILKINSON, P. 2005. Hog Brook Reports: an archaeological investigation of the Roman aisled stone building at Hog Brook, Deerton St, Faversham 2004–5. Kent Archaeological Field School: Faversham. http://www.kafs.co.uk/pdf/hog-brook.pdf

WILKINSON, P. 2006. *The historical development of the port of Faversham, 1580–1780* Archaeopress: Oxford

WILKINSON, P. 2007a. The interim results of an archaeological investigation at Stone Chapel field, Syndale, Faversham, Kent. Unpublished report. SWAT Archaeology: Faversham

WILKINSON, P. 2007b. *The results of an Archaeological Evaluation at the former Shepherd Neame Depot, Belvedere Road, Faversham, Kent.* SWAT Archaeology: Faversham

WILKINSON, P. 2009. *Practical Archaeology*, winter edition. KAFS: Faversham

WILKINSON, P. 2010. An archaeological investigation of the Roman octagonal bath house at Bax Farm, Teynham, Kent 2006 & 2009. Kent Archaeological Field School: Faversham. http://www.kafs.co.uk/pdf/Bax-Farm.pdf

WILKINSON, P. 2012. The Roman Religious Sanctuary at Blacklands, Graveney, Kent. Unpublished report. Kent Archaeological Field School: Faversham

WILKINSON, P. and MUSSETT, G. 1998. *Beowulf: Some topographical Considerations by Dr Paul Wilkinson & Beowulf and the Sheppey Legend by Griselda Mussett.* Faversham Society Paper 64: Faversham

WILLEMENT, T. 1862. *Historical Sketch of the Parish of Davington in the County of Kent, and of the Priory there.* Basil Montagu Pickering: London

WILLIAMS, A. and MARTIN, G. H. (eds). 1992. *Domesday Book.* Penguin Books Alecto Historical Editions: London

WILLIAMS, J. (ed.). 2007. *The Archaeology of Kent to AD 800.* Boydell Press/Kent County Council: Woodbridge

WILLIS, A. J. 1972, *Canterbury Licences 1568–1646* Phillimore: Bognor Regis

WOODCOCK, A. G. 1975. Mesolithic discoveries at Perry Wods, Selling, Near Canterbury, Kent. *Archaeologia Cantiana* 91, 169–77

WOOD-LEGH, K. L. 1984. Kentish Visitations of Archbishop William Warham & his deputies 1511–12, Vol 24. Unpublished. Maidstone: Kent Archaeological Society Kent Records

WYSE, E. and WINKLEMAN, B. 1993. *Past Worlds: the Times Atlas of Archaeology* (ed.) C. Scarre (ed.). Harper Collins: London